Getting it Right for Boys
... *and* Girls

Boys' under-achievement is grabbing headlines in the education debate, and it has never been more important to solve the problem. This book offers clear and practical strategies to headteachers, classroom teachers and other professionals for ways to address the issue. Founded on the very latest school-based research, it provides practical and proven ways of managing the problem which are in the scope of all teachers and heads – in all phases of education.

The book looks at:

- reasons for boys' under-achievement
- ways of adapting teaching styles to maximise learning gains for boys ... *and* girls
- guidance on how to plan successful pyramid, whole school and classroom approaches
- practical strategies for subject leaders and teachers
- examples of successful case studies
- how to introduce ideas through professional development.

After introductory chapters examining whole school issues and strategies there are further subject-specific chapters that advise on particular teaching approaches for individual subjects. English, mathematics, science, modern languages, the humanities, the arts, and design and technology are all covered – as is the design and use of the library. This is a highly accessible book written by experienced professionals and is intended for busy teachers and heads who want to be engaged by practical ideas to work in their school and classroom.

Colin Noble is a PSE Adviser and Raising Boys' Achievement Manager in Kirklees Local Education Authority and has been responsible for publishing a range of packs, videos, leaflets and posters on the subject of raising boys' achievement. **Wendy Bradford** is author of the best selling *Raising Boys' Achievement* packs (1996) and is now Deputy Headteacher at a large and successful 13–19 fully comprehensive school, with a wealth of classroom experience behind her.

Getting it Right for Boys
... *and* Girls

Colin Noble and Wendy Bradford
With a Foreword by Ted Wragg

London and New York

First published 2000
by Routledge
11 New Fetter Lane, London EC4P 4EE

Simultaneously published in the USA and Canada
by Routledge
29 West 35th Street, New York, NY 10001

Routledge is an imprint of the Taylor & Francis Group

© 2000 Colin Noble and Wendy Bradford

Typeset in Goudy by The Florence Group, Stoodleigh, Devon
Printed and bound in Great Britain by Biddles Ltd, Guildford and
King's Lynn

British Library Cataloguing in Publication Data
A catalogue record for this book is available from the British Library

Library of Congress Cataloging in Publication Data
Noble, Colin.
    Getting it right for boys and girls / Colin Noble and
    Wendy Bradford.
    Includes bibliographical references and index.
    1. Boys – Education – Great Britain. 2. Underachievers – Great
    Britain. 3. Academic achievement – Great Britain. 4. Sex differences
    in education – Great Britain. I. Bradford, Wendy.
    II. Title.
    LC1390.N63 2000
    371.823′41 – dc21   99–16267

ISBN 0–415–20884–X (hbk)
ISBN 0–415–20885–8 (pbk)

To David, Jennifer and Henry

Contents

Illustrations

Figures

Tables

Boxes

Foreword

The year is 2020 and I am in a virtual reality shopping centre. It is full of women, with just a sprinkling of older males. In fact, the heavily armed security guards are among the few men one meets and they are only there to protect visitors from the marauding bands of young and middle-aged men who roam the streets robbing passers-by. In the first two decades of the new millennium millions of young men were unable to find jobs, since few were as well qualified as the girls who entered the job market. By 2020, apart from a few men in work, the vast majority of adult males sit passively in their den at home, watching 500-channel television, with a tiny remote control built into the nail of their index finger so that they do not need to leave their chair. The rest are twenty-first-century footpads, lying in wait near food and leisure megastores, or outside storage and delivery centres, revving up their jetshoes, preying on the few unprotected vehicles carrying people or goods. It is a grim and bleak scene.

This nightmare 2020 vision of a stark and hostile urban landscape, blighted by indolent or predatory males, will not come true. It could happen, but it won't. The reason it will be avoided is because something positive can be done about the problem of boys' relatively low levels of achievement, which struck public consciousness so forcefully in the last few years of the twentieth century. In the Leverhulme Primary Improvement Project which I directed (E.C. Wragg *et al.*, *Improving Literacy in the Primary School*, Routledge, 1998) we found boys lagging well behind girls in reading and language throughout primary school. This finding was common, but until the mid-1980s boys used to catch up in secondary school, and eventually more would take A levels or get into university. By the end of the twentieth century the picture had changed dramatically and girls out-performed boys at every level, from pre-school to university finals.

The strength of this book is that it looks at different aspects and explanations of boys' relatively lower achievement and explores practical ways in which it can be addressed. The authors have direct experience of programmes and approaches which seemed to have an impact. Improving the achievement of boys, while not neglecting the needs of girls, is one of the biggest challenges facing teachers, as well as parents. Big issues, like education, poverty, illness, conflict, crime, need many solutions, as there are few miracle cures. The nightmare scenario of a bleak future by 2020 will be avoided through intelligent action, and this book offers many valuable suggestions about what forms that might take.

Professor E.C. Wragg
Exeter University

Preface

This book is not academic, although it is based on extensive academic research as you will see from the exhaustive bibliography. It is an attempt to give the reader practical ideas through an enjoyable experience (echoes of boys' own preferences) rather than a merely worthy plod. Thus it is light and at times iconoclastic, but it is meant to keep the reader engaged.

The title reflects our profound belief that the management, teaching strategies and techniques we suggest for boys will also be beneficial to girls. The latter will benefit in two ways: the boys will be more focused on their studies, thus enhancing the climate of achievement and diminishing the degree of disruption; and the girls will usually find the newly adopted strategies more to their own preference of learning style.

To the reader: how to use this book

This book is intended for a fairly wide range of reader. It should be of general interest to most people in the education world because it deals with a problem which affects us all and suggests ways in which boys' and girls' achievement could be raised. It should also be beneficial to many lay people who have an interest in education, whether they be parents, governors, journalists or are merely interested in reflecting on what goes on in Britain's schools. We have tried to accommodate this in the language of the book which is as free from jargon as possible without jeopardising our credibility with those who discuss these issues daily as part of their professional duties or research project.

Many people will come to this book with a particular interest in certain parts of education: primary, secondary or with a certain subject in mind. *If you are interested in the primary years* you will find that the first six chapters are general, discussing issues of equal relevance to primary and secondary. Chapter 7 has certain elements (such as a discussion of Year 3) which are marked for primary phase interest. Chapter 8 is again of general interest, and the following chapters address specific subjects, some divided into primary and secondary sections where we think it has been appropriate.

Chapter 16 is about working across the pyramid, and the final chapter gives a number of exercises for continuous professional development which can be used or adapted in schools.

If you are interested in the secondary years you may have a subject brief, in which case you can easily pick the relevant chapters using the Contents page, although we would urge you to consider the first four chapters by way of background understanding. If you have a management brief the first six chapters are essential reading, and we would also urge Chapter 16 upon you.

We would be very happy to receive any comments or ideas from readers. Please write to or telephone Colin Noble at 9 Norfolk Terrace, Leeds LS7 4QW. Tel. 0113–2943627.

Acknowledgements

Our sincere thanks to a large number of teachers, pupils and schools throughout the country who have helped to inform our thinking and given us time – both to give and amend ideas.

Particular thanks are due to Andy Green, Keith Williamson and David Bradford for their comments about science and mathematics; Rob Buckley, John Molyneux and Heather Prud'homme about humanities; Gerry Swain about English; Maria Dengate about teaching styles; Elaine Moreton, Ann Skevington and Wendy Redmile on design and technology; and Erica Hiorns about modern foreign languages. Similarly, thanks to Outwood Grange School, Wakefield, and Fulford School, York, for permission to use some of their documents.

Many thanks to our colleagues – Paul Brennan, Gary Wilson, Elaine Moreton and Kathryn Sheard – who have written three of the chapters; to Clive Watkins and John Fowler for their willingness to encourage teacher research at their schools; and to Pat Jones for his support, interest and the contribution of a chapter describing how he went about getting it right for boys – *and* girls.

Introduction

Getting it right for boys *and* girls

> We need to examine, in boys, the complex relationships between the demand on them to be 'real boys' and their attitude to academic work.
> (*TES* 'Opinion', January 1999)

This book is not just about understanding boys' and girls' under-achievement: it's about raising achievement. It is intended to appeal to several groups of people within education. It differs from most other, perhaps all other, books on the same topic inasmuch as we are offering ideas for educationalists to take forward to use in the school and classroom. It is primarily intended to be a practical book offering strategies which can be discussed, used, amended, rejected, passed on and used to help build professional reflection and better practice. Primary and secondary teachers, LEA and TEC officers, higher education students and lecturers will all find insights into the problem of, and solutions to, raising boys' achievement. The strategies proposed are also designed to raise the confidence, quality of participation in learning and achievement of girls. All our suggestions have been revealed through extensive research with school pupils about their preferred learning styles.

How the book is organised and how to use it

Chapter 1 will set out the evidence which suggests how and why boys are under-achieving compared to girls. In general, though, the book is intended to be less a diagnosis of the existing situation in schools and more an essay and description of a range of policies and strategies which whole schools and individual teachers can adopt. Chapter 2 explores the reasons why boys under-achieve; Chapter 3 investigates the favoured learning styles of boys and their relevance to raising achievement; and Chapters 4 and 5 describe the model which schools may wish to adopt in order to plan a coherent and complementary strategy to raise boys' achievement, and gives an example of how one secondary school has gone about it. These first five chapters are generic to education and are equally valuable to primary and secondary teachers alike. The rest of the book is organised differently. The first part of each chapter is an introduction, after which you will find different sections for primary and secondary. We hope and expect that primary colleagues will find the secondary sections of interest and vice versa. At the end of each chapter a summary of key points is given, which could be used as an overhead transparency if leading a discussion with colleagues, or merely as a checklist or reminder of the main arguments or information.

In a recent book David Jackson wrote:

> We need a contradictory, gender-relations model of equal opportunities work that can speak directly and recognisably to both girls' and boys' messy, awkward, lived experiences. And we need that fresh model urgently.
>
> (Epstein *et al.*, 1998, p. 91)

This book does not provide a model of equal opportunities so much as a strategy and a process of professional reflection which helps teachers to ensure that they are getting it right for boys *and* girls in terms of raising achievement.

The book is unashamedly based on the central assumption that it is through good teaching and learning experiences that all boys and girls will be helped to reach their academic potential and, indeed, in many cases surprise themselves by understanding what their potential might be. As 'good' teaching is the main requirement for getting it right for boys *and* girls, 'good' teachers rightly take central stage. Such teachers are the vast majority in every school. They are those colleagues who care passionately about 'their' pupils, sit up and take notice when conversation is about classroom practice and, most of all, are confident or brave enough to try out new concepts in the classroom and to evaluate the brilliant success or frustrating failure of their ideas. The vision of the teaching profession which underpins this book is that which Michael Barber describes as a 'learning profession' – but one which needs to become more assertive about the fantastically creative range of strategies and approaches which every good teacher uses.

Chapter 1

We are facing a crisis

Chris Woodhead, Her Majesty's Chief Inspector for education, has written that the under-achievement of boys is the greatest challenge and crisis facing education. Others have gone further.

> If there is a growing underclass, poorly educated young men are its vanguard. . . . It is certain that one of the critical equal opportunities issues for the next decade is the motivation and achievement of young men.
>
> (Barber, 1994, p. 7)

It is easy to see why this view prevails. The tables in Chapter 2 show clearly that boys are achieving less than girls in most subjects, but particularly so in English and other subjects which demand higher level language and organisational skills. Given that the demand of the modern employer is increasingly for these very skills, the implications for boys, for their future and for society as a whole are very stark. For some boys, their low level communication skills affect their achievement not only in other areas of the curriculum but will also blight their life experiences and chances. Their potential is being left woefully short of being fully realised. There is the likelihood that they will find themselves marginalised and irrelevant to the next millennium's job market.

> Once out of education and with few qualifications, they become trapped in a revolving door of benefits and low-paid jobs. Within months, many fall off the margins and face a lifetime of social exclusion and crime.
>
> (*Finding the Missing*, a report of the
> National Youth Agency)

For society, the prospects of a large cohort of under-employed, unskilled, under-educated and quite probably unpleasant young men is not a healthy one. We have to do something about it.

What crisis?

Practice makes perfect. If the cliché holds true, teachers these days must be almost perfect at balancing the hyperbole against reality. National statistics might worry the politicians, school statistics might worry the headteacher, but it's the progress and results of individual students which concern teachers. They know better than to get swept along with the unthinking panic that could be the product of media interest in the issue of boys. Whatever school improvement strategies are being developed within a school, teachers need to be able to answer the question 'Where are we now?' This must be split into 'How are our girls doing?' and, of course, 'How are our boys doing?' The more delving that takes place at this point the more secure will be the knowledge about particular groups of boys and girls. How are our boys and girls doing in each subject area? How are our boys and girls from different ability groups performing? It is common to find that high and low ability boys are performing about on a par with high and low ability girls – but what about those of average ability? That is often where boys' under-achievement can be found. Average girls often go on to get their Level 4s at Key Stage 2 and their crop of Bs and Cs at GCSE, whereas average boys provide the Level 3s and the Ds and Es, which frustrates the school's effort to hoist itself up the league table. Far more importantly, it limits the training and employment opportunities of the young men concerned.

It is worth remembering, of course, that under-achievement shows itself in many forms. It isn't always noisy, disruptive and unco-operative. It can be also be helpful, reliable and delightfully cheerful! Teachers often use Cognitive Ability Test data, SATs results or a combination of both to establish the starting point from which progress will be measured. In some schools this exercise will reveal many under-achievers, in others it may reveal few. In some schools the under-achievers will be spread across all areas of the curriculum: in some they may be concentrated in, for example, English and French. In some schools, under-achievement will be apparent among students at all levels of ability: in others it may be a certain ability grouping which is faring badly.

And the girls?

> Women never have young minds. They are born three thousand years old.
>
> (Shelagh Delaney, A *Taste of Honey*, Act 1, Scene 2, 1959)

Some teachers express indignation that boys are attracting so much concern now that girls, justifiably in their view, are doing better. But are girls 'doing better'? There are still huge gaps to close and stereotypes to challenge in the A level sciences and in some university courses. In addition, as a recent feminist book on the subject pointed out, the improvement in female achievement has not occurred for all girls, in particular those from low socio-economic backgrounds (Epstein *et al.*, 1998). The world of work suggests that although girls aspire to, and achieve, jobs in the reasonably well-paid professions of law and medicine they rarely appear at the top of those professions – and are still an exotic species in the higher ranks of commerce, finance, the civil service and industry. It may be that the lag effect will take time to shake out; one should not expect good school results over one decade to result in the overnight replacement and femi-nisation of the establishment.

What is more important is the observation by many teachers and parents of how girls succeed and the implications that has for their future life chances and career development. The National Curriculum, the system which has witnessed the relative success of girls, tends to demand a well-organised, compliant, procedure-observing teacher and pupil. It tends not to encourage the radical, the lateral thinker, the bloody-minded, the in-tuitive. Teachers have come to expect (and all teachers who entered the profession since 1988 have little experience of anything else) a curriculum where they do not have to worry too much about the content. The point of education has become, probably subliminally in most teachers' minds, to maximise exam and SATs results. The point of teaching is to ensure that the National Curriculum has been covered. Despite the changes of 1995 and 1998, it is still obese. Whatever the reasons, be they genetic or learned, more girls than boys seem better equipped to slog through the curriculum quagmire. Boys and girls are rewarded for diligence, effort, deadline-keeping, good presentation, organisation and not wasting time. There is nothing wrong with that in itself, but does it properly instruct them about the success of the adult world? Here, school-learned qualities often have to be married to ambition, quick or creative thinking, confidence in one's own judgement and skills, high expectations and occasionally breaking or bending the rules. In this book we suggest that teaching methods which have been encouraged by the National Curriculum could be changed to benefit both boys *and* girls.

We're dealing with generalities

'There are some boys who are very good at work, like yesterday in our form, there's a boy who's good at nearly every lesson.'

(Year 7 boy)

We're dealing with generalities. There are thousands of individuals from both genders who are simply not recognisable from the descriptions we are giving to their gender. Their behaviour, learning style, achievement and demeanour are nothing to do with under-achieving boys or focused, self-managing girls. We are dealing with the problem of under-achievement and many pupils are not under-achieving. We also recognise that achievement is hugely influenced by socio-economic class and, to a lesser extent, by ethnicity. As Epstein points out:

> Overall, the under-achievement of boys at school is a strongly classed and racialised phenomenon. Indeed class and the associated level of education of parents (for both boys and girls) continue to be the most reliable predictions of a child's success in school examinations.
>
> (Epstein *et al.*, 1998, p. 11)

The only problem with this argument is that it does not answer the question of why boys under-achieve relative to girls. This can be answered, to some extent, by a consideration of class and race – but a major thrust of the book is that pupils who begin their school life from a relatively disadvantaged educational position are in greater need of good classroom practice. Good teaching is an escape route from failure: poor teaching practice is more likely to confirm it.

Achievement and pupils from minority ethnic groups

Trying to make sense of national figures for the academic achievement of ethnic minority pupils is not easy, partly because few LEAs effectively collect and collate reliable statistics (Blair and Bourne, 1998). Schools, and departments within schools, should make it a matter of priority that they have a rounded and accurate view of the performance of their own ethnic minority pupils (broken down by gender). It is only by the systematic analysis of the relative performances that patterns of achievement over a period of time can emerge – and this in turn enables more appropriate strategies to be adopted. In general terms, it appears that boys from Afro-Caribbean, mixed race and Pakistani backgrounds are particularly vulnerable to under-achievement. The Afro-Caribbean and mixed race boys appear to be particularly susceptible from Key Stage 2 onwards, whereas with Pakistani boys (and also Pakistani girls) the under-achievement stretches across the phases. But the picture is so highly complex that it largely belies attempts to describe it, let alone diagnose and prescribe solutions. It certainly challenges tabloid images of racial stereotypes:

> African-Caribbean boys have been seen ... as a unified lump, who underachieve academically and are driven by a phallocentric revenge impulse to repair their oppressed maleness.
>
> (Epstein *et al.*, 1998, p. 124)

Tony Sewell (in Epstein *et al.*, 1998) has pointed out that within any one cohort of Afro-Caribbean boys, at least four groups, all with differing attitudes towards school, can be traced. The vast majority of these boys support the idea of education and most support the goals of the school, but schools themselves need to do much more to understand the educational and curriculum needs of minority ethnic groups. Schools need to confront the ways in which they actually *confirm* Afro-Caribbean boys as 'rebellious, phallocentric under-achievers' and to have a clear policy about how to raise their achievement. We shall be returning to this issue later in the book as various strategies are considered for their applicability to minority ethnic groups.

We argue that the National Curriculum has in some respects been hostile to boys. It has also been less than kind to some teachers. In the late 1970s, ignoring Prime Minister Callaghan's Ruskin College speech about the need for change in education, commentators enthused about the variety and richness of the English education system. LEAs, schools and teachers were to a large extent a law unto themselves. It may be a truism to point out that this was very successful when it worked and was a disgrace when it did not; but it does not answer the unexplored question of what happened to the culture of independence, eccentricity and exploration of educational methodologies. It seems to have been largely steamrollered by the National Curriculum juggernaut, and stifled to extinction by the blitzkrieg of SATs, league tables, parental choice and Local Management of Schools (LMS). Who can afford to experiment when failure results in a league table slip, possibly followed by a loss of pupils and finance?

This may be a good thing. It must surely be inappropriate to regard schools as laboratories of educational philosophy and children as the guinea-pigs of badly researched ideas which suit the political prejudice of the LEA, head or teacher. But the present alternative is equally unattractive. The teaching profession, although more accountable and responsible than ever before, has in many ways lost its confidence in its own abilities. There is an accepted culture of receiving thick tomes from the succession of government quangos since 1988 and then debating the organisational headache of how best to implement them. The sheer volume of guidance, diktat, programmes of study, tests, tasks and data which have landed on schools' doorsteps has tended to be overwhelming. When Chris Woodhead, the Chief HMI, cunningly asked headteachers at a 1997 conference if they would like nationally provided units of work to support the National Curriculum, he was almost mobbed. Who could not desire such documents when they would save so much time and effort? If he had asked the question ten years earlier he would have been howled down.

In short, teachers as a profession have been subdued by the advent of the National Curriculum to the point where they have not only lost their resentment of central imposition but have come to expect and welcome it. There is a danger that teachers have become de-skilled. The very heart of the professionalism of the teacher, of understanding their students and how they learn, has been undermined by this new culture of dependency.

This will not do. Teachers have to regain the belief that what they do, how they apply different teaching methods to a variety of learners and situations, not only makes a difference but can also only lie within their own professional discretion. Carol Fitz-Gibbon (1996) writes enthusiastically about how school improvement comes about through trial and error, based on the motivation to make incremental improvements to practice.

There's someone else in the classroom!

Whether they like it or not, there is another new age which will soon be upon teachers. Many will find it initially threatening or repugnant, but by the year 2002 – when the government's first academic targets will be due for delivery – it will have become common practice. Headteachers are beginning to take a very important part of their job seriously for the first time. They are having to show that they really are monitoring the quality of teaching and learning in their school. Arguably, they could monitor learning by analysing the examination results and other data. This gives a partial picture of the quality of teaching and learning, however. To do this they have to get into the classrooms and observe, or 'walking the talk' as one head has dubbed it. Some headteachers have been doing this for some time; most have yet to start in any systematic fashion. As a sense of accountability moves down through the school, middle managers will be centrally involved. It should make a huge difference to the profession. The old privacy will be dead and professional dialogues based on regular observations will be commonplace. It demands a great deal from all concerned. It presupposes a degree of professionalism which the recent changes in education have tended to discourage.

Any move to introduce changes in the context of raising boys' achievement also demands professionalism. The sort of whole school and classroom-specific practices which we advocate are not a blueprint for success. They demand to some extent a willingness to try things out, to observe the outcomes and adjust or even abandon the strategies if deemed necessary. Teachers have to be given, and to accept, the right to fail. Doctors, lawyers, scientists and writers are doing this all the time – often with equally serious issues at risk. The industrialist who said the secret of his success was the willingness to double his failure rate has an important message for teachers. We are, after all, already failing both boys and girls by treading the safe path of doing nothing about the present, growing disparity of achievement. The re-professionalisation of the teaching force should mean a genuine dialogue about methodology, of inviting lesson observation, of asking for ideas and help and of admitting failure. This new-found openness also means the celebration of success. As the dialogue becomes better informed, as the barriers come down and class-room management is opened to scrutiny and discussion, success will inevitably outweigh failure.

Chapter 2

How and why boys under-achieve

For many years teachers have reported that boys are an issue. Chris Woodhead, in his capacity as Chief HMI and columnist in the *Times Educational Supplement*, has been writing about it for some time and quoted a shepherd in Shakespeare's *A Winter's Tale*:

> I wish there were no age between 10 and 23, because young men get wenches with child, upset the ancientry, stealing and fighting.

Woodhead's conclusion is that young men have been exhibiting the same problems for at least four hundred years. Granted, there is little reference to boys' academic under-achievement in Shakespeare, but the behaviour we associate with it certainly is. Arguably it is only the past ten years, with its emphasis on achievement, improvement and gathering evidence that have led to a systematic collection and analysis of the data which enables us to show just how boys do under-achieve. The tables in this chapter clearly indicate that over the last three years boys have significantly under-achieved compared to girls. Just how modern this phenomenon is must be open to question. We know that in the post-war world of the eleven-plus exam, which decided the academic route of most pupils, there was an organised bias in favour of boys, as it was widely agreed that boys matured later and therefore compensation had to be built in at age 11. Just how many women, now in their middle age, were denied a grammar school education for this reason is very difficult to judge, but it is likely to be substantial.

It is a worldwide problem

In 1993 Ofsted began to officially voice its concerns about boys' achievement, but sensibly placed the problem in a worldwide context, as the following shows:

> The gap between boys and girls in language-based subjects has widened because girls' attainment has improved. It is an international trend.

The French are concerned about boys and so are the Germans and Japanese. The Americans have been looking at this area for years. It is not a recent development, nor is it British, nor is it English. But it has become an accentuated area for focus because of concern about boys' employment opportunities.

(HMI/Ofsted, 1993)

Recent research in Ireland and France has revealed that, even without the plethora of statistics which British teachers have at their disposal, the achievement of some boys is a concern to school managers, individual teachers and the state education departments. It may be reassuring or depressing to know that boys' under-achievement is not just another British disease. Nearly every other industrial or post-industrial country in the world reports very similar trends – particularly in the acquisition of language skills. The United Kingdom is probably ahead of many in analysing and addressing the issue because recent reforms have thrown up a mad rush for statistics to inform inspection, league tables and parental choice. A number of European countries, such as Italy, are interested in following the educational trails blazed in the UK and thus their statistics will presumably be honed and examined in the same manner with which teachers here have become familiar. The one country which presently seems to buck the trend is Finland. The Finns tend to start school later than children in the UK, as do many European nations, and literacy is a critical goal in the early years during which classes are comparatively small. Perhaps even more important is the nature of Finnish television, which does not dub the mainly imported programmes but provides subtitles. The hours which the young Finn spends watching television are often spent desperately trying to read Finnish very quickly. The prospect of sitting our children in front of subtitled French and Italian films may have limited appeal to them, the advertisers, and Mrs Whitehouse's Listeners' and Viewers' Association.

The figures

Although teachers are rightly suspicious of the authority and interpretation of statistics, those relating to the relative achievement of boys and girls confirm the observation of classroom behaviour that some boys are under-achieving. Table 2.1 shows the headline figures with which most parents and lay people are familiar: the percentage of students who obtain five or more A*– C grades in GCSE at the age of 16 in Britain.

It is not only at GCSE that the divide is noticeable. The gap continues to A level. As society has given more opportunities to girls they have reversed the previous domination of A levels by the boys. In 1983–84 11.1 per cent of 18-year-old boys obtained three or more A levels compared to 9.5 per cent of girls. By 1994–95 the position had reversed: 20.5 per

Table 2.1 Percentage of pupils gaining five or more GCSE grades A*–C, 1991–98

	1991	1992	1993	1994	1995	1996	1997	1998
Boys	30.8	31.1	33.7	36.2	39.0	39.9	40.5	41.1
Girls	38.4	40.1	43.1	45.2	48.1	49.4	50.0	51.3
Percentage gender gap	7.6	9.0	9.4	9.0	9.1	10.4	9.5	10.2

Source: DfEE (1998)

cent of boys gained three A levels compared to 24.2 per cent of girls. This trend of increasing performance by both genders, but with girls drawing away from the boys, seems to be repeated at all ages.

What is most noticeable in the figures is the huge discrepancy between boys' and girls' performance in English. This is first apparent at the age of 7 in the Key Stage 1 SATs and gently accelerates through the later key stages, as Tables 2.2–2.4 demonstrate.

At this stage, the difference in achievement in English is relatively modest compared to later years. It may well be that both schools and parents are lulled into thinking that there is little to worry about, although these national figures tend to obscure far larger differences within individual LEAs and schools.

The results given in Tables 2.2 and 2.3 show that a very significant gap has opened out between the achievement of boys and girls in English, one which does not close with time but tends to widen. Something peculiar has happened in the four years since the Key Stage 1 SATs. Three years later the gap has been maintained, although in the 'traditional' boys' subjects of science and mathematics it is still minimal.

Table 2.2 Key Stage 1 1998 National Curriculum assessment results: Overview – % of pupils at Level 2 and above in England

	Teacher assessment	
	Boys	Girls
English	76	81
Speaking and listening	80	83
Reading	76	81
Writing	76	79
Mathematics	83	85
Science	85	86

Source: QCA

Table 2.5 shows how boys as a cohort achieved inferior results to girls, particularly in English, over the three years 1996 to 1998. Although the results are not all as bad for boys as English clearly is, it is a worrying prospect – particularly in the light of the critical importance of literacy in other subjects and in key life skills. Students need high level literacy skills

Table 2.3 Key Stage 2 1998 National Curriculum statutory tests: Overview – percentage of pupils at Level 4 and above in England

	Tests	
	Boys	Girls
English	57	73
Mathematics	59	58
Science	70	69

Source: QCA

Table 2.4 Key Stage 3 1998 National Curriculum statutory tests: Overview – percentage of pupils at Level 5 and above in England

	Tests	
	Boys	Girls
English	57	73
Mathematics	60	60
Science	81	80

Source: QCA

Table 2.5 National GCSE results by gender and subject: percentage of students achieving A*– C in individual subjects, England 1996–98

Subject	Boys			Girls		
	1996	1997	1998	1996	1997	1998
English language	41.1	42.8	44.6	60.5	60.9	61.7
English literature	49.2	50.1	50.1	65.5	65.9	65.2
Mathematics	40.4	43.3	43.7	40.8	43.4	44.8
Science (double)	45.1	46.3	47.1	45.6	47.0	48.9
Art	42.4	47.9	48.6	62.9	66.8	69.7
Design and technology	34.6	37.6	43.1	50.5	53.2	50.2
French	33.0	35.3	34.5	49.6	51.1	51.3
Geography	44.2	47.0	48.5	51.2	54.3	55.4
German	39.2	41.8	42.8	56.1	57.9	58.1
History	44.7	48.3	50.2	54.8	56.9	57.6
Music	54.4	58.2	58.6	67.8	69.7	69.3
RE	37.4	40.6	40.5	54.0	56.4	57.6

Source: DfEE (1998)

for academic, social and employment reasons. In recent years employers increasingly demand communication skills in job descriptions and are becoming better skilled in assessing them. Modern economic society demands the swift transfer of information whether it be by mouth, telephone or computer screen. In the great majority of cases these are skills which have been better learned by girls.

Why bother with boys?

> Better build schoolrooms for 'the boy'
> Than cells and gibbets for 'the man'.
> (Eliza Cook, 'A Song for Ragged Schools', 1853)

The topic of gender and achievement can excite a lot of controversy. At conferences, courses and schools all over the country some colleagues will become indignant about this modern concern. Why is there all this fuss about boys when girls were allowed to under-achieve for decades? Why should we be bothered when it seems to most observers that boys are the authors of their own misfortune? The aggression, arrogance and anti-work culture of some boys, the argument goes, do not make them worthy recipients of any strategy, let alone one which unfairly takes the focus of teaching away from girls.

The move towards national and regular assessment of pupils at age 7, 11, 14 and 16 – and the publication of the results – has given educationalists and the public an enormous amount of data to inform them about pupils and schools. It is these figures and their popular scrutiny which has revealed the *relative* under-achievement of boys. This is an important qualification to make. Commentators claim boys are under-achieving because they are not doing as well as girls. This is a poor yardstick. How do we know that girls are not also massively under-achieving? Schools which find that there is little gender difference in the achievement of their pupils cannot afford complacency. Both genders may be massively under-achieving. This is the rationale behind the title of this book: we have to get it right for boys *and* girls. The ultimate focus is on the individual student and his or her learning needs – regardless of gender, ethnicity, social class or even academic ability.

There are other reasons which are worthy of discussion. First, we believe that the manner in which boys under-achieve – classroom disruption, discourtesy, poor organisation – detracts from the achievement of girls. Schools have to convince pupils of the importance of learning; they have to be learning organisations, and this culture or ethos is impossible if a large minority manifestly does not care about learning. Second, boys who fail at school can all too often become alienated, under-employed, unskilled and antisocial. A search of a criminology database revealed 581 studies, worldwide, referring to school achievement or performance (Pease, 1998). A noticeable gender difference, worthy of staffroom discussion, is that dysfunctional women turn on themselves while dysfunctional men turn on others. This is an unwelcome trend for society, but may be particularly unwelcome to girls and women who are more vulnerable.

The reasons why boys under-achieve

Probably the most debatable aspect of the generally controversial issue of boys' achievement is that of the cause of the problem. It is rich territory for the nature versus nurture debaters. Although the arguments normally generate more heat than light it is a valuable one to be had if you are interested in bringing about change. It *does* capture interest and reflection and forces the different sides to focus on the nature of learning, gender characteristics and pupils as individuals. The debate can be a catalyst for change.

In some ways it does not matter what the causes of boys' under-achievement may be. Teachers and the education establishment in general have to work with the situation before them, and its source – obscure, confused and controversial – may be interesting but hardly useful. It is the practical strategies with which teachers are most concerned. However, unless we have some understanding of the background causes, we may be adopting plans and policies which are wholly inappropriate to the problem.

> Much of the response has to be site-specific and based on a thorough, sensitive collection and analysis of local data.
>
> (Epstein *et al.*, 1998, p. 14)

Boys and the anti-swot culture

Some teachers have argued with conviction that we are in danger of over-complicating a very simple fact: some boys don't work as hard as most girls. They tend to be lazier, less motivated, less organised, poorer presenters and less eager to please. In some schools, they positively promote an anti-swot culture which both justifies their own behaviour and challenges the rights of other boys, and occasionally girls, to try hard. This argument is irrefutable but far too reductionist. It leaves two fundamental questions unanswered: first, why is this culture so prevalent when many boys *do* want to work hard and succeed in doing so; and second, where has this culture come from? The simple diagnosis tends to promote a simple prescription – let's change the culture of boys. This is laudable, but without knowing more about its genesis it is impossible to understand the mechanisms and direction of change. In one school we came across a boy who had hidden a large number of books under his sweater. He was on his way home to get on with his homework but dared not display his willingness to work nor his lack of 'cool' in carrying a bag. This is symptomatic of the complexity of the culture that has to be erased.

We are suggesting that there are six main reasons why boys are presently achieving less than girls at school. Not everyone will agree with them or give them the titles we have, but it will help the discussion in your workplace.

The six possible reasons why boys presently achieve less than girls

1 Genetic

This will leave female colleagues cheering and alienate the males. Are women really more intelligent than men? Has their natural superiority been oppressed by centuries of male domination? Is their true potential only showing itself now as we enter an age of generally increasing equality? We have no idea. But there is a certain amount of evidence that women may have an intuitive or genetic disposition to be better communicators than men. Research, mainly in the United States, suggests that new-born babies show clear gender differences in their ability to understand and discriminate between sounds. Surrey LEA found 3-year-olds to have marked differences in linguistic abilities between boys and girls; and the Key Stage 1 SATs show a gender gap at 7 which is not shortened over the next nine years of schooling.

Darwinists have argued that the reason for this gap, for the large telephone bills which are the rites of passage for teenage girls and for the GCSE differences, goes back to the roles which women and men have played for thousands of years. Women have always been the nurturers, the talkers, the makers of homes and occupiers of kitchens where conversation is not only possible but necessary. Men on the other hand have tended to take on more isolated roles, whether it be hunter-gatherers, tillers or herdsmen. It is only in fairly recent times in the span of human history that these roles have changed. It will be some time yet before evolution catches up with the needs of the modern male. There are many more strands to this argument – left and right hemispheres, whole brain thinking, spatial awareness, links to dyslexia – about genetic dispositions which we do not intend to explore. It is an interesting debate, but it does not take us very far forward. There is also a danger that those who take a genetic line become defeatist, arguing that whatever we try to do in the classroom we are predestined to fail.

2 Changes in society

And the men shall come singing from the fields, for they have provided for their own.

(Old English proverb, apparently, quoted in
Heinz tomato soup television advertisement – 1998)

Society has changed so quickly over the last three decades that it has some-times become difficult for us to know exactly how things are different from a generation ago. Most adults, even those in regular contact with young people, often tend to judge present youthful experiences from a twenty- or thirty-year-old perspective. But the environment in which children and young people grow up has changed radically, and looks as if it will continue to do so.

> The social upheavals of the last 25 years – feminist challenges, unem-ployment, the collapse of the male bread winner and the traditional father as head of the household, the emergence of HIV/AIDS and de-industrialisation – have unsettled the traditional models of dominant, white, heterosexual masculinities.
>
> (David Jackson, in Epstein *et al.*, 1998, p. 79)

We have no intention of examining or listing all these changes, but there are some which have had a radical impact upon the life chances of males and affected the way many of them view themselves.

Perhaps the most important change has been in the field of employment. For many boys who were of below average academic ability in the 1960s, there was little difficulty in finding a job, although this may have varied with the economic cycle. Labouring, factory work, the coal-mines, ship-yards and steel mills, semi-skilled jobs on the railway, were all available, sometimes through apprenticeship schemes, and they paid wages which enabled workers to make their way and raise a family. Moreover, there were millions of people doing this. It was an expectation, a normality, and the workers from whom the young apprentices learned were other men who often had a respect derived from their experience and skill. There were few problems in identifying a path to follow. It may not have been a particu-larly exciting or visionary expectation by today's standards, but it was valued by all those involved. This culture pre-dates the revolution of expectation, when the idea that a favourite hobby could be listed as 'shopping' would be incomprehensible. Having a great deal of disposable income, and having the non-essential goods in the shops to purchase, had not yet reached the vast majority of working people.

The shopping, advertising and commercialisation revolutions of the 1970s and 1980s have changed all that. The growth of the importance of image and style has coincided with the demise of millions of engineering, technical, colliery, shipyard and steel jobs. They, and the communities they supported, were bastions of male values and male hegemony. They have largely disappeared and in some parts of the country, for example, South Yorkshire, one can still feel a sense of mourning because they have not been adequately replaced. A film like *Brassed Off* effectively captured the beginning of that process, while *The Full Monty*, underneath the humour and surrealism, says an awful lot about the breakdown of families, the need to be respected and the importance of male role models for boys. Both films were set in South Yorkshire and both depict a society left behind by technological changes.

What has replaced them are millions of new jobs in the service sector. Insurance, commerce, finance, tourism, clerical and other office-based jobs do not need the sort of strength and skills men once used in the old industries. Instead they need good communication skills and, often, good keyboard skills. They are often seen as 'women's jobs', and as most of the staff working in them are women, one can see why. Not only do they demand the sort of skills women have, these same skills are ones which men tend to lack. The old certainties and expectations have disappeared with the jobs, and this has had a dramatic effect upon boys and young men. The under-achieving 7-year-old is unlikely to blame technological change for his reluctance to try harder but, if pressed gently, he may say that the only people he knows who work hard are women. The girls in his class seem to work, his mother, aunts and sister work, but the males in his life resemble resting actors. There are some parts of the UK where for some time the women have been the only breadwinners in the family and the men have come to accept long-term unemployment as a way of life. The sons of these men, who may never have worked, have sometimes adopted a culture which is hard to challenge. This could be viewed as a rational adaptation to the real life chances they have (Kress, 1998). What alternative model is offered by the many critics of boys?

If girls are defined by their work ethic, how do boys define themselves? In the absence of anything else, it may be that boys see that to be a boy means that you don't work. As he gets older this view is confirmed by the popular image of success. The television advertisements, many films of modern life, men's magazines, portray successful men as having fast cars, attractive women, designer clothes and exciting holidays. They are seldom portrayed working (although interestingly women are), and there seems therefore to be a causal connection between success and *not* working. The young man cannot quite rationalise this, but he buys into the image of success without knowing how it is achieved. Perhaps it is achieved by being cool, by not trying too hard. In this context it is not surprising that some boys have developed the idea of effortless achievement. Schools would be ill-advised to use footballers as role models, unless – like the admirable Barrie Horne of Huddersfield Town – they are prepared to talk about the value of their academic qualifications and the possibilities they open up. The age of working smart, not hard, has contributed to the anti-work culture. It is no wonder that the men are no longer singing as they come home from the fields.

3 Changes in families

> My mother cries in the middle of the night, too. She says she's worn
> out nursing and feeding and changing and four boys is too much for
> her. She wishes she had one little girl all for herself. She'd give anything
> for a girl.
>
> (McCourt, 1997, p. 14)

There are now 1,250,000 single parent families in the United Kingdom, and
in the vast majority of cases they are headed by women. Just how much
involvement the fathers have with their children, and particularly their
sons, varies enormously between families. There is no doubt that there are
large numbers of boys who do not have significant adult males in their
lives, and who may not see any male teachers at primary school. This is not
just a case of a lack of a role model, which is important enough. If a child
does not have any form of meaningful relationship with a male adult before
the age of 11, and sometimes after that, what does he or she think about
men and, if a boy, what does he think he will be growing up to be? They
may not actually verbalise the feminist question 'What are men for?' because
other forms of information fill the vacuum. Popular culture has a fairly
lurid or glamorous view of men which has little connection with real lives,
but in the absence of anything more immediate, boys have images and
information which do not suggest that being a man is about working hard.

Questions also need to be asked about the role of men when they *do*
live with their children. Surveys reveal that men are much less involved
with the supervision of homework than women, tend to attend fewer
parents' evenings and hear their children read less than women. Just to
compound the crime, fathers are less demanding of their sons than their
daughters. Girls are expected to be well behaved, well presented, neat,
organised, be keener readers, and clean and conventional. Boys tend to be
expected to be less mature, less responsible, more rebellious, dirtier, sportier,
irresponsible, and to have lower concentration spans. These expectations
are usually met. Many parents feel that there is no need to worry about
their sons' learning until they get to secondary school, by which time it is
often too late.

4 Curriculum reasons

The curriculum has changed. This should be no surprise. Following the
second National Curriculum of 1995, its 'paring back' in 1998 and its
full-scale rewriting for 2000, teachers will soon be tired of change, if they
are not already. One of the reasons why they could be disillusioned with
permanent curriculum revolution has not often been voiced. The new
curriculum tends to be more hostile to boys and this has had an effect upon
their attitude, behaviour, effort and achievement.

In *Key Stage 2* the curriculum is still overcrowded and teachers have generally responded to this problem in the obvious, possibly the only, way. Teaching has become more content and less process oriented. This penalises both genders, but particularly boys, whose favoured learning styles are squeezed out by the exigencies of time and curriculum coverage.

In *Key Stage 3* the curriculum is still crowded and the advent of league tables which reflect National Curriculum success has brought another change. Middle schools are being abolished as LEAs consider ways of making schools more co-terminus with the key stages and therefore more accountable for their results. In many authorities (for example, Leeds and Bradford) the middle school system has gone or is going. The arguments about middle schools are infinite, but there is some evidence that they were good for boys in particular. It is the Year 8 boy in secondary school who is a prime candidate for first losing motivation, but in many middle schools he was in the top class and enjoyed high status.

It is in *Key Stage 4* where perhaps the most obvious boy-hostile curriculum changes have occurred. Many commentators suggest that GCSE courses are appropriate for only the top 60 to 70 per cent of the ability range within any subject. Yet nearly all are forced to follow the full National Curriculum. This is as true for girls as it is for boys, but boys respond differently. When they are bored, alienated or confused, boys are less ready than girls to accept their lot, to knuckle down and work steadily towards their D, E or F grade. Conversely, girls' socialisation often depicts life as being a struggle and that hard work is to be expected. Boys are far more likely to give up, disappear or draw attention by causing chaos. For those within the top 60 to 70 per cent there is more bad news. The assessment methods used in GCSE are often partly based on project work or continual assessment. This suggests organised, long-term planning in a way which was less necessary in the days of end-of-course examinations. The results are plain to see in subjects like design and technology about which boys are often initially enthusiastic. It is interesting to see the results of schools which have adopted modular A levels which give the sort of bite-sized, finite work to which boys relate far better.

In addition to this, there is some suggestion that parts of the curriculum itself are less favourable to boys. Do the set books in English favour stories which are predominantly concerned with relationships rather than action? The tasks set for English, often reflecting on feelings and emotions, seem easier to many girls who have more experience of it in their own lives. Is it not the case that IT across the curriculum, something which boys would have generally found interesting, has in most instances been poorly implemented by schools? When it does exist it has often been little more than word processing, appealing to girls' strengths, rather than spread-sheets, databases and data-handling which are more often favoured by boys.

This is not an argument for changing the curriculum to favour boys, but rather to be aware of the potential effects upon boys – and girls – of changes to the curriculum and assessment methods, and to take account of this in school and classroom management.

> To be fair to both boys and girls it is likely that a variety of assess-ment modes should be used so that all pupils have opportunities to produce their best performance.
>
> (Arnot *et al.*, 1998, p. 39)

5 School management

School managers have had an awful lot to deal with in recent years. Aside from the massive changes to the curriculum, delegation from the LEA, governors, league tables, parental pressure, Ofsted and a school population which mirrors the stresses in society, they also have to manage a revolu-tion in expectation of themselves. They are now monitors of the quality of teaching and learning and managers of change. It is not an easy job. Many also teach, which for some is a blessed relief from meetings, tele-phones, crises and reports. It is thus with a sense of guilt that we write that school managers also have a large measure of responsibility for boys' under-achievement.

It is mainly by a neglect of what they could have done, rather than through what they have actually done, that managers should examine them-selves. The lack, or lack of use in classrooms, of early data about pupil potential is still a large problem despite the huge amount of paperwork devoted to this area. The publication of bench-mark data in Key Stages 2, 3 and 4 might now help schools to focus on the potential of younger age groups.

The acceptance of, or inability to tackle, the anti-swot culture is largely a management responsibility. It will be a recurring theme of this book that schools must be, and must portray themselves as, learning organisations. There should be no place for the anti-swot culture. Schools should treat it as they do racism; there should be no tolerance of it. It is an assault upon equal opportunities and results in misery and under-achievement. We shall address the issue of tackling this culture later in the book.

Another recent phenomenon has been the reintroduction of setting and streaming in an increasing number of primary schools, and its spread to more subjects in secondary schools. We deal in detail with setting in Chapter 6, but in synopsis it is evident that there is no perfect way of grouping pupils and students. All methods have advantages and disadvan-tages, but the most successful have two characteristics: (1) the staff using it believe in it; and (2) the inherent weaknesses in the system are recog-nised and addressed by intelligent and focused use of resources, time and training. Good teachers can compensate for bad grouping, but why make it hard for everyone? The rush towards setting in the past two years has often been at the expense of boys, as we explore later.

6 Classroom management

Most teachers in mixed schools are aware that there are two different genders in the classroom with them. They are also aware that these two genders can exhibit distinctly different sorts of behaviours; that they spend more time telling boys off; that boys tend to be less punctual, reliable, motivated and organised. What is less evident is that teachers realise or accept that there may be two different types of *learner* in the class. Seating policy, display, and teaching and learning styles are addressed in later chapters, but we want to make the point early in the book that teachers have an enormous amount of discretion in their classroom management which can either exacerbate or ameliorate the motivation and under-achievement of boys. There is no blueprint for success but there are techniques and strategies which have been tried in a number of schools and have been found to be successful. Our experience of this work has witnessed the teacher reclaiming his or her confidence and skills as a creative professional who is prepared to try things out, sometimes fail, but more often succeed.

Whether these strategies work in any particular classroom is the result of a complex equation in which teacher belief, determination and skill are the most important factors, as well as the nature of the particular group of pupils. Are teachers aware of the need to force boys, in particular, to reflect on their learning – to think about what they have just learned? Do teachers consciously keep lessons divided into clearly delineated, fairly short tasks and attempt to avoid the long term? Is the teacher concentrating on learning – rather than behaviour – as the major reason why he or she gives boys attention? And is the anti-swot atmosphere eradicated in culture, language and action? We shall be discussing all these points later in the book.

The responsibility of schools

Schools are not responsible for genetics, nor for technology-driven changes in the structure of society and the family. Nor are they responsible for the curriculum which is largely imposed upon them. But they can influence how these changes and their effects are managed. Raising boys', and girls', achievement is largely a management issue – and all teachers are managers. With clear-sightedness, a collegiate style and adherence to fundamental principles of equal opportunities, schools *can* get it right for boys and girls. The remainder of this book will explore how boys' achievement can be changed by schools, teachers and boys themselves.

Box 2.1 Boys' under-achievement

It is a worldwide problem.

Raising boys' achievement also helps girls, both academically and socially.

Why boys under-achieve:

- the anti-swot culture
- genetic reasons
- changes in society
- changes in families
- the curriculum
- school management
- classroom management and practices.

The responsibility of schools.

Chapter 3

The importance of teaching and learning styles

Introduction

In this chapter we discuss the favoured learning styles of boys and the implication this has for achievement and planning. A consideration and adoption of certain teaching styles is a critical part of any strategy which schools adopt to raise achievement. It is, after all, the predominant influence on how students experience education – the actual business of learning in the classroom. At the same time we shall be suggesting in Chapters 4, 5, 6 and 7 that there are significant whole school or departmental strategies that will be needed if classroom-based measures are to succeed. This chapter also suggests it is very important that teachers do some action research, albeit at a very modest level, and introduce the acronym of VEST which should help them to plan lessons which interest boys and girls.

Boys as risk-takers

> It is those who would be recognised as 'natural born warriors' who are the 'right kind' of boy in the context of many schools. This does not mean that all boys are naturally aggressive, inattentive, troublesome beings, but the hegemonic masculinities of most schools are characterised in these ways and schools are particularly difficult places for boys to depart from this norm.
>
> (Epstein *et al.*, 1998, p. 12)

Many parents, teachers and more reflective girls see boys as risk-takers; some see this as their most defining characteristic. Geoff Hannan (1997) notes that boys are more likely to raise their hands in class in a ratio over girls of 6:1. It is a form of risk-taking behaviour and is, he suggests, critical to the understanding of boys' preferred learning style. Being exposed to the possibility, often the probability, of being wrong and the mild ridicule of your classmates is easily outweighed by the glorious benefits of the teacher's and whole class's attention and the nirvana of getting it right. The problem is that boys set themselves up to be knocked down. They are, in this sense, vulnerable learners. In the classroom this may result in boys feeling that their effort, or lack of it, will not materially affect their grades or life. If boys are flattened by getting it wrong all the time they may easily give up, with their main line of defence being a semi-detached scepticism, which in turn can easily lead to an anti-swot attitude as they are forced to scorn those who do succeed. Teachers need to realise that boys often enjoy taking risks, but this needs to be channelled positively rather than tolerated or forbidden. Thus, hands up in class to answer a question could be substituted by a more reflective intermission of discussion and observation before raising hands is allowed. Conversely, girls are generally opposed to taking risks and arguably schools do not do enough to encourage girls to appreciate the positive aspects of this kind of behaviour. One of the reasons why the glass ceiling continues in the world of work, some argue, is that not enough women are prepared to risk breaking through it.

A story about teaching styles

A young English teacher's nightmare scenario: she takes over the sixth out of seven ability sets in Year 11. They are mainly boys. She has to teach them *Macbeth* for their GCSE course. They make it quite clear that they hate Shakespeare; they do not like the work; they have no intention of doing it. They are demotivated and do not care about who they please or displease. Nasty.

During one of her sleepless nights contemplating the coming year she has an idea. Using Gregorc's model, she designs a questionnaire which basically asks the students – boys and girls – about their preferred learning style. She discovers that the boys do like some forms of writing and reading, but not the sort usually employed by English teachers when taking a class through Shakespeare. She tentatively tries out some of her findings on the boys. She presents some of the text in tabulated form, and uses statistics and graphs. She presents *Macbeth* as a play with short, recurring sections of horror, humour, fantasy and action. She sets short, written tasks often presented as games or quizzes. She encourages the class – in small groups – to sort out verbal accounts of what happened. She uses a judicious amount of video – enough to explain and whet an appetite, but not enough to bore. She uses IT to encourage proof-reading, editing and display. She raises the status of oral tasks and introduces a reward system. The students respond, and by the end of the year a close bond has developed in the class as well as an enthusiasm for *Macbeth*. The class begs to be taken to the playhouse to see a live production; for many it is their first time in a theatre. Finally, they take their exams, and many of them gain grades thought very unlikely only eight months previously.

It may sound like a script from *Please, Sir*, but it happened in a Yorkshire school in 1997. The pity of the story is that others in the department were not enthused by the need to research preferred learning styles, nor by their colleague's success. No woman is a prophet in her own faculty.

Asking the students

A survey in Kirklees among Year 11 students showed that many said that it was the first time they had been asked specifically about what worked and what did not work for them in the classroom. This is probably not very surprising in the world of education; but it would amount to criminal negligence in most other sectors. It tends to reinforce the impression that education is something which is done *to* children, rather than *with* them. This may merely reflect how teachers feel about the way they have been treated but it doesn't do anybody any favours. It not only increases the chances of pupil alienation, it is also a very inefficient way of trying to raise achievement.

We found that students from all backgrounds are shrewd observers of classroom life. They are able to remember and recount subtleties and nuances of classroom experience that would hold a par with, or even surpass, many professional researchers. In the appendix to this chapter you will find a model questionnaire which you can use or adapt to discover the favoured learning style of your pupils. But remember: don't bother to use it unless you intend to act on your findings.

It may be a good idea, depending upon the nature of the school, to add an ethnic variable to the questionnaire. Could it be that students from ethnic minority backgrounds differ in their preferred styles from white, indigenous students? We have no evidence from our own work that this is, or might be, the case. However, in Chapter 2 we referred to the idea that students from 'less academic' backgrounds, and boys in particular, are less willing to accept lessons which they view as 'boring', meaningless or which are always the same. Tony Sewell (in Epstein, 1998, p. 123) quotes a confrontation between a teacher and a 'rebellious' Afro-Caribbean Year 10 pupil:

Ms Kenyon: Calvin, will you shut up. I don't know why you come to my lessons because you're not interested in doing any work.

Calvin: I would do if you didn't give us rubbish work. Look around; half the class haven't got a clue what you're on about.

Ms Kenyon: And you have, have you?

Calvin: The lesson is boring, and so are you.

Some teachers would protest that they would not have got themselves into this position. The battle has already been lost, and there is probably very little that Ms Kenyon can do to remedy the situation. The point is that it need not have been like this. If Ms Kenyon and the rest of her colleagues had a clear idea about how to consult with students about learning styles, how to put their findings into practice, and if Calvin and his mates felt consulted about how they were going to learn, a very different atmosphere may have prevailed. Sewell's research of one school in London shows that the vast majority of Afro-Caribbean students value education, a large majority even value the goals of the school – but a majority also have doubts about the way in which schools are trying to achieve those goals.

The preferred learning styles of boys and girls

A great deal has been written about teaching and learning styles, but until recently there has not been much appreciation of the gender differences of preferred learning styles. We offer the list below based upon interviews and conversations with students in, mainly, one local education authority. We believe that it probably holds good for most pupils and students in the United Kingdom but we would encourage anyone who is interested to make use of the questionnaire in the appendix or, much better, design their own to suit the particular culture and language of their pupils.

Marx, stress, and teaching and learning

Much of what we say here is not new; most teachers, if pressed, could probably come up with a similar list. The difference is probably in its application. We have found that Karl Marx, stress management, and teaching and learning styles are linked in a negative fashion. 'The point', wrote Marx, 'is not just to understand the world but to change it.' Similarly, most people have a reasonable idea about the principles of preventing and managing stress. Yet they still work too hard, eat the wrong things, rest too little, exercise rarely and fail to love themselves. So it is with teaching and learning styles. Teachers are often aware that certain teaching styles are more popular with some groups rather than others, but frequently persist with the teaching style which most suits themselves, as teachers, in terms of familiarity and convenience, rather than ones which may be more appropriate to the class which has to learn. They may even persist with the style they most regularly experienced as pupils themselves. It is yet another example of the triumph of habit over thought.

Teaching styles to bring out the best in boys and girls

'I think girls do better because they like to copy from the blackboards and textbooks, whereas boys like to do all the practical work and work as a group.'

(Year 10 girl)

1 Keep it short, keep it sharp, keep it finite

Some boys are not patient creatures, and this often follows them into adulthood. Boys generally need short timespans of learning activities. Lessons which are split into distinct tasks are generally well received. Lessons should begin with very short, motivating, pacey sessions. Lessons and tasks which are split into short or lengthening spans of time, or can be seen to be completed after a discrete task, will generally find favour with boys. This has implications for the lesson itself and how the teacher is approaching the programme of study. We shall be discussing the peculiarities of each subject later in the book, but the breakdown of *Macbeth* to a table for each Act, as discussed above, is a good example. The syllabus is invigorated in the boy's mind by having regular milestones which can be reached and passed. Similarly, the history syllabus can be seen as modules – each one perhaps only lasting two weeks. The horizon is shortened and the work becomes manageable. This method also helps the teacher to develop a well-understood system of regular assessment, perhaps concentrating on a particular skill or set of skills within each module.

It is even more important to think about the nature of the lessons themselves. All lessons should have clear objectives which are known and understood by the students, even if it is a continuation of previously unfinished work. The short input from the teacher, and/or the whole class discussion on the issue at hand, could then set the scene for the activity(ies). The students should know that the activities are time or task limited. They should be aware of the structure of the lesson. A whole lesson on the same task, particularly if it is not obviously interesting, tends to distance all students from learning – but especially boys. If notes *have* to be taken then make these as short as possible, or encourage more creative forms of recording, such as spidergrams. Alternatively, encourage sociably paired working teams to tackle the task.

The end of the lesson should be linked to the learning objectives and can again be short, sharp and exciting. It could be competitive (see below), but it should also have the capacity of making – even forcing – the boys and girls to reflect on what they have learned. We shall be addressing the whole issue of reflection in Chapter 8.

2 Try to make it active

Boys tend to like practical work where they are involved in doing something which is not merely 'book learning'. There is a wide range of active learning strategies which can be used in all subjects. By 'active' we mean that boys like discussion, movement, competitiveness, quizzes, energisers, and – just as importantly – the anticipation of such activities. They have to *do* something to the learning – to demonstrate it or transform it. There is no reason why games, even physical games, cannot be incorporated into subjects sometimes characterised as being cerebral such as mathematics and modern foreign languages.

> 'We want to get on with our Technology and make things, but we can't straight away because you have to write about things. . . . We're always writing and copying off the board.'
>
> (Year 7 boy)

3 What about group work?

A survey of primary schools in Kirklees LEA revealed that there was actually very little proper group work being carried out in class. The fact that pupils were sitting in groups had led to the assumption that they were involved in group work. This was far from the case. It is a pity because boys tend to like group work, where they can collaborate with others or where different, interdependent tasks are allocated. We shall discuss the function of group work in Chapter 8. Suffice it to say that both boys and girls tend to enjoy it if it is appropriate to the learning objective of the lesson. Boys also enjoy working in pairs.

> 'I like it when you can work together in a group of four and help each other.'
>
> (Year 7 boy)

4 The place for competition

Whether boys are naturally competitive or whether it is bred into them is a hoary old chestnut which maintains its interest but not its relevance. Whatever the reason, boys do tend to enjoy competitive teaching strategies, but only if certain conditions can be satisfied. While they are willing to take a risk and get involved, they also need to know that they can protect their confidence against outright failure. They need to feel that they have a chance of winning or succeeding. If this chance is so slim that it is unlikely that they will succeed, they may withdraw from the competition. They are quite happy with group competitions. We shall be returning to this in Chapter 7, which deals with rewards and praise, particularly the idea of group reward and private, individual praise.

5 Oral tasks

Some boys tend to be less good at presenting their written work than girls and more confident in oral tasks. It is to their detriment, and to that of girls who often need encouragement in oral presentation, that the modern curriculum is biased towards the written word. Boys can often describe creative and original ideas in the oral form but struggle to do them justice on paper. Because present assessment techniques depend so much on the written word, teachers have tended quite naturally to place an equal emphasis upon it in the classroom, but for boys already struggling with literacy this can be confirmation that learning is not for them. A fresh look at the value of oracy, and rewarding its positive use, could bring some boys back into the learning orbit. Our evidence is that students delight in being able to talk in the classroom, and Jones (1988) argues that talk is a valuable tool of teaching and learning in primary schools, but is one which falls out of effective use on entrance to secondary school.

6 Information and communication technology

The new economy demands new kinds of thinking, dispositions to flex-ibility and innovativeness, new kinds of hand/eye/brain co-ordination in the visual analysis of quite extraordinary complexity. The new world of communication is vastly more diverse and demanding than that implied in the currently advocated, traditional literacy agendas. And it is, in some important ways, more aligned with what boys do after they hit the start button of their Playstation or computer.

(Kress, 1998, p. 5)

Boys like ICT. This has been accepted by the profession for some years and there is no reason to doubt its continuing veracity. The computer gives boys many of the things they like. It is practical and hands on; it gives instant results in the sense that graphics, DTP, tables, scanning in and other tricks are reasonably accessible with relatively little training. It is ironic that it is the girls who are getting the most out of the workplace revolution in IT. This is perhaps because girls bring different attitudes to it. They use it for set tasks within clear parameters. They use it in conjunc-tion with well-honed keyboard skills and allied to communication. Boys tend to use it in different ways – for creative, undisciplined purposes in which their flights of fancy are in reverse proportion to their keyboard skills. IT can be used creatively across the curriculum, but this is not always the evidence found in schools.

'I like to write on the computers instead of writing by hand.'

(Year 7 boy)

7 Audio-visual aids

'I like it because you have a variety of things you have to use.'

(Year 7 boy)

Pupils who make the transition to secondary schools are often amazed by the sheer volume of equipment at their disposal. Boys like the use of video, CD-ROM, film and slide in the classroom. Obviously, there is skill and danger in its use. Too many teachers have hidden behind the video as a substitute for teaching the class in an appropriate and active fashion. We are not arguing for video *per se* but as a means of stimulating ideas and understanding, as a catalyst for interactive work in groups, for revising the main learning points or for explaining visually those things which are difficult to teach merely by book and word.

8 Questionnaires and quizzes

Both boys and girls tend to like quizzes, particularly if they are not too long, have ability-appropriate language and have a discernible point to them. If they are phrased so that they are challenging or relevant to real or anticipated events in the students' lives, so much the better. Quizzes can be appealing to boys as they are competitive, and boys often enjoy attempting them in pairs or trios. It is important to ensure that the pairs or trios are engaged with the task, and thus the seating arrangements in the class are critical (see Chapter 8 on seating). Questionnaires exploring attitudes and values are very popular with boys, and the same technique could be used for review purposes at the end of a unit of study.

Conclusion

These are only some of the main findings about boys' and girls' preferred learning styles. Obviously there will be many who prefer other teaching styles. We really do believe that the teacher who takes the trouble to find out the learning preferences of pupils and acts upon the results will be vastly increasing his or her effectiveness and job satisfaction and ultimately decreasing the workload. It is not a question of supplying each individual in the class with differentiated tasks to suit their particular preferences, but to be aware of the general trends and within that offering a variety of teaching styles appropriate to the intended learning outcomes.

Using VEST

There is a lot to remember in this chapter and we have invented a memorable acronym to help. We remember our childhood vests as being warm, comforting and supportive. If teachers can make a habit of bringing the VEST described below into the classroom and applying it on a regular basis they may well find the educational vest has a similar feel to it.

V – variety

Teachers should think about varying their teaching style. It is so easy to get trapped into familiar, easy styles of teaching which require – as a result – less thought, effort or preparation. It would be interesting to ask the class, after a lesson or a unit of work, what they thought about the teaching methods. They might initially have little to tell you ('It wor dead boring, sir' is both deflating and of little use) but as they get used to the idea of the teacher as learner, and to become more experienced with a number of learning styles, they may give more specific, constructive feedback.

E – engagement

Boys tend to like to be involved in what they are doing. This may sound like a truism, but there are thousands of classrooms at any one time throughout the country in which the students are required to learn passively. They copy, they listen, they watch. In the next lesson they copy and listen; and in the next they watch and listen. If you doubt this, try tracking a pupil for a day, particularly in secondary schools. These are skills which we want our students to have, but one of the reasons why some are not very good at listening is that they get a huge diet of it, day after day. In kindergarten and Key Stage 1 it is recognised that pupils learn through play. Play is built into the curriculum, although parents are sometimes concerned when their child, when asked the question, reports that 'all we did today was play'. We are not suggesting a home corner for 15-year-olds but a recognition that engagement in the task, of active learning, of enjoyment, of challenge to succeed in a time-limited task is something which boys would welcome. Girls would welcome it too; they are just less likely to rebel against passive learning, but they need more active learning to help them in later academic life, and in their careers, when independent learning skills are vitally important. Other ways of ensuring that pupils are on task are the sharing or negotiation of lesson objectives, time-limited tasks, exercises relevant to students' lives outside school, producing something concrete, working for display, and preparation for a partner.

S – sociable learning

Despite all appearances to the contrary boys are sociable animals. This may sometimes take the appearance of being antisocial animals, but ironically, even when at their worst, boys could be said to be acting socially – within a group. There is some very convincing research that boys, more than girls, have a public and private persona. The private persona is often kept well hidden, even undiscovered, until maturity arrives with relationships and responsibilities. The teenage boy, in particular, relies heavily on the public persona and he gets affirmation and support in this from his male peer group. Boys' friendships tend to be wider, shallower and more relaxed than girls'. This is a characteristic which impinges upon teaching and learning. Boys like working in groups or in pairs. We suggest in Chapter 8, however, that boys should not always be allowed to work in friendship groups. Boys like working with others. This can be used positively if girls and boys work together, at least for a time, when they can learn from each others' strengths.

T – transforming the type of learning

Boys often like to enjoy changing the format in which information or analysis is contained. One example of transformation would be watching a video and making notes under sections indicated by the teacher. This is perhaps not the most popular transforming exercise for boys, who would probably prefer transforming to an oral report or even to a role-play. The important point, however, is that transformation takes place. Apart from the fact that boys and girls tend to enjoy the activity it forces boys to reflect on their learning and to show a partner, a teacher and themselves that they actually understand it. Studies suggest (e.g. Fitz-Gibbon, 1996) that work learned in this way is more effectively kept for recall. It is very difficult to transform information which is not understood, while keeping in the same medium can often result in copying or rote learning.

All these four parts of VEST are important although arguably the first, variety of teaching and learning, is central to the whole issue.

Box 3.1 The preferred learning style of boys

Risk-taking

Short, time-limited tasks

Challenge

Group work

Active learning

Sociable learning

Information and communication technology

Audio-visual aids

Quizzes

Try to use VEST

APPENDIX 3.1[1]

Teaching and learning questionnaire

This questionnaire is not intended to give scientific answers, but to help give the pupils and teacher control over the process of discovering how the class might like to learn together. You can adapt this questionnaire as you see fit, but it is recommended to avoid 'why' questions.

1   What was your favourite X (name of subject) lesson last term?
2   What was your least favourite X lesson?
3   Do you like working in groups?
4   What would be the ideal group?
5   In class, which are your favourite activities: reading, writing, speaking or listening?
6   Which text/aspect/topic we have studied have you most/least enjoyed?
7   What grades do you think you will achieve in your X GCSE?
8   When you get your work back, what do you look at to work out how well you have done?
9   Where do you keep your returned work?
10 Whose work is displayed outside the classroom?
11 Why are you studying X at GCSE?

The answers, and more importantly the classroom discussion which follows, can help to develop schemes of work and a more reflective approach to help boys – and girls – achieve.

Warning: There is no point in conducting the survey unless you feel you will be able to make use of the results!

1 Adapted from Maria Dengate's model at All Saints' School, York.

Chapter 4

How to organise a strategy to raise boys' achievement

Introduction

It is one thing to have a clear idea about the need for change in order to improve boys' achievement. That is a large step forward. It is even better to have strategies in mind, hopefully gained from this book as well as elsewhere. However, in many schools the most demanding challenge will be to introduce such strategies effectively, not because of the intransigence of the pupils but rather the resistance to change of the staff. We are aware that in the many lectures, talks and conferences we have given all over the United Kingdom about the raising of boys' achievement we are only beginning to scratch the surface. What happens after we leave is largely an unknown quantity, although in at least one LEA, where the lecture was received with great enthusiasm, nothing had changed a year later. The boys were still under-achieving and no one had taken on the responsibility of developing the ideas any further.

The careful management of change is a critical factor in planning the success of raising boys' achievement. In this chapter we will be marrying the general theory of how to bring about change in education, based on work by authors such as Fullan and West-Burnham, with the strategy which we have developed in Kirklees which is specifically geared towards raising boys' achievement.

The nature of change

There are a number of ways in which change can be brought about, perhaps encapsulated by the following continuum diagram:

Involve those affected	*Tell* those affected
1 Change attitudes	1 Change structure
2 Change behaviour	2 Change behaviour
3 Change structure	3 Change attitudes

Obviously, involving those affected – both teachers and pupils – is more democratic and participative, and is less likely to cause problems in the longer term. This is the path we favour: indeed it is hard to see that the other option would work at all, but it does mean that a great deal of hard work and planning is needed to change attitudes, which is the first objective. In this instance we are discussing changing the behaviour of staff, but the same principles are true of bringing about change within the student body.

Changing attitudes

It was once said that Japanese car manufacturers spent 90 per cent of the life cycle of any of their models planning and researching its concept, design and engineering and only 10 per cent actually making it. In contrast, the British car manufacturers were said to be the exact reverse of this. The results are well known. There is no evidence to suggest that the Japanese teams were female, but it would have helped our arguments in Chapter 3 about boys' preferred learning styles if they had been. It also throws into sharp focus the critical importance of properly planning for the raising of boys' achievement, and indeed for raising achievement overall.

The three-part strategy

In working closely with schools over the past few years on raising boys' achievement, we have been careful to avoid being over-prescriptive about the strategies which they should use. Schools, staff and pupils differ from place to place and you have to make up your own mind in the light of what they feel would work for you. However, where we have been very prescriptive is in insisting upon the adoption of the three-part strategy. Schools which have ignored it have invariably lost their way or have achieved far less than would otherwise have been the case. The three-part strategy consists of raising awareness, macro (whole school) policies and micro (classroom management) practices.

Part One: Raising awareness

Some commentators have argued that this is the only thing that schools need to do. Once everyone knows the issues they will automatically adjust their behaviour and the situation will have been effectively addressed. It shows a touching faith in human nature and cites the HIV/AIDS awareness campaign as an example of where this has worked. It conveniently forgets the plethora of other social and medical ills about which most of us are only too aware but in which behaviour has changed very little, such as smoking. We feel that much more has to be done to effectively raise achievement, but that raising awareness is an essential first step. If teachers, parents and the pupils themselves are unaware of the issues, they will be reluctant or puzzled participants in any of the macro or micro strategies we describe below. They may resent or even refuse to implement the changes you contemplate. It is axiomatic in the successful management of change that people have to recognise the need to change, and that the measures adopted by the institution are seen as clearly appropriate in bringing about effective change.

Raising awareness of teaching staff

Many teaching staff are already only too well aware that boys are an issue. It is boys who tend to be disruptive in lessons, boys who are more often excluded from school and boys who over-populate the least able sets. None the less, there is a job to be done with teachers in understanding boys as learners, how and why some under-achieve and what teachers can do about it. In short, teachers are too often concerned about boys' behaviour and need to think about them more in terms of achievement.

There are a number of ways in which this can be done. An examination of SATs and GCSE results by gender will, in most schools, throw up discrepancies of achievement. In an era when most teachers are aware of targets to be reached by the school, faculty and subject, the need to raise boys' achievement will soon become paramount. Otherwise schools will simply not reach the targets being set for them by the government and their local education authority: it is a matter of basic arithmetic. Teachers obviously also need to think carefully about the contribution they can make in raising the awareness of those around them – pupils, parents and colleagues – and challenge them to participate in the wider campaign to raise achievement. Teachers may need a course/seminar about the issue of raising boys' achievement. You could run some high-profile INSET as a way into the issue. This may be possible to arrange through the LEA, the local university or freelance trainers. Many smaller schools, or whole pyramids, have joined forces and financed a training day in order to achieve economies of scale.

Raising awareness of support staff

By 'support staff' we mean all those people who work in schools who are not teachers. They are often called 'non-teaching' staff, but this term is inappropriate. It seems odd to define someone's role by what they do not do (would teachers enjoy being called 'non-admin staff'?), and at the same time suggests that these staff have no role to play in learning. Classroom assistants, special needs assistants and some technicians are often directly involved in pupils' learning. Clerical staff, lunchtime supervisors, cleaners, caretakers and kitchen staff may have better relationships with some pupils than do the teachers – and have more meaningful conversations with them. Being local, some are often the mothers, aunts, grandmothers and neighbours of the pupils at the school. They all need to know what the problem is. It may be difficult, although not always impossible, to arrange an awareness-raising course for them so that a different way may be found. Leaflets which set out the problem in both national and school terms would be very useful. In primary schools insights could be given about the topics being taught and the sorts of conversations with the pupils which would reinforce classroom learning. In secondary schools they should be encouraged to talk to the boys about the world of work, the roles of men and how educational success and life after school are linked.

Raising awareness of parents

We believe that the involvement of parents is one of the keys to success in this whole question, as perhaps is the case with nearly all educational problems. It is particularly important in the **primary school**, which may be surprising to some as it is the primary school which generally enjoys much more parental support than the secondaries. However, a closer look at this support reveals that it is to some extent unsatisfactory and compounds the problem of boys' under-achievement. The vast majority of parents who work voluntarily in school are mothers, which is no bad thing in itself but underscores the lack of a male role model. Furthermore, there is ample evidence that parents tend to expect less from their sons until they reach secondary school, by which time it is often too late. After the age of 8, following the Key Stage 1 SATs, parents often spend less time reading to their children and hearing their children read. Boys are often not opposed when they choose to 'play out' rather than read a book. We are not advocating the incarceration of boys while parents force-feed them Enid Blyton – reading has to be seen as enjoyable and rewarding – but we are arguing for a balance which parents are well placed to provide. Parents need to be given much clearer guidelines about how they can help their children, not just with reading,[1] but also with writing, numbers and the application of these skills in other areas of the curriculum and in everyday life. The Level 2 reader, be it a girl or boy, with a hundred-word vocabulary is far from being secure in their skills. They need careful development and encouragement over the next four years.

---

1 *Paired Reading*, a video for parents giving them explicit instructions on how to read with their children, is available from Kirklees LEA, The Deighton Centre, Deighton Road, Huddersfield HD2 1JP, Tel. (01484) 225793.

In **secondary schools** much more could be made of engaging parents to raise achievement. It may not be clear to many parents that boys are presently under-achieving and, even when it is, they are not sure what to do about it other than to resort to rather bland appeals to 'work harder', 'revise' or 'do your homework'. Parents often feel disempowered and alienated from the curriculum. The subjects, with the possible exception of English, often seem to be too technical for parents to offer advice to their children. Parents would benefit from each department producing guidelines laying out how parents could help in raising achievement, particularly with boys who are generally less likely to apply themselves. The school, and the various departments, may also wish to consider how homework could be designed to encourage parents to contribute both to its management and completion. Some high schools have introduced a GCSE information evening for parents, with discussions about the gender gap and an emphasis among other things on the need to have high expectations of boys' effort and achievement. (See Appendix 4.2 at the end of this chapter of a sample leaflet used in one school.)

Raising awareness of governors and the wider school community

It is important that the governing body understands the problems which boys are presenting regarding achievement. It may well have to sanction changes in whole school policy as described below, approve various purchases related to the strategy and be able to respond to those parents who are concerned about the practices which the school introduces. Governors should be made aware of the issue through the annual discussion of the SATs and/or GCSE results, but the evidence that this happens is mixed. In some cases governors may wish to form a specific working party, be briefed by the head or an allotted teacher or include the issue regularly on the agenda.

It is useful to have a variety of awareness-raising activities over a period of time so that a rolling programme can be developed, keeping the issue at the forefront of thinking.

Part Two: Macro (whole school) policies

Following, or possibly running slightly behind, measures to raise awareness, the management of the school needs to implement strategic, whole school plans which are aimed at raising boys' achievement. Perhaps the first step should be to appoint a senior member of staff to co-ordinate and lead the strategy. He or she may wish to form a working party if there is sufficient interest from staff. Arguably, it is better to use existing structures such as heads of department, senior management or curriculum co-ordination meetings. This should ensure that the strategy is not marginalised. It may be better to use both avenues. Whatever the choice, the school needs to ensure that the initiative has clear and accountable leadership and management, and at the same time that everyone in the school sees it as *their* issue. This will be far more secure if staff have been actively involved in the discussions.

The anti-swot culture

In this chapter we will discuss one of the main problems confronting schools as they try to raise achievement – that of the anti-swot culture. In later chapters we shall deal with other macro strategy issues such as setting, the critical Years 4 and 8, role models, praise and reward, and working across the pyramid.

Combating the anti-swot culture

In Chapter 2 we suggested that the anti-swot culture should be treated in the same way as racism, that it should never be tolerated. The question is what to do about it.

Experience elsewhere of attempts to change attitudes suggests that success is far more likely if the message is positive rather than negative. Although there should be a 'zero tolerance' of anti-swot remarks in the classroom and school in general, school managers have to think about the culture they are trying to encourage. Research by the Institute of Education in London (1992) suggested that there are eleven characteristics of effective schools, and two of them are 'a learning environment' and 'a learning organisation'. What should a school do to make sure that it displays itself in this way? When asked why they are at school, only a minority of boys will volunteer the answer that they are there to learn. They will readily agree, if pressed, that it is one of their objectives, but it is not the first one that comes to mind. The need to behave, survive, obey the rules, because their parents make them, because it is the law, to avoid bullies, are all reasons volunteered before that of learning. It is the task of schools to make it very clear that the prime reason why pupils are in school is to learn, and that everything that supports that aim will be encouraged. Conversely, anything which detracts from that aim will be strongly discouraged. But this is not a diktat levelled at pupils and their parents by a teaching staff obsessed with government-inspired targets: this simply would not work. It is the responsibility of *all* – perhaps led by the senior management team – to make the school a learning organisation. Teachers have to be clear that they are continuing to learn: about their subject, about what works in the classroom, about preferred learning styles, about the pupils they teach. In addition, most schools correctly recognise that there are things worth learning which are not reflected in the National Curriculum and league tables.

In the second year of the *Raising Boys' Achievement* project in Kirklees, after the publication of the pack and video,[2] the schools decided that they would like to concentrate on portraying the school as a learning organis-ation and to tackle the anti-swot culture. The teachers wanted something concrete in the school which would help them to do this. It was decided to produce three high-quality leaflets – for parents, teachers and the boys themselves – which explained the problem boys have and introduced the Kolb learning cycle[3] as a model to follow. The three leaflets varied consid-erably in style; each was tested with the client group and consequently amended. In addition, a number of pro-learning posters, addressing the anti-swot issues, were designed and produced with the help of boys. Finally, a conference for boys was organised in which a special emphasis was put on how boys could challenge the anti-swot culture back in schools. This was an LEA-wide initiative but there is no reason why individual schools should not do something similar.

The principles of health promotion have an important point for any anti-swot strategy. Young people, like older people, respond much better to positive messages telling them what they can do and be than they do to negative exhortations to stop behaving in a way which we may regard as undesirable. Hence, although our purpose may be to eradicate the anti-swot culture from school, the path to our objective may lie more with the positive message of championing and modelling the learning school. This can be exemplified in display, in teachers promoting themselves as being open to learning from all sorts of experiences and in establishing a climate in which pupils are constantly encouraged to discuss what they have learned, rather than what they have not.

Part Three: Micro (classroom management) strategies

The final section of the three-part strategy, but in many ways the most difficult to implement, is that of classroom management, including the choice of teaching styles. These strategies can be adopted by whole depart-ments or year groups (which we generally recommend) or by individual teachers. In smaller primary schools the teachers in the whole key stage may wish to join the discussion if they are all to follow a certain strategy. The following are classroom management strategies which will be addressed in subsequent chapters:

2 *Raising Boys' Achievement* – a pack and accompanying video, one secondary, one primary, is available from Kirklees LEA, The Deighton Centre, Deighton Road, Huddersfield HD2 1JP, Tel. (01484) 225793.

3 A fuller explanation of Kolb's learning cycle and its application to raising boys' achieve-ment can be found in Appendix 4.1 on page 45.

- seating policy
- managing risk-taking behaviour
- peer work and peer tutoring
- role models
- lesson planning and feedback.

None of these strategies should be adopted in isolation from that of the school as a whole, nor before the school has implemented plans to raise the awareness of pupils, parents, staff and governors. In many schools, departments or year groups have decided that they would like to trial some of the ideas. This is likely to be more successful than the isolated teacher striking out on his or her own, unsupported by colleagues, misunderstood by parents and finding it difficult to justify individual behaviour.

Supporting the strategy through monitoring the process

Evaluation is not easy. It is particularly difficult in education when there are so many other variables at play. An obvious form of evaluation is through an analysis of exam results. After all, the whole point about the project is that it is intended to raise boys' achievement. However, there are some important milestones to be passed before that stage is reached. If evaluation comes only at the end of what may be a three-year strategy, and you have not succeeded, what do you do? Will you know what has gone wrong? Table 4.1 offers some questions which you may like to consider, with suggested timespans from the start of the strategy together with methods of gathering the data.

Table 4.1 Supporting and monitoring the strategy

Action and key questions	Time	Who involved
1 Do you have a clearly written strategy which all staff and governors have been involved in/briefed on? Do you know *your* boys? Are you aware of how *your* boys are performing in school? Are they performing in line with expectations?: look at input data like NFER tests or SATs. Are you aware how *your* boys are responding to schooling? Have you obtained data about level of involvement in school activities or pastoral problems? Where are the successful boys in your school? Are pupils/students aware of the issue of boys' under-achievement?	After 3 months	By staff meeting By pupil questionnaire or form tutorials

Action and key questions	Time	Who involved
2 Are parents aware of the issues?	After 3 months	By meetings By newsletters By homework-diary/planner By parental questionnaire
3 Have you set in place a management structure of the strategy which staff recognise? Are systems in place in the school which ensure the embedding of the strategies and addressing of the issue in 'normal' school life?	After 3 months After 1 year After 18 months	By meetings By professional interviews or appraisal
4 Have the macro strategies in school got clear leadership and SMART (specific, measurable, achievable, relevant and time-limited) targets?	After 3 months After 1 year After 2 years	By discussion By whole staff discussion
5 Have the micro strategies received sufficient encouragement and support from school management? What is being learned from early trials? Has there been any observation of micro strategies in operation? Have teachers watched each other in these strategies and fed back their observations?	After 3 months After 6 months After 9 months, etc. Every 3 months	Discussion with heads of department Teachers observe good practice Discussion with teachers (they have to know that the SMT really cares about what they are doing)
6 Have you established some sort of baseline for assessing progress, such as: • boys' (and girls') enjoyment of school • enjoyment of specific subjects (could be controversial!) • attendance • parental attitude to school • number of boys/girls reported for behavioural reasons • number of boys/girls recommended for effort rewards • punctuality in lessons • SATs results (tied to CATs scores – in secondary schools) • GCSE results (as above)?	After 3 months Then yearly	By questionnaire By examination of school records By listening to pupils

Obviously there is much more to do in terms of monitoring and evaluation than this. The strategy itself should have in place performance indicators and evaluation methods. The purpose of Table 4.1 is to act as a checklist for management, and as an encouragement to support the strategy and the colleagues implementing it.

> ### Box 4.1 Managing the process of raising boys' achievement
>
> #### The three-part strategy
>
> 1   Raise awareness of:
>   - teaching staff
>   - support staff
>   - pupils and parents
>   - governors
>   - the wider community.
>
> 2   Adopt some macro strategies:
>   - promote the school as a learning organisation
>   - address the magic number 8
>   - examine the effects of ability grouping
>   - introduce mentoring
>   - praise and reward system
>   - role models
>   - target-setting.
>
> 3   Micro strategies:
>   e.g. seating, group work, active learning, managing risk-taking, short-term goals, lesson plans, ICT.
>
> Checklist in place for monitoring the strategy.

Kolb's learning cycle

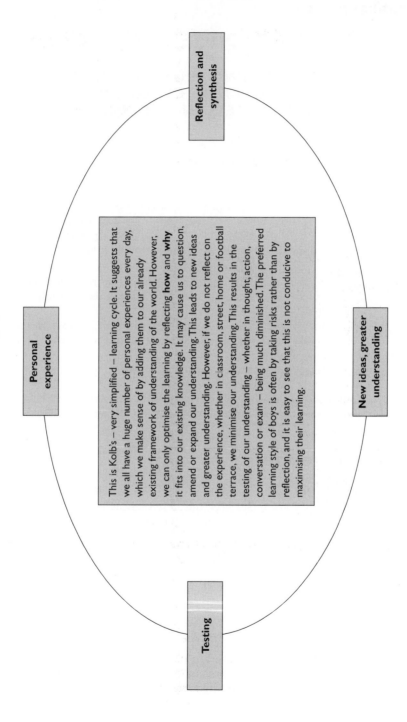

Personal experience

Reflection and synthesis

New ideas, greater understanding

Testing

This is Kolb's – very simplified – learning cycle. It suggests that we all have a huge number of personal experiences every day, which we make sense of by adding them to our already existing framework of understanding of the world. However, we can only optimise the learning by reflecting **how** and **why** it fits into our existing knowledge. It may cause us to question, amend or expand our understanding. This leads to new ideas and greater understanding. However, if we do not reflect on the experience, whether in classroom, street, home or football terrace, we minimise our understanding. This results in the testing of our understanding – whether in thought, action, conversation or exam – being much diminished. The preferred learning style of boys is often by taking risks rather than by reflection, and it is easy to see that this is not conducive to maximising their learning.

APPENDIX 4.2

ST GEORGE'S SCHOOL

– AIMING HIGH IN 1999 –
GETTING CLUED UP
FOR SUCCESS IN EXAMINATIONS

STRATEGIES FOR SUPPORT . . .

Sometimes just *wanting* to offer your son or daughter help with their studies may not seem enough – especially if all you get in response is a grunt or a shrug! The following practical ideas may seem simple but could have a powerful influence on your child's learning over the coming months. We shall be emphasising similar points in school; we hope you will be able to adopt some of these ideas at home.

- Suggest the good sense of dividing work into small, manageable sections. Encourage your child to say in advance what they will achieve in the next half-hour, or next forty minutes.
- Even if it has changed greatly since you were at school, get your son or daughter to tell you what they have been learning. That is a very powerful way of re-inforcing their own learning.
- Offer challenges to test them: 'Right, you've got five minutes to tell me all you know about . . .' or 'Give me five uses for . . .'.
- Be direct and specific to your child with points of praise and concern. This helps to avoid giving the impression that you are just 'generally moaning'.

WORKING TOGETHER . . .

The next few months will need everyone to pull together to give
your son or daughter the best chances of success in
the summer.

Of course, it is the students of Year 11 who have to do the work,
but they will benefit greatly from our joint support –
as teachers and parents.

Much progress can often be made in a short time.
Children keep developing.
There is no reason for your son or daughter to think they have
become as bright as they ever will be!

Please contact school if there are particular issues you wish to discuss,
or where you feel your child has a concern they have been
reluctant to mention.

- Offer *small*, short-term rewards to encourage motivation (a McDonald's at the weekend rather than a new bike after the examinations!).
- Make an arrangement, with your child's best friend and their family, to 'swap children' for a chat. Talk about how work is going and offer encouragement. Sometimes it's good to hear it from another source!
- Have clear guidelines for watching television, playing computer games, going out with friends and (if it hasn't already been postponed for the next few months) weekend and evening paid employment.
- Help your child to stay fit and healthy by having sufficient sleep and by keeping sensible hours. It is important, too, to have some relaxation and recreation – but the balance between study and play needs to be carefully thought out.
- Keep in mind the targets set by your child in school. They are achievable.
- Try not to allow your own concern as a parent that your child should do well to become an additional burden which he or she must carry on top of their studies.

AND WHEN IT COMES TO REVISION . . .

- By Easter your son or daughter should have planned a revision time-table, which should be pinned up – and used.
- It is important that progress through the plan is marked so that your child really feels they are getting somewhere. It is also easier to stick to the plan if everyone in the house knows about it.
- Another reason why a plan is useful is that it is important not to peak too soon. A plan can help young people reach their best just when they need to.
- Sensible use of time will be particularly important after the school leaving date in May. Your child will suddenly have all day and evening available. What are they going to do with it? It is important that they structure it well. The following points may be helpful:

    - Short bursts of revision – up to forty minutes – with small breaks are better for keeping learning fresh in the mind than long periods of concentrated study.
    - Encourage the use of the first few minutes of any session to recap. Without looking at any notes, your child should try answering the question 'What did I learn last time?'
    - Encourage your child to plan a small reward for when they achieve a set goal.
    - Remind them to study the meaning of words and phrases used in examination papers, such as 'Explain', 'Comment upon', 'Discuss', 'Factorise' and 'Evaluate'. Encourage them to study what specific questions are asked.

- Encourage them to be creative in finding different ways to revise. Revision should stay challenging and stimulating. Here are some examples:

    - 'Summarise the topic using ten key words . . .', 'The six things I will remember about this topic forever are . . .'.
    - Make 'spider diagrams' summarising the key points of a topic and the links between them.

- Work with a pen or pencil in the hand and some rough paper or a note-book to jot down new ideas at once.
- The formula 'Study it, cover it, summarise it and check it' can be useful.

• Talking is important – to the mirror, to the family cat, to anyone who will listen! Working with a friend of similar ability can be very helpful. Have them take it in turns to take the role of tutor. *Acting as the tutor and having to explain things to someone else makes for very effective learning.*

Chapter 5

One school's story[1]

It's not what you do, it's the way that you do it ... that's what gets results.

In this chapter I will describe and explain how one school, in a family of schools, set about trying to improve the achievement of boys, the successes we have had so far and the lessons we have learned that might be useful to other groups of teachers faced with similar challenges. In all this I am aware that the job is only part way through, that there is much more to be learned and that we will no doubt be surprised in the subsequent stages of our journey by the twists and turns of fortune that working with human beings in an inexact science can bring. The art of success in school improvement is to employ the canny, hard-won pragmatism of teachers in the face of the wild-eyed certainty of the advocates of short-term quick fixes. I would therefore recommend that the readers of this chapter should be quite prepared to reject the lessons it purports to commend in favour of the lessons you yourselves have learned in the context of your own situation. It is in this spirit that the insights below are offered.

Shelley High School is a large, some would say successful, 13–18 comprehensive school set in a rural area to the south of Huddersfield. It benefits, so the prospectus says, 'from the solid and deep roots of a rural West Yorkshire Community'. The culture of the area brings undoubted plus points to the school: belief in the value of education; strong traditions in music and sport; and home environments that are generally stable and supportive. There are also drawbacks, including a very traditional gender culture, in an area where until relatively recently a far greater proportion of boys than girls continued their education post-16, and stereotypes stubbornly survive of men putting their feet up while the women in the house look after them. A significant proportion of our Year 10 boys

1 This chapter has been written by Pat Jones, Headteacher of Shelley High School, near Huddersfield.

volunteering to do reception duty at the school have to be shown how to wash up the visitors' cups.

It was against this backdrop that our earlier work on gender was undertaken. A policy for equal opportunities was developed in 1988, the main thrust of which aimed to ensure that girls had the same opportunities as boys in the school and were encouraged to see education as a lifelong journey, rather than a staging point before domestic duties took over.

In 1988 the achievement of girls in educational terms at the school was broadly on a par with that of the boys. The boys were generally achieving more strongly in maths, science and technology, but the girls made up the ground in their achievement in the arts, languages, English and humanities. The staying-on rate for boys post-16 was significantly greater than that of the girls both locally and in Shelley High.

During the following few years and into the mid-1990s the climate changed nationally, locally and within the school. Equal numbers of boys and girls were staying on in our sixth form, which had doubled in size. The increasingly sophisticated analyses of our examination results provided by the local authority revealed a pattern of significant improvement in girls' exam results which exceeded the improvement of the boys. In particular the girls had maintained their strong lead in the English/arts/humanities/languages axis while equalling the boys point for point in maths and science (though still lagging behind in technology).

In 1995 we first became acutely aware that it was boys who now seemed to be having serious problems with their schooling, when a 21-point gap between the achievement of boys and girls in the 5+ A–C range was revealed as compared with a rolling average of an 11-point gap in the three previous years. At the same time an increasing number of articles and research findings were emerging nationally which gave consistent enough messages to claim our attention and confirm our own impressions.

The tradition in the school has not been to jump on all the passing bandwagons of educational fashion, but rather to research and develop our own priorities for development, having due regard for national and local developments. Every year in the second part of the summer term all the working teams in the school undertake a review in which they reflect on their progress during the year, set their own priorities for the following year and make suggestions for the whole school priorities. Ideas in these reviews often originate from the personal reviews conducted by group leaders earlier in the summer term.

The reviews are submitted to the school development planning team in July as a basis for the whole school plan, developed and published in the autumn term. In theory the whole school plan should therefore reflect the thoughts, concerns and priorities of all the members of the professional community in the school. The whole school planning team also does its best to take on board necessary legislative requirements of central government and priorities suggested by the local authority in its own planning.

We will not necessarily have as our central concerns the priorities of groups outside the school. In the autumn of 1998, for example, we had to take account of whole school target-setting as dictated by central government, without a shred of substantial evidence that setting whole nation, whole LEA or whole school targets in itself would lead to a rise in standards. We will not therefore do anything else other than carry out our legal obligation for whole school target-setting as professionally as possible. But we *do* see a value in target-setting for individual pupils based on good assessment information and the individual teacher's or tutor's recognition of what each pupil must do to achieve. We have been developing strategies in this area for the past three years. We know it is working. We will not be shaken off course by hasty and unresearched political judgements.

It was therefore the gathering of working group priorities from the whole school review of 1995–96 that stimulated the concerted whole school push in the area of improving boys' achievement signalled in the 1996 plan. The commitment of the staff for that priority has been an essential ingredient in any success we have had so far. Furthermore, we would always wish to carry out further research into the particularities and nuances of the problem of under-achieving boys before proposing what ingredients should make up any whole school strategy. This called for a further period of research, discussion and policy development that characterises our approach to a major whole school priority at Shelley High.

Any major whole school priority generally involves a four-year timescale. The watchword, in a school regarded locally as very successful, is 'change with care'. We have to discover exactly what is broken and precisely what we need to do to put it right before we try to fix it. Fixing it takes time, sustained concentration and resources. The broad pattern is given in Figure 5.1.

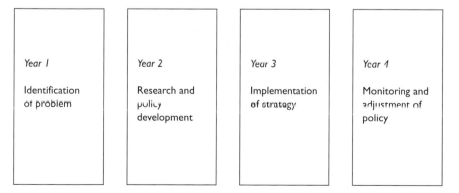

Year 1	Year 2	Year 3	Year 4
Identification of problem	Research and policy development	Implementation of strategy	Monitoring and adjustment of policy

Figure 5.1 The four-year planning strategy.

Having identified the priority in the summer of 1996, the following school year was devoted to further research and to the development of a policy to improve the achievement of boys. The ideal group to take this on board at Shelley High was the teaching and learning group, which had been in existence since 1988 and since that time had carried out a great deal of work on the development, improvement and sharing of best practice in the classroom. It had the added advantage of being a cross-curricular group in membership, led by a teacher with a particular interest in the area of boys' achievement. The research undertaken by this group was supported by senior managers in focusing on the area of boys' achievement in any lesson visits that year, and by the work of the headteacher with the new intake, described below.

INSET monies were targeted on the topic during 1996–97 and a number of teachers attended local and national courses. The teaching and learning group carried out its own researches which included classroom observation and discussions with groups of pupils. Initial discussion papers were distributed at the curricular committee and from there to teaching departments. From that time, the sharper outlines of the policy and associated strategies to be adopted whole school were beginning to emerge. It was a time for raising whole community consciousness about the issue – something that in itself seems to lead to progress. It is as if the very act of the concerted consideration of a problem can lead to some improvement even before precise strategies are agreed.

Pupils at the school were alerted to the priority and involved in the development of the policy at an early stage. In September 1996 the head led a special session on boys' achievement with all classes in that year's Year 9 new intake. A recent video was shown and the pupils were asked to contribute ideas as to why some boys seemed to be more prone to under-achievement than girls and what they would suggest we should do to tackle the problem. The ideas from all the different groups were collected and subsequently published in the school's daily bulletin as a topic for discussion. It is uncanny to reflect how many of these ideas from ordinary 13-year-old pupils reappear in our own, local and national policy statements on this topic. The session has been repeated every year since then. The bulletin item (in the form of a 'Pause for Thought', which is our daily masquerade for an act of collective worship) is reprinted in full below.

> Year 9 pupils have all taken part in a session with Mr Jones in which they have investigated and discussed the reason why in England, Kirklees and Shelley High, some boys seem to fall short of their academic potential. In the past we estimate that two out of ten boys here have not done anywhere near as well in their GCSE exams as they could have. Some girls also underachieve, but not as many.

Below are the ideas put forward by Year 9 English classes after the session with Mr Jones about the reason why some boys tend to under-achieve and what we could do about it. There are a lot of commonsense ideas here for us all to think about.

Reasons why some boys under-achieve

- Some boys get their priorities wrong and give in to temptation;
- Some boys don't think and plan ahead enough – they live for today;
- Some boys can have a shorter concentration span;
- Some boys don't always listen to and take advice;
- Some boys mature later than girls;
- Some boys have a culture where it is not 'cool' to work hard in class and at home;
- Parents are better able to motivate girls as compared to boys;
- Some boys like to show off and joke in lessons to get some kind of status;
- Some boys get easily put off and give up when they find something difficult;
- Some school tasks are too long for boys – they can't see an end to it.

Approaches we could take at Shelley High to improve achievement of boys (and others)

- Encourage career planning at an early stage – careers interviews in Year 9;
- Make sure the boys have goals;
- Give them a talk by well-known young men who have made a success of life;
- Teachers could plan shorter tasks in class and give quick assessments;
- Make the lads sit next to well-motivated girls who would sort them out and set a good example;
- Some teachers could use humour more to make the lesson interesting;
- More practical and varied tasks in lessons would help keep boys interested;
- Teach them to listen and concentrate at an early stage;
- Give boys who underachieve a lot of advice and help. This is better than punishment;
- Make boys realise the value of hard work and good qualifications;
- Use more computers in lessons – boys react well to computers;

- Have a clear structure for everything so we can all see where we are going;
- Use classroom helpers like 6th Formers or Special Needs teachers;
- Make sure everyone knows about it when boys do well;
- Get their girlfriends to make them see sense.

These ideas from the pupils themselves, firmed up by insights from the teaching and learning group and initial reactions from departments, led to the development of our whole school policy, proposed, refined and finalised by the Curriculum and Pastoral Executive Committees in the summer of 1997. It was interesting to note that in the GCSE results published in August that year the gap between boys and girls halved. Was this coincidence or had our concentration on this area affected even the old lags in Year 11?

For the next policy implementation phase in 1997–98, departments were all asked to concentrate specifically on applying the policy to their areas, picking particular strategies from the menu of offered suggestions and developing their own. They would also be asked to incorporate a statement about their particular approach to improving boys' achievement in any future update of their policy documents.

The strategy was launched within the school, but we were aware we also had to think more widely. This was as much a whole community problem as it was a school problem, and any approach which confined itself merely to in-school strategies was only going to be partially successful.

It was clear that the first priority should be to enlist the support of schools within our pyramid for the initiative. During 1997–98 the issue was thoroughly aired at the half-termly meetings of headteachers in the pyramid. Several of the schools were already working on the topic, having detected problems with the achievement of boys in their own assessments at KS1 and KS2. Both middle schools were very interested in looking at the issue. Following an exchange of information and best practice, staff from the teaching and learning group were invited to talk with the middle schools which were beginning to develop their own particular approaches to the issue.

The first schools pinpointed Year 4 as the stage when it appeared that the achievement of boys seemed to stall, whereas the girls began to take off. In particular, the Year 4 boys seemed to lose interest in reading at this stage and all-round progress slowed down as a result. Among other strategies to try to counter this fall-off, we set up a special evening for all parents of Year 4 to promote reading – without overtly signalling this as an evening about boys' achievement. The heads of all seventeen schools attended. The response from parents was very encouraging and, judging by the book sales following the series of talks and readings, the message had got through. This evening was repeated in 1998 with similar success and will become part of our strategy for at least the next few years.

We became convinced that the consciousness of parents about the achievement of boys needed to be raised and that they could make an important contribution to resolving the problem. A substantial article on boys' achievement was written in our monthly newsletter and in the education column of our local newspaper. This was followed up at our GCSE information evening for Year 10 parents, introduced in 1996 to make parents aware of how they could help their children to succeed in GCSE. Again, this was not overtly signalled as an evening about boys' achievement, but the topic was carefully woven into all aspects of the evening. It was clear from responses at the meeting that parents were aware that there *was* an issue. We tried to put across ways in which they can encourage and support *all* their children to make the most of their opportunities and maximise achievement.

Part of the information given out was a grid of all the dates and deadlines for coursework, assessments and major projects in all subjects. The parents found this to be the single most useful aspect of the evening. As one put it: 'I now know that from now on he can *never* say to me he's got no homework tonight.'

After so much activity in the 1997–98 school year we were very relieved to find that the gap between the performance of girls and boys in the 5+ A*– C category, reduced to six percentage points in 1997, was further reduced to five points in 1998. We must now look to, at the very least, maintaining this diminution, and perhaps at best continuing to close the gap while both genders continue to move forward.

As I write this chapter in the autumn of 1998, we are entering the monitoring phase for our policy on improving boys' achievement. We shall be looking at the particular strategies that departments are using and further sharing best practice. The teaching and learning group has continued its investigations with some INSET-sponsored classroom research. All departments will discuss the gender and value-added statistics in the GCSE results provided in October by the local education authority, and further refinement of the strategy will result. We will be having a more careful look at the work of the departments where boys continue to be heavily outperformed by girls, as evidenced by the residual GCSE results. The issue will be kept alive for at least another year.

We cannot, however, sustain the same level of concentration on the topic. Other priorities jostle for attention and demand the kind of sustained push that has led to at least initial success in improving boys' achievement. One of the areas of concern thrown up by our work on boys' achievement will, however, be taken forward. It became clear in our discussions with the pyramid schools in 1997–98 that literacy was a key area in which some boys had fallen behind. This has been reinforced by the gender-based analyses of the KS1, 2 and 3 results in English. The improvement of English has been identified in the 1998 School Review as a key priority for the next three years and a working party is now researching the topic and will present ideas for a strategy later in 1999. We have already had a joint INSET day with our two middle schools on the topic which has resulted in a pamphlet of practical ideas for improving literacy across the curriculum and age range. Without signalling that this is a 'boys only' topic, it is clear that boys will stand to benefit most from any developments and improvements we can achieve. You could say that we haven't finished the topic of boys' achievement – we are just looking at it from another angle. Other angles will no doubt present themselves in our continuing attempts to inch the school forward, year by year.

The approaches described above have in the main been effective at Shelley High. I doubt if they would succeed if transplanted wholesale to a different school in a different context, though there are no doubt individual bits and pieces that can be successfully lifted. The general messages derived from our approach may well apply more widely and could be used when others try to shape their individual strategies to the problem of improving boys' achievement – and indeed other whole school issues.

Decide your own priorities

After two decades of imposed reform it is important that teachers should regain control of their own professional lives and work. Teachers are becoming immune to reform by central diktat. They need to be re-engaged in the examination of the priorities most relevant and urgent to the context in which they are working. Heads and governors looking for substantial progress on the important issues for their schools need to ensure that the professional community of teachers within those schools are able to combine an overview of national developments with a clear insight into the strengths and weaknesses of their own schools, so that they can decide and work on the priorities that will be of most benefit to the children in their school. This means that the issue of boys' achievement might not necessarily be the chosen area for development this year or next year. As and when the issue does emerge it will be more effectively dealt with, and progress made more swiftly, if teachers have ownership of the process. Put another way, the most serious setback to improving the achievement of boys would be if the government of the day were to choose to set gender-based targets for each school to achieve.

Base your strategies on your own classroom research

Following on from the above, it is equally important that each school carries out its own investigation into the problem being addressed. In the case of improving boys' achievement, classroom observation, a study of pupil interests, interviews with groups of boys and examination of learning materials could all play a part. So many central policies are set without substantial research to justify what is being done. There is no more obvious example of this than the government forcing the issue of reading in the early years when there is so much evidence of the harm this approach can do. We must ensure that any work of our own does not fall into the same trap.

Target resources in the area

Our work on boys' achievement involved substantial INSET support – to enable teachers to take part in classroom research, to encourage attendance at external INSET and to give time and space for smaller groups of teachers to put the policy and strategies together. No major development should take place in a school without proper funds being allocated.

Plan over time

The four-year approach to major developments at Shelley High may seem long-winded, but any matters of real importance need time to be carefully examined and discussed, an announced implementation period and careful subsequent monitoring. You cannot do this in under two years.

Involve the whole community

The work on boys' achievement at Shelley High quickly broadened from an issue identified by the professional community of teachers to one that was explained and discussed by the other schools within the family, by parents, pupils and the local community. Not only did this raise the profile of the development and signal its importance, but the contributions of parents, teachers and pupils in other schools helped to shape the agreed strategies.

A continuous seam of developments

Teachers and pupils are rightly suspicious of the 'big-bang' approach to development. Successful ideas for progress do not come out of the blue; they are invariably an organic part of a continuous process of development. Our work on boys' achievement emerged from a careful look at our exam results at KS3 and 4 at a time when the results seemed to have reached a plateau. The boys' achievement initiative will now be ongoing in that certain aspects have woven themselves permanently into the life and work of the school. The initiative on literacy launched this year is a logical development which has arisen naturally from our work on boys' achievement. Teachers and the community as a whole can see the logic behind a natural sequence of developments rather than a crashing gear change as the head attempts to steer the school down yet another side road.

It's not what you do . . .

Above all, to achieve successful change in any important matter, we all need to pay much more attention to the *process* of change rather than its end product – which brings me back to the wisdom of the old song in this chapter's epigraph. I am convinced that the vast majority of our teachers in Britain are at heart altruistic professionals, whose main satisfaction derives from helping the pupils in their care to develop, to learn and to improve their achievement. The school which recognises this and builds the re-empowerment of teachers into its strategy for improvement will reap the benefits.

Chapter 6

Making decisions about setting

As mixed ability teaching is known to reduce the chances of discrimination, the burden of proof that ability grouping is preferable must lie with those who claim that it raises achievement. Despite the wide range of research studies in this area, this proof has not been forthcoming.

(Boaler, 1996)

All classes are mixed ability classes.

(Jones, 1988)

Introduction

This chapter is again about getting it right for both boys and girls. Setting affects the learning and self-esteem of both. What is disturbing is that so many bottom sets contain a disproportionate number of boys, and also pupils from some minority ethnic groups. Just take a look at any English and modern foreign languages sets. Look at your own school.

There are few topics more controversial in education than the way in which students are grouped. Setting, streaming and mixed ability all have their champions and opponents. The basic argument in this chapter is that any system can be made to work, but to do so it needs two things: (1) the whole-hearted support of the staff who have to work within it; and (2) an appreciation of its weaknesses, and a determination to address them. There is no perfect system of grouping which will deliver to schools everything they may wish. In the existing climate of demanding instant results from schools, some headteachers have reinforced the setting system in secondary schools, and primary colleagues are introducing it in increasing numbers. The research evidence is that setting, particularly tight setting, may well penalise the very students schools need to succeed if school-based targets are to be met. However, it need not be this way if schools tell themselves, and their communities, that setting is not a panacea but that they know how to address the flaws.

How to use this chapter

We begin with some background research about the effects of setting and then move on to give suggestions for managing setting (or non-setting) policies in the school. The background is important if you are to have a firm grasp of the issues and if you are to convince others that your decisions are based on a sound understanding.

Background to the debate

In the 1950s students were separated by ability, or supposedly so, both within and between schools throughout Britain. The 1967 Plowden Report recommended the abolition of ability grouping in primary schools, as high-profile research showed a clear link between streaming and working-class under-achievement in the secondary sector. As a result the 1970s and 1980s saw a growth of mixed ability grouping. The 1990s have seen a significant return to ability grouping, particularly fine setting – typically with a hierarchy of groups numbered, for example, from 1 to 6.

Schools' response to the new age of open information

External requirements emerging from the Education Reform Act 1988 – such as SATs and tiered entry for GCSE – have tended to dominate reasons for adopting certain patterns of student grouping. In general, the response to external change has been to increase setting. Now that the external environment is more stable, it is a good time to consider the learning and social implications of the patterns of student grouping which have been adopted for students in your school. League tables have encouraged schools to focus on those pupils capable of obtaining the national expectation of Levels 2 and 4 at the end of the primary key stages, and 5 or more A*– C passes at GCSE. This has led to a growth of setting through a widespread belief that it enhances achievement for high ability students. Open enrolment has encouraged some schools to adopt patterns of grouping which they feel that parents, especially middle-class parents, want to see; this often means more setting. Setting is becoming increasingly common in primary schools and the results superficially suggest that it may have worked. The 1997 SATs, particularly at Key Stage 2, showed some significant improvements. That this often coincided with the introduction of setting is evidence enough for some schools that setting raises achievement. However, there is little doubt that other factors came into play. The realisation that they are also in the league tables strongly affected many primary heads in 1996, and they and their teachers were more thoroughly geared to preparing their children for SATs in 1997. There is no firm evidence that children in setted schools did any better than those in the non-setted.

In 1993, the National Curriculum Council and the DfEE (Circular 16/93) explicitly encouraged primary schools to introduce or reintroduce setting. In 1997, the White Paper, *Excellence in schools*, advanced the presumption that setting will be the norm, at least in secondary schools, but there is also the important view that teachers will be expected to develop further, innovative approaches to grouping. Certainly it is noted that 'no single model of grouping pupils should be imposed on secondary schools' (DfEE, 1997, p. 39, para. 3).

What is clear, in the apparent reversal of thinking concerning the grouping of students by ability, is that there has been no attempt to argue against the powerful research of the 1960s which outlined the detrimental effects of setting and streaming on educational equality. Rather, attention has moved away from equality towards academic success, particularly for the most able.

For the purposes of this discussion the equality issue relates to gender, although it obviously interacts powerfully with other aspects of stratification such as class and ethnicity. Just as in the 1960s it was noted that, through setting, working-class students sink to the bottom, so in the 1990s research shows that, through certain kinds of setting, boys sink to the bottom, realising they are probably there to stay, with their subsequent behaviour, motivation and achievement reflecting that realisation.

Table 6.1 outlines the advantages and disadvantages of setting by ability; the preponderance of advantage from setting accrues to the teacher, whereas most of the disadvantage affects the pupil.

It is not often appreciated that there is *no British-based research evidence supporting the idea that setting advances achievement*, particularly for high ability students. There have been a number of international reviews of the literature on grouping pupils by ability.

1 Slavin: setting does not affect achievement

Slavin (1990) produced a review of all the research that contrasted setted or streamed ability grouping with mixed ability grouping. Across the twenty-nine studies included in the review, Slavin found that the effect of ability grouping on achievement was, statistically, indistinguishable from zero for students of all abilities in all subjects. Slavin's study included four British-based pieces of research and these showed no difference in achievement between ability grouped and non-ability grouped classes.

2 Linchevski: setting does affect achievement – negatively

A recent piece of research conducted in Israel (Linchevski, 1995) compared the achievements of two groups of students at the same school assigned either to setted or mixed ability classes. This showed that the average scores

Table 6.1 Suggested advantages and disadvantages of grouping pupils by ability

Advantages of setting	Disadvantages of setting
Students make progress which fits their abilities.	Less able pupils need the presence of more advanced students to stimulate and encourage them.
Learning strategies can be adapted to the needs of the group.	A stigma is attached to being in a low set, which has a negative effect on motivation.
Interest and motivation are maintained as high ability students are not held back by those of lower ability.	Most teachers do not like teaching the bottom sets.
Slower pupils participate more when not eclipsed by those who are much brighter.	Ability grouping discriminates against pupils from ethnic minorities and lower socio-economic groups.
Teaching is easier.	Pupils in the lower streams or sets tend to receive instruction at a slower pace and of an inferior quality than pupils in higher sets. They get less than their fair share of good book resources, rooms and teachers.
Individual or small group instruction for the less able becomes possible.	The accurate and fair placement of children into ability groups is difficult. Often a difference of one mark between two students will lead to a future of very different learning experiences.
	Setting can be an excuse for ignoring the need for differentiation *within* a setted group.
	Once ability groups are established, movement between groups is limited, both for practical reasons and because the self-fulfilling prophecy takes root.

of the most able students placed in setted groups were slightly, but not significantly, higher than the able students placed in mixed ability groupings. However, the scores of students in the two lower setted groups were significantly lower than similar ability students in the mixed ability classes. Linchevski found that low ability students in the mixed ability classes coped well with tests because they were used to high demands and expectations.

3 Boaler: setting does not raise achievement but penalises the very pupils in most need of help

Most recently, publication of a summary of a three-year study by Boaler (1996) has stimulated a debate on these issues in the *Times Educational Supplement*. Boaler concludes:

> There was no qualitative or quantitative evidence that setting raised achievement, but there was evidence that setting diminished achievement for some students. . . . There was much evidence that the students who were disadvantaged by this system were predominantly working class, female or very able. . . . It seems fair to assume that if a student is middle class, confident, thrives on competition and pressure and is motivated, regardless of limits on achievements, they will do well in a setted system. For the rest of the students success will probably depend upon their ability to adapt to a model of learning and a pace of working which is not the most appropriate for their development of understanding.
>
> (Boaler, 1996, pp. 14–15)

Effects upon boys' achievement and reaching the national education targets by 2002

It is clear that research into setting as it has been experienced in the UK and abroad strongly suggests that setting, particularly tight setting, militates against the achievement of boys, ethnic minorities and pupils from working-class backgrounds. Its positive effects upon those in the higher sets are measurable but very marginal, as these pupils generally achieve just as well in a mixed ability or broad setting. If the country is to reach its targets for academic achievement by 2002 it is not the high ability students who have to be helped – they are already succeeding – but the very pupils which setting penalises most.

Effects on self-esteem

There is much research evidence to show that decisions taken about grouping of students will have a central impact on students' self-esteem, social mixing and consequent levels of motivation and behaviour. Classic studies in the 1960s and 1970s showed the negative social effects of certain kinds of student grouping. Such studies have been augmented by more recent work. Generally, the research suggests that students in higher groups have more positive academic and personal self-concepts, while those in lower groups have lower academic self-esteem (Hallam and Toutounji, 1996). Similarly, on a whole school level there is substantial evidence that the self-esteem of Year 7 pupils in a selective grammar school is far higher than their peers in the neighbouring secondary modern.

There is also evidence that students in highly placed groups accept and adopt the school's norms, whereas students in lower groups may resist or even subvert the school's rules. Not surprisingly, evidence relating to friendship grouping shows that students make friends with those with whom they are taught. There are therefore more friendships cutting across ability, class and gender lines where groupings are mixed. This is often viewed as 'a good thing', preparing students for the realities of life in a pluralistic and multicultural society.

There is clear evidence that students tend to be labelled and stereotyped according to the ability grouping they are in. Descriptions such as 'thick', 'slow', 'difficult', 'bright' and 'quick' can become self-fulfilling prophecies. The Elton Report (DfEE, 1989) suggested that bad behaviour can occur in low groups because of students' recognition of their place in the scheme of things – at the bottom. This seems to be particularly true of boys who are found in disproportionate numbers in the bottom sets.

Boaler's study, looking at perception of and performance in mathematics at two secondary schools, found that setting created pressure and anxiety – particularly for girls in top sets – and anger and a sense of disappointment among the rest. The boys in particular felt that the set they were in reflected their behaviour more than their ability. Could this possibly be happening in your school? Boaler reported that students could not see any point in working in mathematics for the grades that were available to them. She notes:

> Feelings of despondency were reported from students in set 2 downwards and many of the students suggested that the limits placed upon their attainment had caused them to give up on mathematics. The students believed that they had been restricted, unfairly and harmfully, by their placement into sets.
>
> (Boaler, 1996, p. 19)

We believe very strongly that if boys and girls are to play the game in school the game has to be kept open for them.

Why not have sets and move pupils between them?

It is now widely acknowledged in educational and psychological research that students do not have a fixed ability that can be determined at an early age. This would suggest that, within a setted situation, there would be a need for regular movement, as children develop skills in different ways and at a different pace. In practice, however, evidence shows that movement between sets is restricted. Where there are different paces of learning, transfer becomes difficult because of the increasing gap in completed work.

Where movement does occur, moving upward produces better than expected performance, whereas downward movement produces worse than expected performance. There is also evidence that middle-class children are more likely to move up, whereas working-class children are more likely to move down. In the absence of research, it is interesting to speculate the movement patterns of boys from ethnic minority groups between sets.

The practicalities

Looking at the practicalities relating to teaching and learning in the classroom, there is evidence that teachers prefer teaching high ability groups and dislike teaching lower ability groups because of the latter's negative attitude towards school and their poor behaviour in the classroom. High ability groups tend to be taught by more experienced, more qualified teachers. There is also significant evidence that students of different ability grouping receive different kinds of learning activity in the classroom. For lower groups there is a higher concentration on basic skills and worksheets. In contrast, higher ability groups are given more critical thinking tasks, opportunities are provided for discussion, pupils have more choice and independence and are allowed to take responsibility for their own work. It has been suggested that the differences in teaching and learning may be a means of classroom control, with lower ability groups being perceived as more difficult to manage.

Ways forward – not back

In the conclusion to her research paper, Boaler argues:

> The consequences of setting . . . decisions are great. Indeed, the set . . . that students are placed into, at a very young age, will almost certainly dictate the opportunities they receive for the rest of their lives. . . . Slavin (1990) makes an important point in his analysis of research in this area. He notes that as mixed ability teaching is known to reduce the chances of discrimination, the burden of proof that ability grouping is preferable must lie with those who claim that it raises achievement. Despite the wide range of research studies in this area, this proof has not been forthcoming.
>
> (Boaler, 1996, p. 15)

Similarly, in the conclusion to her review of research evidence, Hallam suggests:

> That turning the clock back . . . will not provide an effective solution to the problem of underachievement in our schools and may lead to

the increased alienation of some pupils exacerbating current social problems. . . . In considering the available options schools will need to take
account of what will be acceptable to and most appropriate for their
staff, pupils, parents and the wider school community.

(Hallam, 1996, p. 6)

Some practical suggestions

Whatever the composition of the group in front of you, be aware that you
have the power to effect change through effective teaching and learning.
As Hallam notes:

> Different grouping procedures depend heavily for their effectiveness on
> the ways that they are implemented by teachers.

(Hallam, 1996, p. 7)

Consideration of the importance of the process in the classroom must remain central

Accepting that any move forward should take the form of small steps rather
than giant strides, the following ideas are suggested for consideration.

Take stock of the existing situation

Be clear what kinds of groupings currently exist in your school. If there is
setting, what form does it take? Compare the grouping policy adopted by
each subject area with the results that subject achieves. What link is there
between the form of grouping used, the strength of results and the 'gender
gap' in results? Regardless of the form of grouping, if it is giving students
a good experience, and allowing students of both sexes to develop to their
full potential, it may be best to leave well alone. If there are signs of under-
achievement, the composition of groups should be examined. How can you
find the evidence? Have you or colleagues produced scatter diagrams
measuring achievement against ability – and compared how they might
differ in different sets?

Make colleagues aware

Take time out to talk to colleagues about what the research evidence
shows – it will not agree with many teachers' prejudices. Any new
grouping policy will work best if teachers are committed to it and can
see the benefits it will bring. If there are areas of good practice within
school, make sure that the doubters see this and talk to students working
in that area.

Be discriminating

Students could remain in mixed ability groups for the greater part of their curriculum and be regrouped by ability only in subjects in which reducing the spread of ability in the group is particularly 'important'. What criteria would you use to identify this limited number of subjects? Is it really that the subject is different and demands setting, or is it that the teachers are concerned about change? It is not always easy to separate the two.

Delay setting until later

As happens in one of the schools in Boaler's study with regard to mathematics, ability grouping could be delayed until the last possible moment.

> In mathematics lessons the students work in mixed ability groups from the beginning of Year 9, when they start the school, to half-way through Year 11. At this point, the students are moved into one of three 'examination' groups according to the level of examination they have been entered for.
>
> (Boaler, 1996, p. 5)

Ensure easy movement between sets

If there *is* grouping by ability, subject areas should frequently assess pupils' progress and be flexible enough to allow for easy movement between groups, but be aware that the research strongly suggests that this is very difficult to maintain.

Plan over five years

Take a longitudinal view of student grouping in a subject through the years covered by the school in order to avoid movement from mixed ability to setting and back to mixed ability, as currently occurs in some subjects. For example, in history, groups may be mixed ability in Years 7 and 8, setted in Year 9 and back to mixed ability in Years 10 and 11 as students choose their GCSE courses.

Use parallel groups

Remember that within the term 'setting' many variations are possible. Broaden setting arrangements so that there are parallel groupings, in place of a strict hierarchy; two higher, two middle and two lower groups rather than 1 to 6, for example.

The menu system

If the point of setting is to achieve a more appropriate curriculum for pupils, differentiating between their needs and favoured learning styles, primary schools may want to consider the benefits of a menu system which has many advantages in this context. This can be particularly effective at Key Stage 2 in helping to stretch the more able while assuring a balanced curriculum for the class as a whole and giving extra help and support to the less able. (For more details, see Kirklees LEA, 1995.)

More promotion than relegation

Structure sets in such a way that more students move up than down. Indeed, could you avoid moving students down at all? Carefully monitor the academic progress of those who *are* moved down to ensure that they are still aiming appropriately high. Make sure that recommendations for set changes go through a rigorous process of consultation which should certainly involve pastoral heads.

Focus on achievement

Ensure that no child is ever moved down for behavioural reasons. Ensure that pupils are initially setted according to potential as revealed by, for example, NFER/CATs scores.

Where are the boys?

Monitor the gender balance of those moving up and down.

Independent study and shared learning

Reduce the 'weight' of the academic curriculum so that there can be an increased emphasis on independent study and use of library and computer facilities to support learning. A useful corollary here would be to encourage parents, other adults, or other, older students to assist younger learners at these times. This would support whichever system of student grouping is chosen, and would allow all students to place emphasis on skills for transforming and using their learning.

Conclusion

Setting is in a state of flux. Some schools have increased setting in response to target-setting and the *Excellence in schools* White Paper in 1997. Others have moved back to mixed ability after experimenting with setting. Leeds LEA published research suggesting that the introduction of mixed ability in English sets significantly increased achievement. The two most successful English departments in Kirklees LEA are firmly wedded to mixed ability. What all these schools have in common is a belief in the system they are using. You need to look carefully at the types of grouping you are using in an open-minded way. Whatever system you are using, your VEST will still be required.

Box 6.1 Making decisions about setting

Research suggests that setting does not raise achievement *per se*.

Historically, setting tends to depress boys' achievement.

Whatever the grouping policy, be aware of its weaknesses and take steps to address them.

If you decide to set, bear the following in mind:

- take stock of the existing situation
- make colleagues aware
- consider discriminating between subjects
- delay setting until later
- ensure movement between sets
- plan over five years
- use parallel groups
- consider the menu system
- more promotion than relegation
- focus on achievement
- monitor the placing of boys
- encourage independent study.

Chapter 7

Other whole school strategies designed to raise boys' achievement

Introduction

In previous chapters we have dealt with the need to raise awareness across a broad front, the impact of setting and the need to counter the anti-swot culture in school. In this chapter we will suggest some more whole school strategies. We would not recommend that schools adopt all of these, as too many will dissipate the effect of others. School managers need to decide which strategies most closely fit existing practice or potential of their school, and also to consider the extent to which such strategies would complement each other in their institution.

The magic number eight

The main reason why boys have become an issue for educationalists is that schools' Ofsted reports have invariably pointed out the gender differences in achievement in GCSE results. This is still the headline story carried by the mass media. There is little public discussion about what goes on before the beginning of the GCSE course. There are still secondary schools which are not involving themselves in the schemes of their primary feeders because they cannot see their relevance; and there are many primary schools where the touching belief that the big school will sort the boys out is still prevalent. This view is often reinforced by parents who sometimes think it is in the secondary school that 'real' learning starts.

The 8-year-old

Research (Bleach, 1998), observation and anecdote strongly suggest that there are two key years which schools need to address if they are to reverse the under-achievement of boys. Eight-year-old boys, or more accurately those in Year 3, and those boys in Year 8 of secondary school show certain common characteristics. Year 8 of the few existing middle schools is a slightly different issue. The 8-year-old boy has completed his Key Stage 1 SATs and he has over three years (a lifetime in junior terms) before his next public tests. Moreover, his parents, as discussed in Chapter 2, are less likely to encourage his reading and general work than they do his sister's.

Added to this is the often less than interesting, very overcrowded and too content-based Key Stage 2 curriculum. The boy finds himself having to do more writing, more copying and more reading than seems comfortable. There is also the possibility, although the boy probably would not protest very much, that his teacher is a little more relaxed about progress than the previous year when the teacher had to get the pupils through SATs and felt very accountable to parents. This new teacher may well feel that his Level 2 in English was a little flattering and probably feels that a period of consolidation is in order, besides which there is a huge curriculum to plough through. Just as well, she says to herself, that it's not me who has to get them to Level 4 in four years' time. The momentum of progress is slowed. The girls – much happier in the repetitive tasks of writing, copying, drawing and presenting well-organised, neat work – begin to draw further ahead of the boys. This is, of course, a gross stereotype which is very unfair to thousands of skilful and aware Year 3 teachers. However, it is also a scenario which many teachers recognise. The question is what to do about it.

To some extent there are good things already in train. The peremptory slimming down of the curriculum in Easter 1998, initiated by schools' demands for extra time for the Literacy Hour, may result in a lighter curriculum and encourage teachers to use VEST, discussed in Chapter 3. Schools will need to be careful to ensure that the texts to be used in the Literacy Hour are not too heavily weighted towards relationships/emotions/feelings. This will be discussed in more depth in Chapter 9.

Boys are bored by worksheets. Schools may want to think about how to use them less, or at least more imaginatively (e.g. the more structured worksheets suggested by Geoff Hannan which help to teach skills in organising ideas) so that individuals within groups take on different but mutually supportive tasks, and to build in elements of challenge, not just completion. The advent of the Literacy Hour with its very structured approach and short-term tasks should help boys disproportionately compared to girls. The plenary session at the end, with its accent on short-term learning achievements and feedback should be particularly helpful to boys if done well. Similarly, those schools which are using the First Steps scheme which has recently arrived in the UK from Australia may benefit. They should find that its emphasis on a developmental continuum and the use by the teacher of a checklist of learning behaviours in order to assess will also benefit boys. It is believed that both of these initiatives will help reduce the differential between the genders without disadvantaging the girls, which as stated before has to be a prime consideration of any strategy. Anything which results in the boys becoming more work-focused and less prone to disrupt is good news for the girls.

Schools may also wish to consider what else to do about Year 3. It may be a good idea to use this year to have a renewed blitz on parents, supplying them with a specially written leaflet about the issue and their role in continuing to encourage reading; to use this year, particularly, to invite male role models into school (see elsewhere in this chapter); to ask staff to think about planning short-term, quick-reward learning objectives/challenges for boys and girls; to analyse the content of the library or ask the boys themselves to analyse it. More controversially and possibly less welcome, schools could decide to undertake the voluntary Year 4 SATs – although what exactly you wish to get out of it should be clear. Merely putting pressure on teachers, pupils and parents is not a very laudable objective. Having clear targets, learning objectives and teaching strategies which the SATs could be used to support is another thing altogether.

The annus horribilus – *Year 8 boys*

Are Year 8 boys horrible? Traditionally, Year 9 has been the time when boys exhibit most troublesome behaviour in greater numbers, but there are good reasons for regarding Year 8 boys as inhabiting a critical time, when many show the initial tendencies to reject the rules and norms of school and to become more questioning of the worth of learning.

In many ways, this is only to be expected. They are no longer the new Year 7 kids on the block. They have a confidence and an understanding of their place in the school institution. They are also more independent of their parents, not just because the maturing process and the hormonal revolution is upon them, making peer approval often more influential than parental pressure, but because at the age of 13 they are more able to find paid part-time employment. It is the age when paper rounds can legally be undertaken. Year 8 is also the time when many boys – and girls – find themselves setted for the first time. This should not be underestimated. They may have done less well than their peers in the Key Stage 2 SATs, but setting means that many feel they have officially been recognised as having failed, and as a result they are to receive a different educational experience from their peers.

Barbara Walker's research into boys and young men suggests that boys, much more than girls, are working to build both a public and private self.

> Within their private selves these boys were exploring concepts such as doubt, independence, fear, romance, uncertainty, academic pressure and anxiety – building a personal moral code. Within the group they appeared to be learning solidarity, trust, judgement; learning the banter of affability; learning to be part of a team.
>
> (Quoted in the *TES*, October 1996)

Walker goes on to suggest that the two personae tend to narrow as boys get older, but for 13-year-olds it is very important that the public front is accepted and supported. Schools do not always recognise the nature of boys' development and sometimes try to oppose or suppress its manifestations rather than to channel its energies. Kevan Bleach (1998) has suggested that the boys' changes in attitude in Year 8 are substantially rooted in educational challenges, the quality of teaching and the nature of pupil–teacher relationships. What is crucial about Year 8 is that if boys do adopt a public scepticism towards learning and academic achievement at this age it is very difficult for them to change back in time to affect their school career.

A Norfolk headteacher, when asked to explain why his GCSE results consistently showed boys achieving as well as girls, commented, 'I talk to my Year Eight Boys.' He did more than talk to them. The following is a list of possible ways of keeping Year 8 boys interested and alert to academic success. It is not rocket science, and reflects some of the things we have discussed before.

1   Encourage/insist that teachers in Year 8 take VEST (see Chapter 3, pp. 31–33) seriously. Practical investigations, oral work and role-play are much more interesting, and will capture peer group approval.
2   Plan with heads of departments so that active teaching and learning is championed, supported (with INSET if desirable) and monitored. Ask each department to offer and share a strategy.
3   Focus even more closely on literacy. Have visiting male readers, writers-in-residence, book weeks, library competitions. Ask Year 8 boys to review the library and make recommendations for change. Use ICT to encourage word processing and better presentation. Place more value on non-fiction and science-fiction, magazines and comics. Ask students to share their books. Ask them to give books a mark and compare the marks given.
4   Design homework so that it involves boys working in pairs or groups on active or investigative work. Try to design homework that helps the students to practise the skills learned in the classroom, but avoid setting work which is merely completion of work started in class.
5   Think carefully about the way the school praises boys. Is it generally public or private? What sort of praise do boys prefer? Has the school got an *effective* reward system in place (see p. 87) and how do Year 8 boys respond to it? Celebrate achievement in display, both of individuals and teams.
6   Introduce mentoring, possibly targeted at boys who staff feel are particularly at risk of losing motivation (see pp. 74–76 on mentoring).
7   Establish exciting events to anticipate and enjoy, and which are connected to learning; for example, skiing trips (do schools connect

this sufficiently to learning?), field trips, exchange visits, historical primary evidence gathering.

8   Introduce the Internet, e-mail and ICT as important tools to learn through, not as an enjoyable off-task addition to 'real' or 'normal' learning.

The general message has to be that Year 8 boys are in need of a specially vigilant eye, and that as they embrace adolescence with its peer pressure and questioning of previously accepted authority, the school has to move to a culture which accepts the development and seeks ways to work with it.

Mentoring

Mentoring is a fairly new addition to the strategies at a school's disposal, and it can take a number of forms. The idea of mentoring is that the student has a regular discussion about his or her learning with a significant other, with whom they can share their problems, ideas and progress. Just what sort of mentoring a school chooses is largely a matter of resources as much as educational principle. Another problem is who should be mentored. Some schools have chosen 'twelve students of concern' in each year after consulting year tutors or class teachers. Others have decided to concentrate on certain year groups, and some ensure that all boys and girls have access to it. In secondary schools Year 11 is often targeted for mentoring because of the proximity of GCSEs, although there is plenty of evidence that this effort could be better spent in Year 8 (see above). Exactly what should happen in a mentoring session, and how it is organised, is described below. Don't be afraid to mentor initially on a small scale: the key is that it must be manageable and sustained.

Mentoring by the senior management team and/or all teachers

The coverage and depth of any mentoring scheme will depend on the number of staff available. Some schools are reaching the conclusion that all form tutors in secondary school must become mentors. This has meant that the personal and social education (PSE) curriculum which they used to teach has had to be picked up by subjects or by a timetabled block. The form tutor's main task becomes much more specific. He or she is the academic mentor for all the students in the form. This involves a highly structured and well-supported schedule in which students are interviewed on a regular basis, either alone or in carefully chosen pairs. The interview will be supported by information or reports from subject teachers. The interview may start with the sort of general questions such as the following:

1   How are things going at the moment? Are you enjoying schoolwork more or less than last year?
2   Which subjects are you enjoying most? What is it about those subjects which you enjoy? Which subjects are not going so well? Why is this?
3   Do you understand the work you are doing in each subject? Is the work explained clearly?
4   What is the classroom atmosphere like? Is it friendly? Do you enjoy being there?
5   Are there any individuals or groups who mess about in class and stop you working?
6   Does the teacher tell you how you are getting on?
7   Do you think you are working harder this year than last year? Why do you think that?
8   What would make you work harder than you do now?
9   What do you think this school could do to help boys/girls do better?

Obviously there have to be clearly understood rules concerning the discussion of specific colleagues. This has to be kept on a professional basis if the scheme is going to work. The mentor would also be using the school's statistics regarding NFER/CATs scores and predicted grades (in the older years) to help the student agree academic targets. (See target-setting, p. 79).

If the mentoring is undertaken by only a fraction of the staff, possibly the senior team, the school will have to be more selective about the students it wants to see. It may want to think about the following as possible cohorts:

1   Year 11 boys and/or girls
2   Year 11 boys and/or girls who are suspected of under-achieving
3   Year 8 boys and/or girls who are under-achieving
4   Boys and/or girls from all years who are under-achieving
5   Boys and/or girls from all years who are seen as 'culture-setters', those whose opinions and behaviour often lead others.

Peer mentoring

The idea of peer mentoring is that it is more time efficient than that done by teachers; that peers can effectively continue the mentoring in their own time if they wish; and that the language and discussion may be more comfortable and meaningful to the students. However, if it is seen by teachers as a method by which responsibility is passed to the students and they can have a chat together while the teacher gets on with something else it will not work. The school has to value the system, and to show that it values it. This means that a great deal of investment has to be put into its planning, preparation of teachers and training of students. Students should be involved in the planning; it should not be something that happens *to* them. Students should be asked to pick a mentor who is not from their normal cohort of close friends. It would be helpful to both genders if they had to choose someone of the opposite sex. This would give them an opportunity to understand the thinking of their opposites, and would also expose them to a more critical scrutiny than might otherwise be the case. In some schools mentoring has been one way, with older students mentoring younger ones (e.g. sixth form with Years 7, 9 and 10 in a Kirklees school) while other schools have chosen horizontal paired mentoring (in another Kirklees school), where the partners mentor each other. There are a number of variations which schools will want to consider and trial.

Industrial mentoring

In some areas, particularly in Norfolk LEA, schools have established partnerships with local businesses – factories, offices, banks, etc. – in which male employees have come into school to work as mentors for boys, particularly under-achieving boys. This partnership has a number of benefits. The boys, who in some cases may lack an adult male role model, are given the chance to talk to a male – who is not a teacher – about the world of work, its disciplines and its benefits. He can also see how life may look in a few years' time. It gives him a longer term perspective which is not easily dismissed. The mentor may talk to the boy about the questions listed above, about his targets and about his ambitions outside of school. Businesses are usually quite happy for their staff to become involved. They view it as a form of personal development and of establishing a meaningful relationship with the local community. In some places, particularly in primary schools, the mentor is more of a reader or a listener of reading than strictly mentoring. In all cases, using outside mentors throws up questions of child protection and training. Both of these require time and effort, but they should not be barriers to what can be a very rewarding experience for all involved. In the case of child protection, co-operation will be needed from the police who will have to check criminal records. Policy may vary between forces, or even between divisions within the same force, so it may be wise to seek political support via the chief constable or the chair of the police authority. This support may be more likely if the local police themselves are involved in the mentoring. The appropriateness of this will vary enormously depending on the age of pupils, local attitudes to the police and the suitability of individual officers.

Training is available from a number of sources. In many LEAs the National Year of Reading Co-ordinator – if still in place – may be an ideal supplier of training. If not, the LEA may have other ideas, or literature is available from Norfolk LEA.

Display

It is a generally observable fact that display of work in British primary schools is of a very high quality, certainly compared to equivalent schools in other parts of Europe. Display in secondary schools tends to be more mixed, with less effort and care taken over its quality and presentation. What is not so clear in either sector is that there has been a carefully thought out philosophy of what display is actually meant to do, particularly in the way it may affect achievement. Most teachers, even in the primary phase, are sceptical about the idea that pupils actually learn very much from display. It is intended much more as a valuing exercise, to raise the pupils' self-esteem and to encourage them to maintain or increase their efforts. Schools may wish to ask themselves the following questions about display:

1   Are boys as well represented as girls on the walls? (Often they are not.)
2   If they are not, is this because their work is scruffier, shorter, torn or lost?
3   If their work is less well presented are there any ways in which they could be helped, for example, to word process it, or ask a well-presenting girl to help them?
4   Is presentation the only criterion we use for display? What do we do about creative ideas? If boys are good at doing rather than recording why not use photographic displays of them achieving? Ensure that a broad range of experiences is celebrated, not just sport.
5   How can we make displays more interactive and less passive?
6   What does the display say about the roles/career choices/leisure time of the two genders? Is the display opening up possibilities or closing them down?
7   Does the display give positive messages about the opportunities open to pupils from minority ethnic groups?

Celebrating achievement in display

Many schools are very good at capturing extra-curricular achievement on photographs and displaying them. The expeditions, sponsored walks, skiing trips and parachute jumps are there for all to see. Not so much is made of achievement within the mainstream curriculum. Photographs of Year 11, 12 and 13 students in earnest debate, working on a science experiment, heads down with pages of essay written, will be informative to Year 7 and 8 boys. It may well be that their normal images are of sports players, bullies, smokers, and car and motorcycle drivers who get free periods, more independence and little work.

Similarly, a photo display of last year's leavers, with information about their successes, will be read and discussed by boys. In Kirklees, schools have designed two large sheets: 'This is what boys do' and 'This is what girls do', with every subject contributing photographs of boys in the school achieving and hard at work. Display plays an important part in the school showing itself to be a learning organisation. Why not display pictures of teachers, men and women discussing their favourite read? Photographs of students in work experience show boys and girls succeeding in a variety of contexts, and will be all the more valuable if they are in a non-gender stereotyped context.

Role models

As we discussed in Chapter 2, one of the reasons why boys are under-achieving may be a lack of adult, male role models at home or in their community. This can be exacerbated in primary schools which are pre-dominantly staffed by women. Boys can be denied any living clues as to what it might be like to be an employed, contributing man. Some primary schools have organised programmes of male visitors to come into school to talk to the children, but care needs to be taken over who is invited. Ideally boys should see men who, as well as having a worthwhile career, are reason-ably articulate and can discuss how important education was and/or is to them. Having the leading players from the local football league club will always be popular with the boys, but it will not always say very much to them about education. In fact, it may prove to them beyond all reasonable doubt that education is a waste of time. Seek out the growing, but still small number of graduate footballers instead.

Having male mentors from industry working with them, or hearing them read, is also a very good model. Other schools (for example, in Kirklees) have invited grandfathers, fathers and ex-pupils to come in and help with reading and listening. Whatever they actually do in school, their primary purpose should be to clearly state that education is a male concern, and that real men are into learning. Schools which organise a 'bring-your-dads-to-school' day, involving them in the classroom, should obviously be careful that those children without fathers at home do not feel left out or second rate.

All schools with boys have already got role models, of course: the older boys in the school. They should be viewed as a resource to be used appro-priately. It is important to remember that the younger boys never see them in the classroom, and probably do not look upon them primarily as learners. They may have many other images, positive and negative, but learners is not one of them. Portraying older boys as learners – in display, celebra-tion, or even a tour of the school as part of their induction – will leave the younger boys with a powerful impression. Even more effective is the practice of working across age groups on schemes of shared working or shared reading. We shall be discussing shared reading in Chapter 9. It is worth emphasising, however, that older boys helping younger boys with their work has immense potential benefit for both partners. Not only can it raise achievement, it has a remarkable effect on self-esteem and introduces or confirms to boys that they have a role as carers which begins to prepare them for parenthood. It is not always easy to organise boys to have time away from their own lessons, especially if they have exams looming. Any such project should be time limited from the start to a maximum of a term. Boys will welcome such clear parameters. It may also be interesting and productive to use older volunteers who are not necessarily high achievers, or whose public image is very far from being a swot.

Schools should also ensure that as many boys as girls are visible in responsible roles; for example, receptionist in school entrance, escorting guests around school, making refreshments at parents' evenings, and so on.

Target-setting

All schools have targets for academic achievement. Whether they be the government-inspired targets at Key Stage 2, the number of A*– C passes at GCSE or each subject's or key stage's internally driven targets for their cohort, the age of target-setting is upon us. And it is unlikely to go away. The now medieval-sounding tips on classroom management given on PGCE courses in the 1970s ('If it moves, belt it') have been subsumed by the more scientific approach of 'If it moves, measure it'. The targets set by the government for itself have been translated into targets for each LEA, which in turn have negotiated targets for each of their schools. Many schools, quite naturally, feel that their targets are unfair, too ambitious or just impossible. But like it or not, they will be judged by their success in meeting them.

The principle of subsidiarity, not often used in education, comes into play here. If the government targets depend on LEAs, and the LEAs depend on schools, the schools depend on individual students. If schools are going to meet their targets they have to talk very intensively with their students about their own, individual targets. Most primary schools already target those pupils who, in Key Stage 2, are on the verge of a Level 4 in English. Most secondary schools are very aware of those students on the cusp between a C and D grade. This targeting of a pass grade is probably detrimental to many other pupils, high and low achievers alike, and the likelihood is that a new system of calculating academic success will be introduced – perhaps something like the existing points system for A level grades, in which each grade carries a number of points. This should mean that it is in the schools' interest to raise the achievement of all, not just those near the 'pass' grade.

The following gives an example of how one high school has tackled the challenge of target-setting. What has been done here is equally applicable to primary schools.

How can I move ahead?

What follows is an outline of one tried and tested way of using the data which is collected in most secondary schools to set up a system of target-setting. While the focus will be on individual student target-setting, the same data can be used in a different way to produce the information needed for departmental and whole school target-setting. Working with this process in schools has shown it to be well received by tutors, who find it clear and easy to present to students, and by students themselves, who like the personalised nature of what they are being offered.

The example which follows is based on the mock exam results of a group of Year 11 students. It could just as easily have been an exam within Key Stage 3 or even Key Stage 2. If target-setting is to make a difference it needs to be embedded from an early stage.

Results from the mock exams were loaded into Lotus 1–2–3 and converted into a number score (A* = 8 down to G = 1). Bar charts were created within Lotus 1–2–3 to show the results of individual students. Each bar chart contained a summary entitled 'Total points score'. A horizontal line across the chart showed the level of that student's average performance. For example, a line across at the level of 4 meant that the student was scoring on average 4 points in each subject, or, in other words, was averaging a grade D.

A copy of all relevant charts was printed for the tutor and a single bar chart was given to each student. Each student had the bar chart printed in colour. That definitely seemed to make a difference to students' perception that the exercise mattered.

On the copies of the graphs given to tutors, the NFER/CATs score and a target points score had been added. These two pieces of information were not put on to the student's own chart. The target points score was derived from looking at the performance of previous cohorts of students with the same NFER/CATs score in the same school, the LEA and nationally. Targets were set towards the upper end of what previous students had achieved. It was hoped that, in this way, targets would be both fair and challenging.

Tutors proceeded to discuss the information with each student who had, first, to agree a target points score through negotiation with the tutor, and second, make a clear declaration about *where* and *how* the extra points would be produced to enable the target points score to be reached.

The exercise of comparing the students' actual points score in the exams against their target points score was illuminating. Of course, there were a few troublesome boys who were shown to be dramatically under-achieving, but there were also some very pleasant, co-operative girls and boys who were shown to be quietly getting on with under-achieving. Interestingly too, in this school, there was significant under-achievement at all levels of ability. For boys, this was mainly in the middle. It was the boys scoring an average of 90–110 in NFER tests at age 11 who were going on to under-achieve. These were the students who were moving forward to collect a list of grades D and E at GCSE, while girls with similar NFER scores were leaving with grades B and C. Looking at the performance of girls, the under-achievement seemed to be at both extremes: at the very bottom – where surely one couldn't possibly expect more from such quiet and conforming creatures, who, after all, were always so reliable – and also at the very top, where some girls seemed unable to fulfil their potential.

Figure 7.1 shows a student who is performing well, even 'over-performing', based on an NFER score of 285 gained at age 11.

Target-setting for this student becomes a positive experience of being praised, discussing the kinds of learning strategies which are obviously being used to such good effect and ways in which further progress can be created. The school felt that the student should be aiming for sixty-two points in the GCSEs. In fact, following negotiation with the tutor, the student actu-ally set the target of 'Every grade to be at least a grade B with two scores of A or A*'. In unpicking this overall target to develop precise strategies for improvement the student wrote:

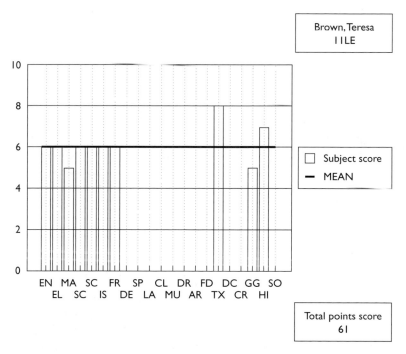

Figure 7.1 Individual target-setting – Example 1.

I was let down in Geography because I kept giving an example, but not explaining it. I need to collect some examples of answers which were better done than mine, and then have a go at some new examples myself. In Maths, I missed a page out of the booklet, probably because I was rushing. I need to practise working under timed conditions and making myself check that I have covered all the right bits.

The next two examples (Figures 7.2 and 7.3) show a rather different story. Both students were shocked to see the gap between what they had achieved and what the school thought they should be achieving. (That is why target-setting needs to start early – four months before the GCSEs is a little late to start being shocked.)

The first 'under-achieving' student (Figure 7.2) was seen as 'bright' – top sets all the way – but certainly not fulfilling expected potential. He had gained an NFER score of 358 at age 11. You will notice that, in the mock exams, he scored exactly the same points score as the student in Figure 7.1, and yet from a much higher level of measured potential. Through discussion with the boy's tutor it was seen that the student needed to develop a clearer approach to note-taking and keeping files organised.

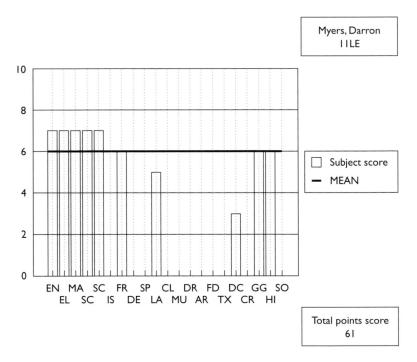

Figure 7.2 Individual target-setting – Example 2.

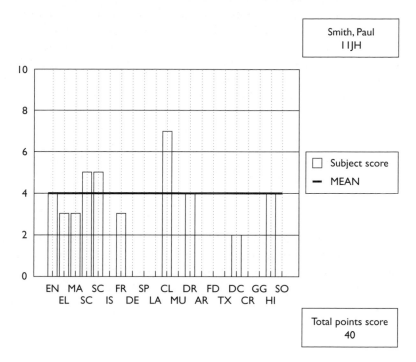

Figure 7.3 Individual target-setting – Example 3.

Homework needed to be more clearly focused and more attention needed to be given to meeting deadlines for coursework – particularly in design.

The second student (Figure 7.3) was 'a really nice lad' – he played football for the school, was always on hand to help out, and was quietly getting on with failing to obtain the grades which would move him into his chosen sixth form college. He had achieved an NFER score of 300 at age 11. His mock performance showed he had only 'passed' three subjects at grade C or above, yet he needed six passes to move on to sixth form college. Failure here would mean another boy closing down his opportunities for the future. Through discussion, a target points score of 50 was agreed. English grades were lower than expected as the boy had not taken the opportunities offered to re-draft coursework assignments. French had suffered through under-preparation of topics for oral assessment. In maths he had simply given up, through the sense that everyone else was moving ahead of him and he could not keep up. In order to chart a way forward, the boy devised a work schedule which would be checked by his parents and best friend on a weekly basis. His best friend also agreed to work with him on a specific maths topic each week, with the emphasis on testing each other, working through past questions and preparing a twenty-minute revision session for the rest of the class.

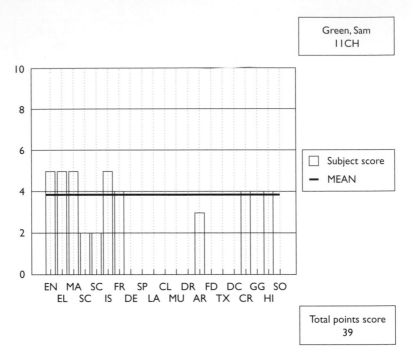

Figure 7.4 Individual target-setting – Example 4.

Not only were students put in charge of deciding the precise nature of their targets, and how these were to be achieved (no more bland statements of 'I must work harder' were allowed), but these were shared with family members so that all parties knew what the 'game' was, and were regularly reviewed to see how progress was being made.

A sheet was prepared so that each student could attach the bar chart and declare the way forward. Students were also given the fictitious performance of Sam Green so that they could learn how the process worked (Figure 7.4.)

Where can I improve?

This bar chart (see Figure 7.4) shows the grades my teachers judge I am likely to achieve if I continue to work as I am currently doing (I know that 8 points = grade A*, 7 points = grade A, 6 points = grade B, 5 points = grade C, 4 points = grade D, 3 points = grade E, 2 points = grade F, I point = grade G. I also know that some colleges will only count GCSE points which are scored at grade C or above).

Having discussed my learning with my tutor, I feel that I should be aiming for ... GCSE points. I know that this points total can be achieved in various ways. I am planning to get:

.... points in .... subjects
.... points in .... subjects
.... points in .... subjects
.... points in .... subjects
.... points in .... subjects

Looking at each of the subjects I am taking at GCSE, my targets are as follows:

Subject	Target grade	Number of points
		Total:

Looking at individual subjects, here are four *practical and precise* steps I will take to help me to move towards my targets for GCSEs:

1   ....
    ....
2   ....
    ....
3   ....
    ....
4   ....
    ....

I will share this information with my family, but I know that the responsibility for moving towards my targets lies with me.

Setting SMART targets

The really significant work in individual target-setting, however, is not the production of coloured graphs, impressive and motivating though they are. It is the negotiating and agreement of targets with the students. It is very easy to do this badly. The two principles that should guide you are that the individual student must feel that they are *genuinely* his or her targets, not imposed by a harassed class teacher who gives off messages that he would really prefer to do something else. This means that sufficient planning, time and training have to be given to it by the school. The second principle is that the targets should be SMART, not sloppy or soft (see Table 7.1).

Note the change of verb in the SMART target. 'Will' suggests less coercion and more certainty than 'must'. A variation on this theme is to use a form of neuro-linguistic programming to create more visionary targets. Thus the first SMART target could be changed to 'I'm pleased that I'm taking six spellings home every week, and testing myself on Tuesdays and Thursdays for the next two months.' The verb has changed to the present, and the sentence has been injected with emotion. You should be aware that the emotion has to *genuinely* come from the pupil (risible laughter from the sceptics), but they may be surprised. Many pupils welcome the chance to find a way, *their own way*, forward in their work (Pacific Institute, 1997). Obviously, most students will need help to

Table 7.1 SMART target-setting (**S**pecific, **M**easurable, **A**chievable, **R**ealistic, **T**ime-limited)

Sloppy target	Soft target	SMART target
I must improve my English	I must improve my spelling	I will learn six spellings each week and test myself on them at home on Tuesdays and Thursdays for the next two months
I must be better behaved	I must improve my behaviour in history and French	I will sit apart from Andy in French and Gaz in history I will not talk when the teacher is talking I will get off yellow report by the end of term
I must do better in science	I must improve my practical work in science	I will carefully plan five steps for each practical I will ask questions if I'm unsure what to do next I will put away the apparatus at the end of the session

find appropriate strategies, and Appendix 7.1 (pp. 89–92) has a number of suggestions which can be adapted and used as a starting point.

Praise and reward system

We use the word 'system' very deliberately. One of the complaints which students, but particularly boys, have about schools is the lack of consistency between different teachers' methods and generosity of rewarding. Schools need to structure and support a system which is manifestly fair and clear to use. Whether it is based on effort merits, on target achievements, on social and community grounds or on adherence to simple tasks like punctuality and uniform, pupils and staff need to know exactly how it works in each class. To this end it would be advantageous if the system were designed with full participation of staff and students. If both feel that they have ownership of the system they are more likely to use and value it properly.

Some teachers have observed that boys do not like public praise but would much prefer private praise or a letter home. If that is the situation pertaining in the school they not only need to be aware of boys' sensitivities, but also that such an attitude is usually the result of an anti-swot culture, discussed in Chapter 4.

We know that boys tend to respond well to short-term, time-limited challenges. We also know that they tend to be sociable, and like learning in social groups. A rewarding experiment in some schools has been that of group reward, based on group achievement. Whether it be punctuality, attendance (not always an advisable measure), uniform, inter-form sports, inter-form quizzes, problem-solving challenges, cycle rides or anything else which can be done collectively, some interesting developments take place. The performance of the group often depends upon the strongest helping the weakest to achieve, and the dynamics this can produce among the competitive boys is too complex to describe, but can quite easily be imagined. Most boys, like girls, soon realise that the weaker 'players' will do better with encouragement and support than being shouted at – although that can help as well. It is important to design such competitions so that the same form or class does not win all the time. One way around this is to make the winner the class which shows the most improvement from last time. This should encourage them all. Obviously schools could tie in this form of competition to academic achievement (reaching milestone targets or gaining effort merits) but would probably capture the support and involvement of more pupils if they widened the activities.

Box 7.1 Other macro (whole school) strategies

Year 3 and Year 8 need special treatment:

- mentoring
- target-setting
- display
- role modelling
- praise and reward.

APPENDIX 7.1

Examples of action points to move towards target grades

Punctuality

- I will get to school by 8.25 a.m. each day.
- I will arrive promptly at each lesson so I am ready to start work.
- I will get up by 7 a.m. so that I am not so rushed in getting to school.

Attendance

- I will make every effort to attend school each day.
- I am aiming for full attendance over the next month.

Organisational skills

- I will make sure that I have checked and packed my bag the night before school, so I have homework to hand in and books for the day.
- I will get out all the equipment promptly at the start of each lesson.
- When I have completed a piece of homework in a subject, I will spend ten minutes checking and sorting my notes and making a note of any gaps I need to fill.

Listening in class

- I will make sure that I listen intently to what is said in . . . .
- After the teacher has spoken I will check that I understand what point is being made.

Responding in class

- I will ask and answer in class at least three times a day.
- In . . . . I will use questions to check my understanding.

Work partner in class

- If I am being distracted in class I will ask the teacher if I can move.
- I will continue to work well with . . . . in . . . .
- I will not sit with . . . . or . . . .

Seating position in class

- In . . . . I will ask to sit nearer to the teacher.
- I will sit well away from . . . . and . . . .

For the most able

- I will extend my work in . . . . by thinking about . . . .
- An interesting part of my work in . . . . is . . . . and I will now find out more about it.
- An academic skill I will develop in the next few weeks is . . . .
- A personal/social skill I will develop in the next few weeks is . . . .

Use of the student planner

- I will enter all set homework into my planner.
- I will record all deadlines for coursework into my planner.
- As I sit down to start my homework I will check what is to be done that night and which section of longer assignments I need to work on.

Drafting/preparing work

- I will spend the first ten minutes of each homework checking what I have to do and setting time allocations for each piece of work.
- In . . . . I will spend ten minutes planning the shape of my work before I start to write it up.
- In . . . . I will plan the paragraphs of content before I start to write it up.
- I will try brainstorming lists of ideas and then group them together before I start to write up work.
- I will use spider diagrams to link together ideas.

Adding more detail to work

- In . . . . I will give an example to illustrate each major point I make.
- In . . . . I will comment on why the example I have given is a useful one.
- I will find one extra book to consult for my work in . . . .

Homework: time spent on it

- I will spend . . . . hours on homework on four nights per week. I will also do . . . . hours at the end.
- In . . . . I will spend an extra half hour on work every Wednesday.
- For the next two weeks I will log the time spent on homework and speak to my teacher/tutor about it.

Homework: use of resources

- For each piece of homework in . . . . I will consult two sources before I start to plan my answer.

- I will use the school/town library once a fortnight to help to get resources to support work in . . . .
- I will ask my teacher for extra resources to help with homework in . . . .

Homework: organisational skills

- I will make my best effort to work in a place without distraction.
- On longer assignments I will break them up into at least four separate tasks and enter them in my planner as such.
- For longer assignments in . . . . I will spend two sessions planning and two sessions writing up.

Revision strategies

- I will revise . . . . for forty minutes, break for twenty minutes, and then spend ten minutes testing myself on my learning.
- I will put answers to past questions on to cassette tapes, then check for gaps using my notes.
- I will spend one session per week looking at exam terms such as 'explain', 'comment upon', 'factorise', 'evaluate'.
- I will keep my revision stimulating by making such notes as 'ten key words from this topic are' or 'the six things I will remember about this topic forever are . . .'.

Revision: organisational skills

- I will draw up a revision timetable seven weeks before my exams and show it to my tutor.
- I will have a copy of my revision timetable in my planner and one at home.

Outside activities: employment, leisure, commitments

- I will have one evening each week and one full day at weekends away from school work.
- I will cut my job down to . . . . hours per week until my exams are over.
- I will limit outside commitments to two per week until my exams are over.

Presentational skills: spelling, handwriting, paragraphing

- I will cross out planning notes and mistakes with one neat line.
- In . . . . I will make it a priority to write in paragraphs.
- In . . . . I will cut down the length of answers I give to questions worth only one or two marks.

Getting help with work

- I will talk to . . . . each Thursday about the successes I have had in . . . . during the week.
- I will talk to teachers as soon as possible if I am having problems with home-work assignments.

Keeping motivated

- Every Sunday I will briefly write down the main areas of learning which have gone well this week.
- Every fortnight I will tell my teacher/tutor about three things which are going well with my learning and one area which needs further improvement.
- I will talk to people at home, and my friends, about my targets and will share strategies with them.

Chapter 8

Getting it right for boys *and* girls in the classroom

Introduction

> A strong message seems to be emerging: in running all but the most simple systems, there is complexity beyond the reach of most theories and predictions. The way forward in such unpredictable circumstances lies with trial and error. Actions must be taken and the outcomes monitored. In particular, this monitoring should uncover problems, for it is by solving the problems that the system is improved.
>
> (Fitz-Gibbon, 1996, p. 49)

The strategies described in this chapter are those which individual teachers, or even whole departments or year groups if they so choose, can try in the privacy of their own classrooms. Except, of course, classrooms are not as private as they used to be. Special needs assistants, classroom assistants, monitoring heads and all manner of previously unheard of beasties have made the classroom their new habitat. There is a climate of change in education and increasingly exotic fauna can be found on the sunlit glades beside the blackboard. It gives teachers the chance for a really in-depth, professional discussion about their teaching and classroom management. It is a golden opportunity in all sorts of ways, not least in thinking about how boys react to classroom management techniques designed to raise their engagement and achievement.

It may be surprising that we have not broached this issue until Chapter 8. The reason reflects how we advise schools to tackle the issue: start wide and focus down. Awareness-raising is the first, and ongoing, priority followed by whole school strategies which everybody understands. These first two strategies create the supportive climate to carry through the micro strategies. The initiatives of individual teachers in the classroom do not need to wait for the completion of whole school strategies, but the first of them should at least have begun. This leaves time for planning and a shift of understanding and empathy by colleagues and pupils. It is the changes in the classroom which will actually make the difference to student performance. If nothing changes in boys' – and girls' – experiences of learning, their achievement will not change either. Obviously many of the whole school strategies discussed in previous chapters will be implemented in, or have an impact upon, the classroom. The micro strategies described in this chapter are those which individuals may choose, or not choose, to implement.

Hands up in class

We have already touched upon the 'hands up' issue elsewhere, but it is so important that it is worth expanding upon. Hands up can be an excellent way of getting a lesson off to a brisk and even exciting start. In the right classrooms, with good banter, it can lead to humour, relationship building and the cementing of knowledge. We do not suggest that it should be banished, but merely relegated to become *part* of a teacher's menu rather than the mainstay – which it often is – of assessing whole class understanding.

The problem is that boys love it. It appeals to their preferred risk-taking learning style: unfortunately, they often don't learn very much from it. 'How many people work for Dewsbury Healthcare Trust?' its Chair recently asked the pupils of a junior school. The boys' arms were out of their sockets. Answers ranged from 'a million' (crestfallen look from the boy) to 'none' (which may have been a sarcastic response to the verb in the question). It turned into one of the world's longest question and answer sessions as the boys hit the mega-speculation button, trying all the numbers they could think of as they played the Dewsbury Healthcare Trust lottery. The girls wisely sat on their hands. Five weeks later no one had the least idea what the correct answer was.

Geoff Hannan points out that boys putting up their hands in class is disadvantageous to both genders. The boys are encouraged to speculate but not to reflect, and therefore do not. The girls, whose preferred style is to reflect, do not have that strength recognised nor are they really encouraged to speculate because it is often too risky for them. If the teacher starts the lesson by asking 'What did we learn in the last lesson: no, don't put your hands up now. Turn to your partner(s) and discuss it for thirty seconds. Then put your hand up', then four things happen which would otherwise not have done:

- boys reflect in their discussion
- girls reflect and discuss, and are then more confident to put their hands up because they know that at least one other person agrees with them
- the *whole* class is considering what they learned, probably in a meaningful way, which helps embed the learning
- the correct answer is far more likely to be forthcoming.

Seating policy and learning zones

'It was almost as if they were wanting the teachers to take charge of seating in the classroom. They know they can't coast. They have to be on their mettle all the time and are expected to work.'

(Head of English)

A habit has evolved in many British schools of allowing students to sit in self-selected seats. It is in the traditions of a liberal, empowering society that this should be so. Unless you interfere with others, why should you not sit where you want? It is a sloppy habit, though, if held up to examination. If children are in school to learn should we not do all we can to assist the process, even if it means going against their initial wishes? After all, we impose uniform, school rules and assemblies on children. Why do we think that a seating policy, which is central to their learning, should be different? A pupil in a classroom occupies what we have come to call a 'learning zone'. This zone is fairly flexible. Most of the time it consists of the desk of the learner, plus the desks and personalities of the other one, two or three pupils in the same block or pair. Occasionally the zone will change shape completely as the teacher engages the individual or the whole class. The zone could take the shape of a corridor of learning or widen out during whole class discussion to be a hall of learning. But its most enduring features will be dominated by the shape and character of the learners in the immediate vicinity. If pupils have a free rein about choosing their friends as neighbours they will invariably choose those who share the same values. Thus an under-achieving boy will choose to sit next to another under-achieving boy, and the same with girls. These will naturally support each other's lack of effort, initiate each other into the anti-swot club and be unchallenged by any competing values – save that of the teacher. The classroom will soon become pockmarked with burgeoning ghettos of under-achievement. Schools should thus regard the learning zone of individual pupils as a manifestation of the learning school. The classroom is principally the place to learn.

Seating Plan A (Figure 8.1) shows how a class might arrange itself if left to its own devices. The under-achieving boys have sought each other out, as have the girls. Their ghettos may not be disruptive; they may be very quiet and easy to manage – but they are under-achieving.

In Seating Plan B (Figure 8.2) the teacher has paired them off so that no under-achiever is sitting next to another one. Not only that, and what is not indicated on the plan, the teacher has carefully considered which learning styles would be complementary. He or she has paired a verbally confident but under-achieving boy with one who is reflective and would benefit from some of the confidence his new partner has; another under-achiever who is a poor presenter of work with a girl who is excellent at this; and a girl who is under-achieving in mathematics with one who has

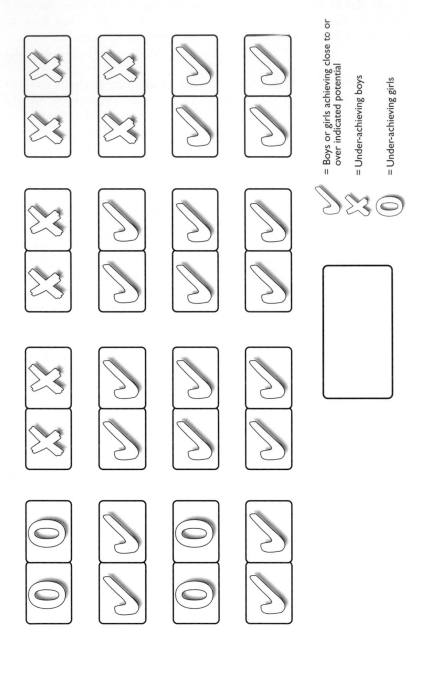

= Boys or girls achieving close to or over indicated potential

= Under-achieving boys

= Under-achieving girls

Figure 8.1 Seating Plan A: Pupils decide where they sit.

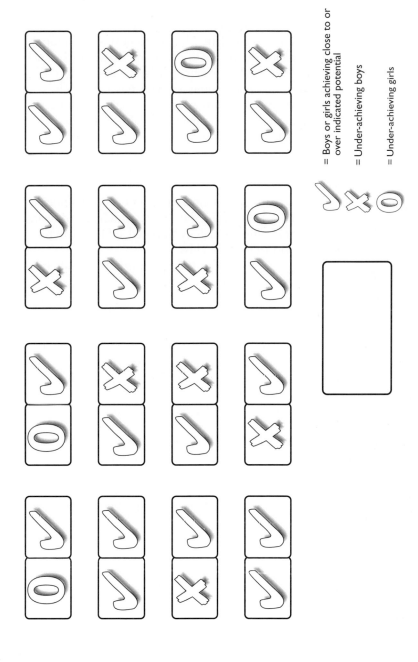

= Boys or girls achieving close to or over indicated potential

= Under-achieving boys

= Under-achieving girls

Figure 8.2 Seating Plan B: Teacher decides on pairings.

the skill and patience to help her through it. All have been placed for reasons of learning, not of behaviour, and that is a vital distinction to make when introducing it to the class. Pupils will be much more willing to accept the former rather than the latter. This seating pattern is not fixed. One headteacher has suggested that 'students should be entirely comfortable in working with everybody else in the room'. It is an ambitious but achievable goal. It would necessitate the regular, perhaps half-termly change in seating positions but, as one head of English who has used such a system stated, 'It means there are no cosy corners where people are just coasting.'

Teachers will make mistakes in seating plans, although less frequently with experience. It will soon become an accepted norm in the school and is ideally started at the beginning of the academic year, although some schools have introduced it as late as Christmas in Year 11.

> 'Initially it did cause some questions, but it soon became fine. In the past I sometimes felt that you have one table which was drawing my attention – and it was often a male-dominated table – whereas now my attention is around the whole class.'
>
> (Head of art, northern comprehensive)

So much depends on the way it is introduced and adherence to a rigid rule that you are primarily concerned with learning. This helps to emphasise the image of the school as a learning organisation. Some teachers announce to the class at the beginning of the year that by the end of it they will have worked intensively with every other student in the room. In other words, seating positions are regularly shifted around. The result of this has generally been beneficial. It has cut down the amount of teasing, taunting, name-calling, poking and bullying, as for the first time pupils get to know *all* their classmates – or anticipate having to work with them. For youngsters growing up in multi-cultural, pluralistic Britain the more they have to work with different sorts of people the better for all concerned.

The system is not a panacea. Some teachers, surveying their hard-working, well-behaved girls, quite rightly want to protect them and their work from a bunch of wild boys who they just cannot see would be influenced for the better. Raising the achievement of boys should never be done at the expense of the girls, as we have been at pains to make clear, but girls are under-achieving as well, sometimes in different ways from the boys. We would argue that the glass ceiling will continue until girls get more used to taking risks, speculating and causing upsets. The present National Curriculum, with its rewards for patient hard work, may not do many favours for girls in the longer term.

In Seating Plan C (Figure 8.3) the teacher has decided to place the desks together in groups of four, a common strategy in primary schools. The advantage of this is that it gives more scope for planning a stronger

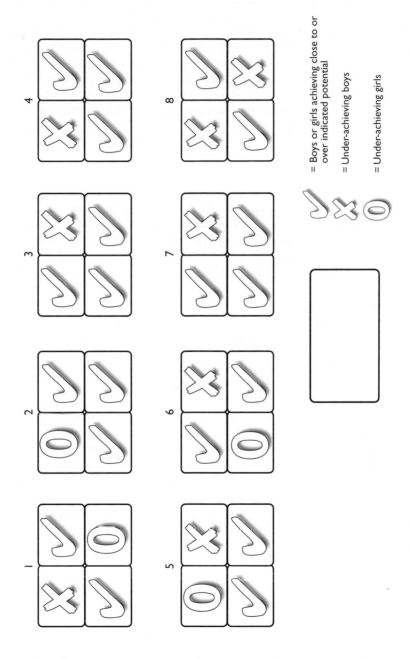

Figure 8.3 Seating Plan C: Teacher decides on foursomes.

influence upon the under-achiever. The teacher may now have three achievers exuding good practice as can be seen in 2, 3, 4 and 7. The disadvantage is that – if the numbers don't work out – you can be left with two under-achievers on the same table (1, 5, 6 and 8). There is nothing wrong with this *per se*. It all depends on where the balance of influence lies and is a decision that has to be the product of professional reflection. The other advantage with this plan is that the students are ideally placed for group work (see below).

Teachers should be aware that seating plans in the manner described above can be controversial, which is one of the reasons why it is so important to have an effective awareness-raising strategy. Parents do not always like the idea of choice being taken from their children, nor that their little Marie-Louise is forced to sit next to Sam-who-keeps-ferrets, never mind that Sam is terrified of her. An important aspect of any seating policy is that it is flexible. It can be changed if things do not work out. The pupils know that, they know why they have been asked to sit in a certain place and they know their role there – whether it be to learn from, or to show and encourage, another. It is accepted that the teacher is in charge of managing learning in the classroom.

Group work

A recent survey of primary schools in one LEA revealed that, despite the fact that the pupils were sitting in groups, very little group work was being done. By group work we mean learning when the pupils have to work together, not when they are sitting together but engaged in individual work. Boys, as we discussed earlier, tend to prefer being social learners, and group work will help them. Group work also helps to optimise the effects of having a planned seating policy. Under-achieving boys who have been placed in groups for specific reasons – of which they are aware – may well find that the very aspects of learning where they are weakest are regularly exemplified for them. The sorts of areas where group work is at its best are:

- problem-solving, particularly something concrete like tower-building;
- group opinion on a controversial subject, such as capital punishment or school uniform;
- conducting an experiment or survey where group members have different tasks which build to a coherent whole;
- production of a multi-faceted piece of work, such as a newspaper or a display;
- a quiz or challenge based on teams.

It can be interesting to ask individuals their opinion, of each other as learners, or of an issue, both before and after the group work. Teachers may well build objectives into a lesson so that the pupils come to realise the function, benefit and potential of group work. As when thinking about a seating plan, the teacher needs to be careful about the composition of the group and also that the task is appropriate to group work. In one school the teacher wrote comments on the board about the quality of the group work going on. 'Group A working well together', 'Group B listening well to each other', 'Group C making good use of resources' both reinforced the fact that co-operative working was one of the learning objectives and also gave positive messages to all the groups. The students really enjoyed and responded to this immediate feedback. At the end of the lesson the teacher gave them a score on the quality of their group work. Thus the process of learning, as well as the outcomes, is being valued in the eyes of the students.

Some teachers have reported that boys prefer working in pairs rather than groups. This is fine if they are in productive, achieving pairs but care needs to be taken to ensure that the pairs are more than a social or comfort zone: they have to be learning zones as well. Pairs can be a precursor to a group of four, with the comfort zone provided of working with another of the same gender.

Lesson plans which work for boys and girls

Lesson plans which work for boys have got to be good. Lesson plans which work for girls can be much looser, as experience and research suggest that girls are still willing to work despite poor teaching. Girls may be more co-operative about copying from a book or the board, but is that really a good learning experience? We feel that in this light boys' achievement can often be viewed as a barometer of good teaching. The wider the gap between boys' and girls' achievement the more a school should be monitoring the quality of teaching. Many boys may well have been disenchanted by inappropriate lessons, which do not stimulate the girls either but who persevere with boring and confusing tasks.

In general we feel that it is important to start with reasonably short spans of activity at the beginning of the lesson which gradually lengthen out as the lesson progresses until the processing at the end. Thus a sixty-five minute lesson may run as follows:

1   Look for a 'smartstart'. Praise those who have their books and materials out, but don't dwell on those who have not.
2   What did we learn in the last lesson? Discuss in your pair/trio/group for thirty seconds. The *rapporteur* must be alternately boy/girl. – *Two minutes.*
3   The objectives of this lesson: How it relates to the unit of study/course as a whole. Explain any other objectives which may come out of the

way we are going to learn. What exactly are we going to do in the lesson? – *Three minutes*.

4 Teacher input on the subject, setting the context of the Siege of Paris/irregular verbs/mosquito reproduction/role of the clearing banks/ algebraic equations, etc. May use board/refer to specific pages in textbook or whatever. – *Five minutes*.

5 Explanation of their task and where they can find all they need for the work. Give strategies for the successful completion of their task, for example, spider diagrams, find five key words. – *Three minutes*.

6 Main lesson activity, divided up into four parts totalling forty minutes:

(a) Ten minutes on collecting, planning, deciding the shape of the activity. This is a good opportunity to drive home the importance of preparation.

(b) Five minutes with the whole class asking how they have progressed, ironing out any problems, etc. Ensure that the task set is so designed that even the slowest will have achieved something in ten minutes. In some situations the teacher may find it useful to model to the class what they could or should have done, or what they should do next.

(c) Twenty minutes for the main part of the activity.

(d) Five minutes to set any homework due.

This main part of the lesson will obviously vary considerably depending upon the nature of the lesson and how well teachers feel pupils are learning from it.

7 Processing activity: how has it gone? What have you learned? Have you managed to fulfil the learning objectives? What still causes you concern? Can you see how this links in with what else we have done? If not, do you realise that it will in the future when we do x, y and z? Set any homework due. – *Seven minutes*.

8 Processing the teaching: how else would you like to have learned that? Do you think it was the most effective way? What would have improved your learning? – *Three minutes*. This activity is a sign of a confident teacher. It is usually something to aim for when relationships have been established with the class. There is an enormous payback from such an activity. It not only creates trust in the classroom; it confirms the school as a learning organisation, allows the students to make honest mistakes and will inform the teacher about possible amendments to teaching strategies and style.

9 Time to clear away. – *Two minutes*.

Obviously, this will have to be varied for the very many lessons which are not sixty-five minutes long, and there should be no slavish loyalty to the contrived times in this model – but the principle ingredients are clear enough. It is important that teachers do not adopt the strategies which have often been reported when facing classes of difficult boys: keep them busy, keep them writing, don't give them time to mess about. They are surviving, not teaching. It may be a natural reaction to fill the time of the nuisances with boring tasks, but it is doing favours to no one. You should try to keep clear in their minds that although there is a strong link between classroom management and discipline, they are not the same. As classroom managers you have to manage the learning of all the individuals in your class. To penalise the whole class with boring, repetitive work is unfair, unproductive and eventually *counter*-productive. This could be discussed with the class. If individuals in the class still refuse to work despite being given the kind of work which we know and they have said they prefer, it is a matter for the wider disciplinary procedures of the school. Most boys will react positively to the sorts of measures we have described in this chapter – but remember: it is essential that any work in the classroom is taken in the context of awareness-raising and the whole school strategies discussed elsewhere.

Feedback

Feedback and marking play an important role in raising the interest in success of all students. Unfortunately, it has often played the role of confirming students' more negative suspicions about their abilities. This is particularly true of boys who may find that their areas of weakness – tidiness and presentation – are commented upon, even scorned, by teachers. Tell anyone enough times that they are untidy, sloppy or lazy and they will soon feel obliged to live up, or down, to this image. The general rule should be that students need to be moved forward from where they are, not bogged down by repeated failure. Hence when marking, teachers should:

1   Be very clear when the work is set exactly what they will be looking for. It is an unwise teacher who tries to mark all aspects of every piece of work – that way madness lies. It may be an idea to ask the students to write at the top of their work the aspect which is being marked. *Never* have more than three aspects or 'things' which are being marked.
2   Try to avoid commenting on presentation unless really necessary.
3   Try to give more positive comments than negative ones. This does not mean that mistakes or poor work should be ignored, but feedback is an opportunity to ask the students to question the whole relationship they have with their work and, if necessary, to challenge the image they have of themselves as learners. If a mistake is pointed out it should be made clear why it is wrong. If it is a first or unusual mistake in this aspect of the work, make it clear that it is unlike the student to make it. If it *is* typical of them, tell them they are too good to make such

errors. In other words, the teacher is building an image in the students' minds of them as successful learners. Specific ideas for improving their work are also much more useful than 'try harder' (e.g. count the number of sentences; count the number of full stops; is either 'winning'? It should be a draw).

4   In many cases peer assessment may be a good idea. Not only does it give boys time to reflect on their work, and that of others, it should lead to a discussion about what exactly good work is and what gains high marks.

5   Show the class a previously completed example of good work. Photocopy it. Homework could be to find five good things about it.

6   Consider using another sort of pen. Some teachers are very keen that a red pen is not used, and suggest that a green pen is far less aggressive.

7   Remember that some boys do not like public praise, and a private word is more appreciated. If this is the case the school is probably in the grip of anti-swotism (see Chapter 4), in which case there is a considerable amount of work to be done.

8   Try setting homework which actually favours boys and stretches girls; for example, observe the reaction in class when an essay, notes or all the answers to the comprehension must not total more than ten lines. Boys will go home smiling; some of the girls will be beside themselves.

The effective use of talk to produce gains in learning

Linked to the area discussed above, but more focused on a specific strategy, it is suggested that teachers need to give more attention to ways in which talk can be effectively used in the classroom to progress learning. One of the clearest outcomes from student responses in both questionnaire and interview, from both boys and girls, but particularly strongly from boys, was that they enjoy using talk in their learning. They find it enjoyable, effective in learning and checking learning, and motivating as a basis for further learning.

In discussing the use of expressive talk for learning, Jones (1988, p. 139) comments:

> the way schools and classrooms work at the secondary level, pupils are deprived of this most valuable tool for learning. Until teachers undergo a fundamental change of heart, a radical shift of attitude, this will continue to be the case.

Jones outlines learning contexts which encourage or discourage the effective use of talk in classrooms (see Table 8.1). Responses from both questionnaire and interview suggest that students enjoy talk and feel motivated by

Table 8.1 How to encourage educational talk in the classroom

Context	Encourages learning-talk	Discourages learning-talk
Physical	Desks in groups or U-shape Good acoustics Cassette players available Extended time available	Desks in rows Poor acoustics No equipment Limited time available
Personal	Warm, open relationship with teacher Secure, non-competitive relationships with peers Relaxed, accepting atmosphere Pupils have strong self-image as learners	Distant, suspicious relationship with teachers Insecure, competitive peer group relationships Tense, aggressive atmosphere Pupils have low self-image as learners
Task	Open Active involvement sought A purposeful outcome Real objects and tasks at the centre Tasks require collaboration	Closed Passivity expected No clear purpose or outcome Purely abstract exercises Tasks done individually
Pedagogy	Pupil's contribution most important Small groups, pupil-led Learning to do things Process-based curriculum Talk a valid part of learning Starting where the pupils are at Teacher as learning expert Pupils have autonomy Pupils influence agenda for learning Clear, understood approach to talk	Teacher's contribution most important Whole class, teacher-led Learning things Content-based curriculum Talk peripheral Starting where the teacher is at Teacher as subject expert Pupils have no autonomy Teacher dictates agenda for learning Teacher confused

Source: Jones (1988, p. 130)

it. They are certainly capable of separating the use of 'talk for learning' from 'talk for purposes of sociable interaction'.

Teachers within the schools participating in this action research project were keen to create situations in which 'talk for learning' could take place. Much attention was given to strategies for encouraged paired conversations, the results of which could then be fed back to a larger group or the whole class. This led the participating teachers to turn their attention to the organisation of the classroom, as has been discussed above.

In the following chapters we go into deeper discussion about raising the achievement of pupils within individual subjects. We shall not stray far from a formula which has clear, time-limited tasks, active learning when appropriate, sees boys and girls benefiting from social learning and the teacher being very aware of using the class to its full potential, including advising him or her about what works best.

> ### Box 8.1 Micro strategies – getting it right for boys and girls in the classroom
>
> Hands up in class
>
> Seating policy and learning zones
>
> Group work
>
> Lesson plans which work for both genders
>
> Feedback
>
> Effective use of talk

Chapter 9

Raising achievement in English

Literacy is a critical issue

Not only is English the subject in which boys show most signs of under-achievement; it is also the key to further learning, and helps to explain why boys under-achieve in other areas of the curriculum. Tables 9.1–9.3 show how boys have been out-performed by girls since 1995.

In Chapter 2 we touched upon the possible reasons why boys were under-achieving so markedly in English. These included genetic disadvantage, the lack of literate role models, the changes in the curriculum and assessment methods, lack of appropriate parental support and unsympathetic classroom management. In this chapter we look more closely at some of these issues and how schools might redress the balance. Some of the methods we suggest may have been mentioned already, but in a general context. We want to discuss them now in the way they apply to English.

Raising achievement in English in the primary school

No discussion of primary school English achievement can ignore the impact of the Literacy Hour which most schools adopted from October 1998. In March 1998 the National Literacy Strategy was published, which describes in detail the composition of the Literacy Hour. It is interesting that the hour follows quite closely the VEST model (Variety, Engagement, Social Learning and Transformation) we covered in Chapter 3, although arguably

Table 9.1 Percentage of 7 year olds achieving Level 2 or more in the Key Stage 1 teacher assessments in English

	1995	1996	1997	1998
Boys	76	74	75	76
Girls	80	79	80	81

Source: DfEE (1998)

Table 9.2 Percentage of 11-year-olds achieving Level 4 or more in the Key Stage 2 statutory tests in English

	1995	1996	1997	1998
Boys	42	50	57	57
Girls	71	62	69	73

Source: DfEE (1998)

Table 9.3 Percentage of 14-year-olds achieving Level 5 or more in the Key Stage 3 statutory tests in English

	1995	1996	1997	1998
Boys	45	48	48	57
Girls	64	66	66	73

Source: DfEE (1998)

not closely enough. For both key stages the hour is split into four parts (see below). It is important to acknowledge that each part is also divided to some extent. For instance, the first fifteen minutes should deal with what was learned in the previous hour and what the learning objectives are for the next hour.

The Literacy Hour

1   Whole class: Key Stages 1 and 2 – shared text work (a balance of reading and writing). – *Fifteen minutes.*
2   Whole class: Key Stage 1 – focused word work. Key Stage 2 – a balance over the term of focused word work and sentence work. – *Fifteen minutes.*
3   Group and independent work: Key Stage 1 – independent work while the teacher works with at least two ability groups each day on guided text work. Key Stage 2 – independent work while the teacher works with at least one ability group each day on guided text work. – *Twenty minutes.*
4   Whole class: both key stages – reviewing, reflecting and consolidating teaching points and presenting work covered in the lesson. – *Ten minutes.*

The question is: To what extent will this help boys? The guidance in the pack makes it clear that teaching should be:

(a) discursive with plenty of high-quality oral work. This will suit boys in many ways but will be jeopardised if teachers rely too heavily on 'hands up in class' and do not give boys the opportunity to reflect;
(b) interactive – which again should suit boys;

(c) well paced, 'characterised by a sense of urgency, driven by the need to make progress and succeed'. This again should suit boys and reflects what we have previously written about boys responding well to short-term challenges;

(d) confident, 'teachers having a clear understanding of the objectives', which are very well laid out in the framework. This is fine, but teachers also need to be sure that the pupils are similarly aware of the objectives;

(e) ambitious, 'creating an atmosphere of optimism about high expectations of success'. This is excellent, and could be supported by some of the suggestions made earlier regarding the school as a learning organisation, together with the celebration of success.

In short, the Literacy Hour, despite or perhaps because of its prescriptive nature, should be viewed by teachers as a positive opportunity, but only if they apply their professional expertise in moulding it to the needs of their pupils, and particularly to their boys. What will be the nature of the text to be discussed? The framework sets out the types of texts to be discussed for each term, but it may be a good idea to ask the pupils themselves if they have preferences for any particular text. Some teachers feel that the politically correct 1990s, although in many ways 'a good thing', have deprived boys of the sort of fiction they used to relish with nothing replacing it. Perhaps boys are incapable of being satisfied by the alternatives on offer. Why is there no male equivalent to the female teenage magazines *Bliss*, *Sugar*, *More* and *Just Seventeen*? The publishers, normally so keen to exploit a market, certainly feel that boys would not be interested, although recent, unpublished research in Kirklees suggests that some boys are desperate to find a 'Junior FHM'.

There are a number of other strategies which primary schools can adopt.

The library

Schools should be able to consider exactly how the library could be organised to benefit boys. Boys often have less understanding than girls about how a library works. Interestingly, they can be seduced by the organisation and technology of libraries and enjoy spending time in them. This means that they may be busy 'doing' things in the library but do not spend any more time reading. Giving boys responsibility within the library, of explaining its functions and organisation to younger boys, showing how the library can help them in their interests, are all useful ways of raising its profile and attractiveness. This can be further enhanced if the library enjoys a wider role as a resource or information centre. Boys are attracted to ICT and the library can be made synonymous with excitement and fun, which is not the image it presently enjoys in most boys' minds.

Libraries can be used to encourage boys to read if their needs are catered for. Give it some VEST! Find some books about dinosaurs, which say three similar and three contrasting statements about them. In accepting this challenge, or an infinite number of others like it, the boys will read a great deal.

Boys and reading are not all bad news; it often depends on what has been prepared for them. Kim Reynolds (1996) from the Roehampton Institute found that 93 per cent of boys at Key Stage 2 enjoyed reading adventure stories. They preferred to read about sport, were more likely to choose a book because it was about their hobby, and selected sport, science-fiction and hobbies as their preferred choice of reading matter.

Having avoided certain stock for its focus on typically male stereotypes and interests, has the school and its library replaced it with books which boys want to read, will ask to read, will be excited to read? Boys are attracted to cult/fashion reading like *Goosebumps* or, more recently, *Animorphs*. The latter makes good use of boys' – and girls' – interest in pets and animals. Boys are interested in a fantasy world (a taste later carried forward to science-fiction) but one where, importantly, they can see themselves in the stories.

It is interesting to ponder the mirror which boys provide for the adult world. Highly literate male authors tend to write from plot whereas their female equivalents tend to write from character. Perhaps we should not be surprised that boys display a different approach to literacy compared to girls.

The LEA's library support service will probably have ideas about the 'right kind' of stock to attract reluctant readers – which will probably be predominantly boys. Boys *do* judge a book by its cover! Choosing books with good covers showing boys as central characters is a good idea. Some schools have asked the boys themselves to recommend reading matter – books, magazines, comics – which they think might be interesting. These are sometimes non-fictional and represent boys' interests in sport, computers and hobbies. Asking the boys themselves has the added bonus of resulting in peer group approval.

Preparation for transfer to secondary school

Secondary schools often complain that the pupils they inherit from the primary schools are not up to the standard suggested by their transfer information, and in particular that they cannot read as well as had been claimed. This is often based on the introduction of a completely different menu of English by the new school which, as Graham Frater (1997, p. 16) notes, could almost be a different language entirely:

> except in English, most subjects immediately make heavy new demands on that (the new pupils') literacy. They provide a diet of reading

material that differs quite sharply from the staple of the primary years: it is not predominantly narrative; it is formal in style; it seldom uses dialogue; and it does not always, or even commonly, follow simple chronological order. Moreover, most subject departments require pupils to write in these unfamiliar genres with little explicit instruction. In short, stiff new challenges face the pupil whose literacy is secure.

To say nothing of those whose literacy is insecure. Although this observation implies that secondary schools have a lot of work to do there is also plenty of scope here for primary schools to liaise with their local high schools and introduce and explain some of the different types of English which may be encountered within a few weeks. The introduction of the Literacy Hour with its insistence on a wide variety of fiction and non-fiction texts should greatly assist with this situation.

Partnered reading

The idea of partnered reading is not new. The value of an older pupil reading with a younger one has been well recognised for some time. Prospective pupil tutors are trained with very precise instructions about exactly how to support the younger learner. In the best schemes,[1] when and how to follow, lead and intervene are all very carefully explained – as is the importance of allowing the younger learner to choose the book and discuss its story and pictures. Partnered reading as a concept was not developed with the under-achievement of boys particularly in mind, but some schools have made very good use of it in this context. The pairing of Year 6 boys who are themselves low or under-achievers with Year 3 boys has been very interesting. These older boys are revealed to the younger ones in roles they had not suspected. They are no longer the kickers of footballs, cock o' the school and potential or real bullies – but instead are students with skills which they are willing to share and pass on. Some schools have claimed remarkable results, but perhaps the comments of the pupils involved are just as revealing.
     From the tutors:

> 'I couldn't read very well but I am improving as well. I'm reading more books with George [his pupil]. I didn't like reading but now I do.'
> (Boy, aged 11)

> 'Sometimes when he [his pupil] has a bad day I don't enjoy it. He's made progress. When he started I thought he had to concentrate more

1 See *Shared Reading*, a video instruction pack to train pupil-tutors, from Kirklees LEA.

and now he does. He reads library books without a lot of help. It helps me too.'

(Boy, aged 10)

'My partner is learning quite quickly . . . now he whizzes through. I think it's interesting and I like to help him.'

(Boy with behavioural problems, aged 11)

'When I have been learning him I have picked up some words, and when I used to read I was very slow, but now I can read more faster. How I learned to do it I watched a video and the video told me how to do it and be a tutor.'

(Boy, aged 11)

'I do my tutoring with Class 5 on their mat. I ask him to read a page and if Thomas (my partner) doesn't know a word then I break up the word or ask him to look at the picture. If there is not one and he can't read the word still I tell him the word. At the end of a page I ask Thomas to read the word he got wrong to see if he could remember the word. When there's only a minute or two left I ask him to read all the words he got wrong to make perfectly sure that he remembers the words.'

(Boy, aged 11)

It is apparent that there are gains to be made through the partnered reading scheme that go beyond literacy. Boys find themselves in the role of carers and teachers, and the vast majority of them say they like it. This is a wonderful opportunity to challenge the vicious circle of boys who, denied their caring role, may go on to become outwardly uncaring partners and uninvolved parents, in turn producing more uncaring boys. The organis-ation of such a scheme is more difficult in a secondary school because of the disruption to a complex timetable, but some schools do manage it.

The initial training of tutors is crucial. Potential tutors love watching the training video because it gives them a chance to be critical of 'model tutors' who show them what to do (which is the intention), and to build up their own idea of good practice and self-confidence.

Parents

Elaine Millard (1996) has found that some boys expressed a strong dislike of reading – 'They represented their reading as a hypothetical construct. That is they could read but chose not to. In other words they were allit-erate rather than illiterate and their reading skills were being allowed to stagnate.' Perhaps this is not surprising given that the same researcher found that the boys described their fathers as reading mainly the football results, sports reports and newspapers, but not very much fiction. Primary school and parental reading, or listening to reading, has been dominated by fiction. One of the welcome aspects of the Literacy Hour is its insistence that different types of text, including many non-fiction varieties, should be used. Parents should also be aware of the need to encourage such interest and be prepared to listen to articles about sports, fishing, ICT, animals and cars.

As discussed previously, parents as a cohort tend to exhibit some fairly sexist behaviour. They will invariably expect less of their sons – in terms of behaviour, effort, appearance, organisation and presentation – than their daughters. This is reinforced by fathers' relative under-involvement with their children. Research by the NSPCC suggests that 50 per cent of children reported doing homework or reading with mothers, but only 34 per cent did so with their fathers. Nearly 80 per cent said they wanted their fathers to spend more time with them, but only 2 per cent wanted more time from their mothers. Perhaps we should not be surprised that a nation of under-performing dads results in under-achieving boys.

This tolerance of boys' lack of application is born of a number of factors: the boys' greater tendency to rebel against things which do not interest them; a parental belief that real learning starts in the secondary school; and a parental satisfaction with the progress indicated at the end of Key Stage 1. These factors, combined with the fact that parents often get more feedback and enjoyment from their daughters when they help them with reading and writing, adds up to a benign and unintended conspiracy against the achievement of boys in primary English. Schools need to form partnerships with parents about continuing to hear their sons read. Newsletters home, instructional videos or specific leaflets about exactly *how* to hear them read (available from a number of LEAs[2] and also in bookshops) are a good start, but in some areas they are not enough. Some schools have held special literacy evenings where the problems and techniques of helping reading are explained. Not all parents will attend. The school should make it clear to parents that teachers, classroom support assistants or others will be visiting them if they cannot attend. Parents are sometimes embarrassed by their own lack of literacy, either because English is not their first language or because they failed at school. Great sensitivity must be shown, but the achievement of the pupil cannot be put to one side. If the parent(s) would like help in tackling their literacy the school may be in a position to help, or at least put them in touch with helping agencies listed at the end of this chapter. Meanwhile, if the parents feel that they genuinely cannot help, ask them to find a neighbour, friend or relative who can. All this sounds like a great deal of effort. It is. But it is probably a great deal less

2 E.g. *Paired Reading* video, available from Kirklees LEA.

than the effort the school, and the secondary school after it, will have to invest in mopping up failure as the maturing pupil, failing and alienated, begins to express himself in a more destructive fashion. Research into the effectiveness of reading recovery, for example, shows clearly that the earlier the intervention the more effective it is likely to be, certainly more effective than statementing later on.

Role models

There is no greater potential than in English for the creative and effective use of role models. Primary schools can use relatives, friends and neighbours of the school to talk to the pupils, but particularly the boys, about the importance of reading and to read to them. The visiting males should have a job, a personality or an appearance which will appeal to boys – and be able to talk about reading enthusiastically. They could perhaps talk about their favourite book or the book they are reading at the moment. It does not have to be fiction. Some schools ask their visitors to bring a story to read to the children; others have a reading week or fortnight when perhaps as many as twenty male visitors come into school to read. Schools should also be aware that they have a number of visitors anyway, independent of any reading strategy. How could they be used? Can the road safety officer, police officer, fire officer, chair of governors be asked to read? What about the caretaker or groundstaff? Some would be excellent at such a task.

Some schools use role models who can come into school to read, or listen to reading, on a regular basis. They have to be careful that these are not all older, retired people. The emphasis must be on the role model rather than their availability. The release of staff from local factories, offices and commerce – discussed in Chapter 7 – is a possibility for some primary schools.

Raising achievement in English in the secondary school

> 'As a former Head of English, I was aware that boys and girls functioned in quite different ways in regard to literacy. It wasn't simply the question of different rates of maturation, but different styles of interacting in the classroom, which, perhaps, was more obvious in the context of an English lesson than it might be in some other sort of subjects, with different traditional pedagogies in place.'
>
> (Headteacher)

Working in partnership

It is necessary to breathe to stay alive. Night follows day. The Pope is a Catholic. Bears stroll in the woods. English departments need to work in partnerships with their feeder primary schools. It may be obvious to some, but in that case why is it so often marked by its absence? The complaints from secondary schools that their students arrive semi-literate in Year 7 are legend. 'And he's got a Level 4 in his SATs! He's illiterate and his teacher is innumerate. What's the matter with them down there?' These types of comments are not symptomatic of a united profession working together in the interests of developing the potential of the pupil. The English department should be fully aware of the real strengths and weaknesses of new students before they arrive. It is in English, marked out more than any other subject by its continuity and progression of skills, that true partnership has its greatest potential. When partnerships do exist it is often, quite naturally, the secondary school which leads them and administers them. It is the secondary school which is the common link, the secondary school which inherits the pupils, and the secondary school which has most to gain from effective partnership. We shall be dealing with partnerships in a more generic fashion in Chapter 16, but there are certain aspects about English which are worthy of specific consideration.

Earlier in this chapter we referred to Graham Frater's research about the transition from primary to secondary school (see pp. 110–111). We suggested that there were certain things the primary school should consider. Similarly, the secondary school should ensure that its English teachers have helped the primaries to develop the concepts of the different forms in which English can be written before they change schools. Colleagues in other departments can be asked to develop with their students (*not* given) writing frames and guidelines about how to teach them to students. These should help the newly arrived student to realise what a report, an observation, an experiment, a discursive essay, notes, actually look like. It may also help to focus the assessment criteria of the different departments.

There are obviously many other activities which an active and empathetic partnership can develop. Partnered reading and role modelling (see above) are obvious examples. Some schools have produced Theatre In Education (TIE) plays and workshops about health or bullying issues, and then toured their primary schools with it. This brings home the point that literacy is about more than reading. The subject of the TIE could be achievement or literacy or boys. Shared artists-in-residence, shared INSET, shared leaflets to parents or parents' evenings, shared book or reading weeks and shared theatre visits are other ideas. Some primary schools like their old pupils to come back to talk to their Year 6 about how English is different. The possibilities are almost endless. Just how much can be done by teachers from across the curriculum is not apparent until they sit down and talk over the issues. The onus lies with the English department of the secondary school.

Setting

We have already discussed setting at some length in Chapter 6, but there are particular reasons for discussing it in the context of English. We discovered that there is no research we know of in the United Kingdom which shows that setting increases achievement. There is, by contrast, recent research which suggests that setting can militate against the very students whom schools need to encourage more – ethnic minority pupils and underachieving boys. The rationale for schools to adopt setting is a combination of misinformation and teachers believing, sometimes correctly, that it is easier for them to teach students grouped by ability. Those subjects which are more linear in knowledge acquisition and understanding, such as mathematics and modern foreign languages, are particularly enthusiastic about setting. English is not one of those subjects. It may still take more classroom management skill to teach a mixed ability class in English than if it were setted, but the nature of English and the methods of text reading and discussion make it a prime candidate for VEST (see Chapter 3). Research in Leeds LEA strongly suggests that results in GCSE English could be improved by the use of mixed ability. This comes with our previously stated health warning, namely that every system of grouping students is imperfect and those that work best satisfy two conditions: that all the staff involved believe in it, and that the inherent weaknesses in the system are recognised and *meaningful* steps are taken to address them. See Chapter 6 for more detail.

Role models, partnered reading and challenges

We have already discussed the importance of role models (p. 114). It is just as important for the secondary student. Whether it be the staff themselves (there tend to be far more men in secondary schools) who go out of their way to portray themselves as readers via a 'What the teachers are reading this week/month' display, or having a male writer-in-residence or organising residential writers' weekends, the school should be giving the message that writing and reading are fun, cool and male activities. It may be that the nature of what is read and written becomes far wider than the set books, and this is discussed below. The school should also ensure that it provides a literate environment through a variety of events and devices. Making imaginative use of notice-boards is a start (can you make them interactive?). Other schools have tried suspending assemblies for a week and using written notices instead. Another school has a reading tutorial every term when the whole school (office staff included) stop what they are doing and read silently for twenty minutes.

Partnered reading, with help from sixth formers, might be possible to organise in some schools. It will be a telling experience for, say, a Year 8 student to be given time by the cool, car-driving, non-uniform-wearing

sixth former who talks to him about what he is reading and the importance of education.

Boys also like challenges. Who can find the scariest story? Who or which
team can read the most books? Provide frameworks for book reviews, reading
outcomes (e.g. mapping the topography of a narrative, or altering key words
in an article to make the tone funny rather than scary – or vice versa),
perhaps in pairs or threes, and send them to the author and/or publisher.
You will often get a reply. Give them team quizzes about the set texts and
marry this to competition (e.g. races to the blackboard to write the correct
answer to the questions given).

Champion the width of reading

Boys do read (albeit less than girls), but they tend to read non-fiction.
Their comics, football, sport and hobby magazines, technical journals and
Internet or Encarta information all involve the reading of English. This is
not always recognised by schools, and rarely celebrated. Encouraging
those boys who are interested in any kind of reading – it may not be this
year's set book – to set up a display, form a small club with like-minded
others (they may have done so already, but schools may be able to help),
present to the rest of the class their understanding of their genre and why
they like it – all these things may lead to more commitment to reading
from boys. There will be many school staff whose primary reading is not
a novel or a book of poetry, and it is perhaps unfair to expect boys, and
girls, to reflect a different image from the one which society presents to
them. Diversity in reading should be expected and welcomed, but schools
need to go out to find it with enthusiasm rather than tolerate it when it
does appear.

Computers

We have noted elsewhere that boys tend to like ICT and audio-visual work.
The former has an image which tends to appeal to boys, even if they find
the reality of ICT is more about word processing than the more technical
or creative potential of computers. ICT gives boys the chance to transform
(downloading information, cutting and pasting, typing up work), to be social
(sharing a keyboard and ideas with one or two others) and to be engaged
(boys find that time flies when they are working on the computer). The
computer's ability to correct spelling and grammar is, on balance, to be
welcomed, although teachers need to be careful that it does not result in
similar effects to the indiscriminate use of calculators, which is said to have
impaired the mental arithmetic of some students. The use of the new (Word
95 and later) spellchecker, which highlights misspelled words immediately,
has been singled out by some teachers as a benefit as it gives instantaneous

assessment and easy correction. Boys enjoy the challenge of finding information whether it be on Encarta or the Internet, but teachers need to set tasks which expand their organisational and reading skills (e.g. find three differences between the backgrounds and influences of Wilfred Owen and Siegfried Sassoon; or download the information on Shakespeare and write a twenty-line précis of his life. Even better, do it in threes). Not only do boys enjoy their time on the computer, it is preparing them for the future.

The importance of oracy

Some boys do not always enjoy reading, and they often dislike writing just as much. One secondary English department, which enjoys the best GSCE results in a high-achieving school with no significant difference between boys and girls, withdraws all pupils in small groups of six or seven from its mixed ability sets once every few weeks for intensive language and vocabulary work. Nothing is written down. The department is convinced that oral confidence and enrichment of language is the key to a more highly developed awareness and pleasure in using the written word. The key point is not the minutiae of organisation, nor the details of timetabling which enable the system to thrive, but the belief by the whole department in the merits of the system and the high expectations they engender for each other and their students.

Box 9.1 Raising attainment in English

In the primary school

The Literacy Hour

The library

Transfer to secondary school

Partnered reading

Parents

Role models

In the secondary school

Working in partnership

Setting

Role models, partnered reading and challenges

Champion the width of reading

Computers

The importance of oracy

Chapter 10

Raising achievement in mathematics and science

'They always tear in to the room asking if we're using the bunsen burners this lesson, and if I say "no" they get very disappointed.'

(Key Stage 3 science teacher, Bristol)

It has been suggested that mathematics is a male fantasy searching for control, that the path to rationality, displayed best in mathematics, is a path to omnipotent mastery over a calculable universe.

(Hilary Povey in Clark and Millard, 1998)

Introduction

In many ways mathematics and science are different from the other subjects in the curriculum. Girls have yet to out-perform boys in any meaningful way in these subjects, as the figures in Tables 10.1 to 10.3 show. However, there is a wide difference in the relative achievement of the genders compared to fifteen years ago, when girls consistently under-performed compared with boys. The widespread belief was that mathematics and science were 'boys' subjects', and that in general girls were not destined to succeed in areas which carried the scent of engineering oil.

Although the results shown in Tables 10.1 to 10.3 suggest that there is not much national difference between the achievement of boys and girls in mathematics and science, there is a considerable body of research (e.g. Levine and Geldman-Caspar, 1996, and many more) which suggests that the two genders have very different views on these two subjects, and that they bring to them some differing learning strengths and preferences. Although the 1990s have witnessed the erosion of boys' superiority in science and mathematics, at least up until the age of 16, there is evidence that both girls and boys could be under-achieving. The girls may have caught up with the boys in terms of raw A*– C grades, but their residuals (comparative grades to their other subjects) show that maths and science are still generally among their weakest. More worryingly, only 40 per cent of science entries post-16 are girls. Only 21.5 per cent of A level physics

Table 10.1 Percentage of 7-year-olds achieving Level 2 or above in teacher assessments in mathematics and science

	1995	1996	1997	1998
Mathematics				
Boys	76	80	82	83
Girls	79	82	83	85
Science				
Boys	83	83	84	85
Girls	84	84	85	86

Source: DfEE (1998)

Table 10.2 Percentage of 11-year-olds achieving Level 4 or above in statutory tests in mathematics and science

	1995	1996	1997	1998
Mathematics				
Boys	44	54	62	59
Girls	45	54	61	58
Science				
Boys	71	62	68	70
Girls	68	63	69	69

Source: DfEE (1998)

Table 10.3 Percentage of 14-year-olds achieving Level 5 or above in statutory tests in mathematics and science

	1995	1996	1997	1998
Mathematics				
Boys	57	57	61	60
Girls	58	58	60	60
Science				
Boys	80	82	84	81
Girls	80	84	83	80

Source: DfEE (1998)

entries are girls which is less than it was ten years ago. Whereas girls make up over 90 per cent of the modern apprentices taking hairdressing, child-care, and health and social studies they contribute less than 5 per cent of engineering modern apprentices. Girls appear to have improved their achievement in maths and science *despite*, not because of, viewing the subjects with little long-term interest or planning. If girls have caught up with boys by dint of hard work and application in subjects which they still, generally, do not view with any great favour, it suggests that boys should be doing much better than they are. After all, they are supposed to be interested in maths and science.

Why boys are under-achieving in mathematics and science

'I don't like science because every time we have done a practical we always have to write a plan for it, a conclusion, and then we have to write up how we did it afterwards.'

(Year 7 boy)

Many boys come to maths and science with a similar degree of anticipation and excitement which they show for design and technology (see Chapter 11) and for similar reasons. Science in particular appears to offer practical, hands-on learning connecting to many of the things which excite their imagination such as space, cars, aeroplanes and even dinosaurs. The prospect of messing around with chemicals, bunsen burners, explosives and experiments is very seductive to many boys.

Science, as it is manifested in many boys' imagination, also appears to satisfy at least three of the VEST elements (see the end of Chapter 3): variety of learning, engagement in task and social learning; and rather than *transform* information (the fourth element) science offers the chance to *discover* it. Unfortunately, the actual experience of science for many students is nothing like as seductive. Focus groups of 16-year-olds told a Wellcome Foundation (1998) research team that if science is so interesting and important, why do they spend so much time copying and memorising all the 'facts' and repeating so much work? The overcrowded National Curriculum has resulted in a science educational experience which:

has lost its interest for too many pupils as they are frog-marched from one feature of the scientific landscape to another, without time to stand and stare, or discuss the implications of the ideas.

(Osborne, Millar and Collins, *TES Science Extra*, 1999)

The main attraction of mathematics for boys is that it constantly poses short-term challenges which appeal to their sense of competitiveness and satisfaction of attaining time-limited goals. In addition, it has the merit of discarding descriptive writing, of writing around the point, and instead appears to demand the answer without any recorded, intellectual foreplay.

There is a limited amount of physical writing which many boys dislike, and which – we have noted elsewhere – tends to follow them from lesson to lesson. Mathematics has the attractiveness of also appearing useful at times. A large amount of measuring and drawing can take place in a maths lesson, and is often organised in a social way by the teacher. It is a subject where pupils who may be linguistically challenged – more often boys than girls – have the opportunity to shine in a very different discipline. Moreover, there is the chance to use gadgets, the most obvious one being the calculator. This way of working tends to appeal to boys. So why aren't they doing as well as they should?

Some teachers have pointed to the onset of coursework in secondary school, where problem-solving is the key. Pupils have to write down how they produced a formula, or why that formula works: mathematics is no longer 'right' or 'wrong'. Communication, the old Achilles' heel of boys' academic armoury, is a very important strand when it comes to assessing coursework. As in science, boys often don't enjoy 'writing up' coursework. In addition to this, new government proposals, acting on concern with the over-use of calculators, are lessening the opportunities for using them in exams. An increasing number of exams over the last few years demand explanations of why an answer is correct, which tends to help girls' strengths of reflection but to highlight boys' weaknesses.

Boaler (1997) noted that in her research in secondary school mathematics a clear difference in favoured learning styles emerged between the genders. She characterised girls' approach to learning mathematics as 'a quest for learning', whereas the boys' style 'involved playing a kind of school mathematics game . . . the aim for many of the boys was not to understand, but to get through the work quickly' (Boaler, 1997, p. 115).

Boaler believes that this desire to understand mathematics lies at the heart of the gender-differentiated response which can be seen both in the classroom and in results.

> I became convinced that it was this desire to understand, rather than any difference in understanding, that really differentiated the girls from the boys. The girls knew that they needed to understand mathematics, but they felt they had limited access to understanding within their fast, pressurised textbook system . . . 91% of girls regarded 'understanding' as the most important aspect of learning mathematics, compared with 65% of boys . . . 5% of girls regarded 'getting a lot of work done' as the most or second most important aspect of learning mathematics, compared with 19% of boys.
>
> (Boaler, 1997, p. 113)

Boaler goes on to suggest, as we have noted elsewhere in this book, that girls have a tendency to lack confidence and often attribute their failures to a lack of ability, and need to become 'less anxious, more confident, in essence more masculine'. At the same time boys tend to rush towards answers without seeing the need to properly understand or reflect *why* they were right or wrong. In essence they are not learning, and this has implications for teaching and learning styles, discussed below. This chapter is concerned with suggesting methods of teaching which try to optimise learning experiences for both genders.

By and large, the researchers have found that girls think and write about science with a degree of practicality, building on their everyday experiences and suggesting how these could be improved by science (Table 10.4). They also inject their thoughts with emotion and build a relationship with scientific objects, real or fantasised. Boys, on the other hand, tend to be less practical, more imaginative and creative, and – when invited to describe science-related experience – are more confident than girls in writing about personal, out-of-school events as well as classroom experiences. Many boys are also interested in science-fiction, which may help to fuel their imagination. Most girls, and most women, have a very negative view of science-fiction. Have a look at the gender balance in the science-fiction writing evening class, or look in at the Star Trek conventions. Wall to wall testosterone. Perhaps we should not be surprised: most popular science-fiction books present very negative stereotypes of women, if they are there at all.

If boys and girls view science in different ways, they bring to it some different preferred learning styles, but they also share some interests both in terms of topic and in learning style.

Table 10.4 How do boys and girls differ in their attitude to science?

Most typical writing of a boy	Most typical writing of a girl
If I were a scientist I would invent a fuel that one eye drop will power a 50' spaceship to Jupiter and back safely. This super fuel would help us to get to far off places very cheap. I would make this fuel from an explosive material found in space and there would be a lot of this material in the universe, so it would be very cheap. It would be useful because we could fly to a far off galaxy with about three gallons that would cost $3. (Boy, aged 13)	I would invent a robot that could do anything. He would be really cute. He would be small and look like a regular robot. He could clean and do things. He would clean my room and wash my clothes and he could do my homework. Whenever I needed him he would come and if I had a problem he would fix it. I could talk to him too. He would be a good friend. (Girl, aged 14)

Source: From Levine and Geldman-Caspar (1996)

Getting it right for boys and girls in mathematics and science

Building on pupils' earlier experiences

Children do not come to science and mathematics as empty vessels, either in terms of understanding science or in the nature of scientific investigation. Many pupils will have attended reception and nursery classes where they will have had opportunities to find out and learn about the world in which they live. These experiences are likely to have included:

- asking questions about why things happen;
- investigating a wide variety of objects and materials in the natural and man-made world;
- learning about themselves and living things;
- looking closely at similarities and differences, patterns and change;
- talking about their observations and sometimes recording them.

The differing backgrounds which children have in scientific learning offer a significant challenge to teachers. By observing children's developing understanding of scientific knowledge and ideas, teachers will be able to ascertain what tasks and expectations would best support their learning. It also means that the way in which lessons are structured, in both primary and secondary schools, may need to change. The initial activity at the beginning of a topic/lesson may be to find out – perhaps by pair and then whole class discussion – what the class may already know. There will be a great deal of misconception and misinformation as well as proper understanding. It is fascinating, for example, to ask groups to draw around the shape of a body on some sugar paper and then to insert the bones and organs. This sort of activity has a manifold effect: it is active and interesting; it totally engages pupils in learning; it is social, and it involves transforming information. In other words, it has all the characteristics of VEST (see Chapter 3). In addition, it has a relevance to the learners and at the same time informs teachers about the level of knowledge and understanding of the class before moving on to the physiology of the body. Unfortunately, when the science National Curriculum was introduced, its emphasis on content led many primary teachers away from this type of investigative approach to acquisition of knowledge. We may now be approaching another challenge to primary science as the emphasis on literacy and numeracy encroaches upon its curricular time.

Building on Key Stage 2 in the secondary school

> 'By the sound of it some people have done this before – that's a bit of a shame.'
>
> (High school maths teacher)

'It's a bit too easy. We've got more things to do now because we have more lessons, but the work isn't all that hard.'

(Year 7 pupil on science lessons)

On the same theme as the previous section, there is evidence to suggest that some secondary schools do not value what has been taught, and learned, in the primary school. An investigation by Suffolk LEA found that in some schools, failure to build on previous attainment in mathematics meant that pupils' progress was set back by a year or more, and the same report found that most schools were only 'partially successful' in building on pupils' previous attainment in science. The relevance of this to boys' achievement in particular is that some boys will not see the point of repeating work, which is a reasonable perception, and are more likely than girls to be alienated from the learning process.

'I have had several parents ring me up after the first few weeks of Year 9 to ask if their child (mostly boys) can move up a set because they find the work too easy because they maintain they have done the work before. I address this problem every year and try and encourage my teachers to believe the middle school and their assessment.'

(Head of maths, Yorkshire high school)

Similarly, research by Bunyan (1998) into the comparative science gradings at Key Stage 2 and 3 SATs found that secondary school science departments were not sufficiently cognisant of what had been taught in primary schools, and that as a result there may be lower expectation of students. He recommended that:

- Key Stage 3 science departments must develop a mechanism to receive and note information on children's attainment in science at the end of Key Stage 2. Such information is a valid component of any value-added analysis which could be done at the end of Key Stage 3.
- The scheme of work for Key Stage 3, and especially Year 7, should not be so inflexible that it cannot adapt or be modified to take account of pupils' prior knowledge and understanding.
- Teachers in Key Stage 3 should ensure that they are fully familiar with the programmes of study for Key Stage 2 which pupils are both being taught and evidently learning. It is no longer appropriate to discount Key Stage 2 by reference to variability of practice in different schools. It is thus very important that Key Stage 3 teachers are fully cognisant with the National Numeracy Strategy, as it appears in nearly all primary schools, and to understand both its mathematical content and its teaching methods.

- Teachers in Key Stage 3 need to monitor pupil progress throughout to ensure that enough progress is being made. This challenge has been taken up by Huntingdon School, near York, which subdivides National Curriculum levels in mathematics, science (and English) to 0.25, with the overall aim of adding two complete levels to the Key Stage 2 SAT result for each pupil. During the ensuing year, Year 7 pupils are closely monitored using effort and performance grades awarded three times per year. Targets are realigned in the light of progress made. This system, which is designed to be accessible and informative to teachers, students and parents, gives pupils short-term, achievable and *personal* goals, making them 'grade-hungry'.

The effect on learners of a new school discounting previous learning is very demotivating. There is scope here not just for carrying out Bunyan's suggestions, but for some taster learning in the summer term of Year 6 when pupils could be introduced to the sort of writing within science (and mathematics) which will be expected of them in secondary school (see section below on literacy). Perhaps the best solution, however, is to instigate bridging projects between primary and secondary schools, as has occurred in parts of Kirklees. A mathematics or science project beginning some time after SATs could be continued in the first part of the autumn term of Year 7. Some heads have objected that they have so many feeder schools that it would be impossible to organise, but here there is scope for making use of another strategy we have discussed – that of shared learning. If some of the new Year 7 intake have not taken part in the bridging project, they are assigned to pupils who have, and whose responsibility it is to bring the uninitiated up to speed.

> 'There has been a marked change of attitude of Year 9 students since we implemented Spotlight Science as a common course starting in Year 7 in the middle school. The students see from the textbook that it is a continuation of the work they did in middle school, and it has given science a clear identity across the divide of changing schools. They are comfortable with the approach because they are used to working in a similar way and see the relevance of the work they did in the middle school.'
>
> (Head of science, Yorkshire high school)

Literacy is a key issue

Many observers of the science education scene have commented that literacy is a key issue in trying to improve understanding and raise achievement. We have written elsewhere about the need for clearly explaining the key, and often troublesome, words which pupils are expected to understand and manipulate in a subject-specific context. Mass, weight, pitch, orbit, revolve, conduct and insulate, along with hundreds of others, have general as well as scientific meanings – and it is unreasonable to expect pupils to learn these by osmosis. Science co-ordinators and subject leaders need to plan specifically for the teaching and learning of the scientific vocabulary. This is probably best done socially, with pairs or groups given the task to investigate and explain to the rest of the class the common and scientific meanings.

In Key Stages 1 and 2 it should be possible for teachers to find science-based texts to be used as examples of non-fiction activities within the Literacy Hour. Science, like literacy, can be used in a cross-curricular way and stories can also be used to exemplify the usefulness and relevance of science in everyday life, which will particularly appeal to boys.

Practical science

In the debate about the desirability of more practical science, one of the considerations which is often not discussed is the effect on language development. Practical science usually involves social learning, which is an excellent arena for language development as pupils are engaged in working together on a shared, enjoyable activity. Research by the ASE (1999) with teachers found that they regarded practical work as 'an essential part of learning in science', and that the main benefits were that it:

- is motivating;
- enhances and consolidates knowledge and understanding of concepts;
- should be used to demonstrate scientific ideas;
- develops transferable skills, planning, logical thinking, teamwork, measurement and systematic enquiry;
- helps learners to become confident users of scientific language;
- helps learners to develop a critical point of view, particularly when evaluating evidence;
- gives learners the opportunity to handle specialised equipment;
- is important in exploring and solving problems in the environment.

Seating policy

In Chapter 8 we went into some detail about the importance of a seating policy and how the teacher should manage the learning atmosphere in the classroom. You may wish to read this again with science or mathematics in mind. Some of the most effective and immediate changes we have seen in classroom atmosphere and motivation took place in a science laboratory in a Dewsbury high school when the teacher introduced 'revolving benches'. However, some recent action research by Goldsmiths College (quoted in *TES*, 1 January 1999) in Key Stage 3 science has taken these ideas further. The class was divided into five groups, four to work on science and one to observe their interactions. The observers recorded who talked, who interrupted, who listened and who was supportive. At the end of the session all the students had to estimate how much talking and listening had been going on and to write down their perception of the lesson – and this led to a whole class discussion of who had done what and what had been learned. Teachers have found the science classes much more pleasant to teach, and this reflective approach has seemed to eradicate gender differences.

> 'Work is more interesting because you can talk about your feelings and someone else's.'
>
> (Female student)

> 'You get to meet different people and get to know them, and sometimes people have a lot more in common, but they don't know it.'
>
> (Male student)
>
> (Both quoted in *TES Science Extra*, January 1999)

Researchers believe that by making science more social to girls it will encourage fewer of them to abandon it after GCSE. At the same time boys are encouraged, and enjoy reflecting upon and discussing what they have learned – one of the major weaknesses in the learning style of the typical under-achieving boy.

Effective teaching and learning strategies

> The teaching methods used in mathematics can also create barriers to women's participation. We know that women express much less preference than men for competitive or individualistic approaches to learning and a greater preference for a co-operative mode. ... The traditional style of mathematics teaching is authoritarian and teacher-centred, and tends to encourage a competitive atmosphere.
>
> (Barnes and Coupland, 1990, p. 74)

What feminist observers of mathematics (of which the above is an example) failed to grasp is that this teaching method is not very efficient at helping most boys achieve either (although some teachers claim that very able boys *and* girls prefer the challenge, and that it is what they most enjoy about the subject). We have written elsewhere about the benefits of challenge for many boys, but only in the context of the ability to succeed, of social learning, of reflecting on their learning, and in experiencing a variety of teaching and learning styles. The mathematics classroom which Povey describes as being good for girls is one which, to a large extent, would be good for boys as well:

> A mathematics classroom in which girls might thrive is likely to be one in which learning takes place through interaction and co-operation, where group work and discussion are encouraged and validated, where experience, activities and ideas are shared, where individuals' contributions are welcomed and where creative and imaginative thinking is valued.
>
> (Quoted in Clark and Millard, 1998)

This very much reflects what we feel boys also need: the encouragement to discuss, reflect, to work socially and to contribute. We do see the need to give challenges as well, both in groups and individually, in order to engage boys and to encourage girls to take risks in a situation where they feel safe and can succeed.

Research suggests that teachers are well aware of the teaching and learning styles which are most favoured by pupils and are more effective. However, teachers tend to feel that the volume of work that has to be covered jeopardises their ability to teach attractively. The ASE consultation with teachers (1999) asked them to identify activities which frequently occur in classrooms and those they would wish to develop further.

The situation is that teachers frequently ask learners to:

- listen to explanations;
- take part in question and answer sessions;
- participate in whole class discussions;
- complete worksheets;
- carry out practical work;
- consider evidence from experiments and investigations.

Given more time and resources, teachers would create more opportunities for learners to:

- put forward their own ideas/models;
- discuss ideas with peers/whole class;
- plan, carry out and consider investigative practical work;
- use secondary sources to read and reflect;
- use drama/role play;
- become independent learners.

However, when looking at the effectiveness of different teaching styles in conveying information that was retained (Chapter 3), we found that the more active the style the more likely was retention. It may therefore be a poor investment to forsake the admittedly more time-consuming active learning styles, which the teachers prefer, for the more passive styles which are largely less effective in retaining information and which are often resented – particularly by boys.

The advent of the National Numeracy Strategy

During the autumn term of 1999 most primary schools will be implementing the National Numeracy Strategy, the most obvious sign of which in school will be a daily numeracy lesson of between about forty-five to sixty minutes' duration. The main changes in primary school mathematics teaching are intended to give:

- a framework to give much clearer learning and teaching objectives;
- a greater emphasis on mental calculation and oral discussion – both to understand numbers and figure them out;
- more whole class teaching, with whole class discussion and interaction;
- better use of assessment to inform learning weaknesses and appropriate interventions;
- more pace and challenge;
- more varied work for differentiation, and less repetition;
- a delayed use of calculators until later in Key Stage 2.

These are largely in line with the type of mathematics teaching which we feel will help both boys and girls. The signs from the pilot schools are that the strategy will make a significant, positive difference to the mathematical, and possibly the *literacy*, achievement of primary schoolchildren. The 1998 Key Stage 2 SATs results brought higher than average improvement in both mathematics and English to those pilot schools which were using the numeracy lesson (*TES*, 26 February 1999). Just why this should be is not clear, but success in teaching and learning in one subject may well breed extra confidence and effort in another – both for teacher and pupil. It may also be that the emphasis on oral work, one of the characteristics of the strategy, benefits children's spoken English which in itself gives greater access to language.

The National Numeracy Strategy also makes it clear that the use of mathematics, particularly numeracy, has enormous cross-curricular potential and that it should be used quite explicitly in that way. Some schools have reported that they normally do not make explicit reference to mathematics skills in science because 'science is seen as a discrete unit, with the national curriculum teaching in science being very focused' (*TES Extra Special*, 1 January 1999). However, when the pupils were encouraged to regard the maths they were using as actually mathematics, and which they had previously learned elsewhere, the quality of their work improved. It is perhaps a comment on pupil perception of the curriculum that they did not expect to find that what they had learned could have a use, a relevance, outside the subject classroom.

Box 10.1 Raising attainment in mathematics and science

Why boys are under-achieving.

How boys and girls differ in their attitude to mathematics and science.

Getting it right for both:

- building on experience
- building on Key Stage 2
- literacy is a key issue
- practical science
- seating policy
- effective teaching and learning strategies
- the National Numeracy Strategy.

Chapter 11

Raising achievement in design and technology

Introduction

Design and technology should ostensibly be a 'boys' subject', or at least one where boys should achieve as well as girls. At first glance the characteristics of design and technology totally satisfy the VEST formula discussed in Chapter 3 – Variety of teaching style, Engagement on the task, Social learning and Transforming. Nothing could be more likely to please and interest boys. Boys like *doing* things rather than listening, copying or writing. Boys like clear, short-term goals. Boys like working in groups. Unfortunately, the figures show that in recent GCSE results the boys have been considerably out-performed by the girls. What has gone wrong, and what can be done about it?

Raising achievement in design and technology in primary schools[1]

There are no figures to inform us of the achievement of pupils in design and technology in primary schools but we are able to make some observations about design and technology lessons and the standard of the outcomes achieved. In an early years setting both boys and girls respond to the active learning on offer such as making models, collages or products using construction kits, reclaimed materials, wood, clay, paper, card, textiles or food. Where there is explicit teaching and time allowed to practise, many very young children become proficient users of a variety of tools including those used for resistant materials; for example, saws to cut wood. However, emphasis is rarely placed upon children communicating their ideas, either verbally or graphically, before (or after) making, and so the interactive nature of the design element is often absent and valuable connections between designing and making are lost at an early age.

---

1 This, primary, part of the chapter has been written by Elaine Moreton, literacy consultant with Surrey Local Education Authority.

Young children are very able to put their ideas on paper and are often under-challenged in this area. Note that we use the term 'ideas on paper' as opposed to 'draw a picture'. This is because the language we use is important in establishing fundamental differences between 'design and technology' and 'art' in order to encourage pupils to produce 'designs' rather than 'pretty pictures' by the time they reach the end of primary education. Observations and experience within an early years setting have shown that young children can not only communicate 'ideas on paper', but also refer to them as simple plans during the making process, thus beginning to develop the important balance between active and passive learning which underpins the design and technology process.

Obstacles to learning

As noted elsewhere in this book, primary aged boys tend to be less organised, less prepared and less able to plan their work than girls. Perhaps they feel that these stages of the design-and-make process are too open-ended and seemingly unconnected to the making. Ofsted frequently flags up the imbalance between designing and making skills, with design/planning skills frequently seen to be underdeveloped and poorly understood by both pupils and teachers alike. Pupils tend to want to skip the designing/planning stage in order to get on with 'the making'. Their approach can be a bit 'bull in a china shop' and in some cases over-ambitious and unrealistic in terms of the techniques and materials available.

This lack of a disciplined, structured approach to design and technology is often inadvertently reinforced by teachers who do not actually 'teach' any skills or techniques or lack an overall awareness of the design-and-make process itself. This is reflected in planning where there are few clearly defined learning objectives notably within the design element, such as annotation and quick sketching. There are many reasons for this, not least of which is teachers' general lack of confidence and subject knowledge. The many changes that the National Curriculum for design and technology has undergone have not helped to instil confidence or embed good practice.

Expectations

Pupils are very quick to sense a teacher's lack of knowledge or confidence and this can devalue the learning in the eyes of the pupils. This is perhaps magnified by the gender issues that have evolved within design and technology, namely the fact that most primary teachers are women but that design and technology has traditionally been considered to be the domain of men. It is arguable that boys see the 'making bit' as 'what men do' and the writing and drawing as less important and often not valued by the teacher anyway. Boys in particular often expect (and are expected) to be able to use tools such as saws and hammers, but some are surprised to find that the skills involved need learning and practice. Girls (and many female teachers) often do not expect (and are not expected) to be skilful when using certain tools but many are pleasantly surprised when, through opportunity and practice, they become quite proficient.

If the 'design' process becomes detached from the 'making' process at the primary school stage then a range of related language skills development is also lost for all pupils, especially boys. The loss of this stage of development makes for shaky foundations in the secondary phase of a pupil's education. It simply reinforces the learning style 'do first and think about it afterwards'. This learning style is favoured by boys but is not one that encourages carefully presented written plans, recorded design ideas or reflective thinking. If, on the other hand, the design process is carefully linked in a structured and purposeful way it can provide a rich source of motivational factors that can persuade more pupils and especially boys to want to put pencil to paper in a meaningful way, thus developing the learning style of 'think first and then do', as favoured by girls. Design and technology therefore offers a unique opportunity to plan for work that gives a balance of both reflection and activity, not only offering access to pupils' favoured learning style (teaching to their strengths) but also addressing their weaknesses, thus offering real equality of opportunity for girls and boys alike!

Learning to enjoy the journey

Emphasis on the design-and-make process, including opportunities for real team work rather than just the outcomes, needs to start at an early age if pupils are to see themselves as real designers and makers. If pupils are encouraged to view tools, materials and techniques as simply a range of skills, knowledge and understanding that make ideas possible, this might go some way towards changing the gender-biased choices and attitudes at GCSE level in the minds of both pupils and teachers.

Careful planning of the process is essential at the primary stage. By providing scaffolding or writing frameworks for pupils' planning and designing and by further refining them with clear, short-term and timed goals, teachers can enable pupils (particularly boys) to structure their thinking and recording. By using a 'campaign' approach teachers can exploit further language opportunities to develop a range of writing models. Let us look at a Key Stage 2 (Year 5/6) primary school design-and-make assignment, to be completed over a term that involves pupils working in teams, designing and making a model of an adventure playground (Figures 11.1 and 11.2). The teacher may include certain success criteria in a design brief in order to cover specific skills that must be taught or the use of certain materials, in this case wood.

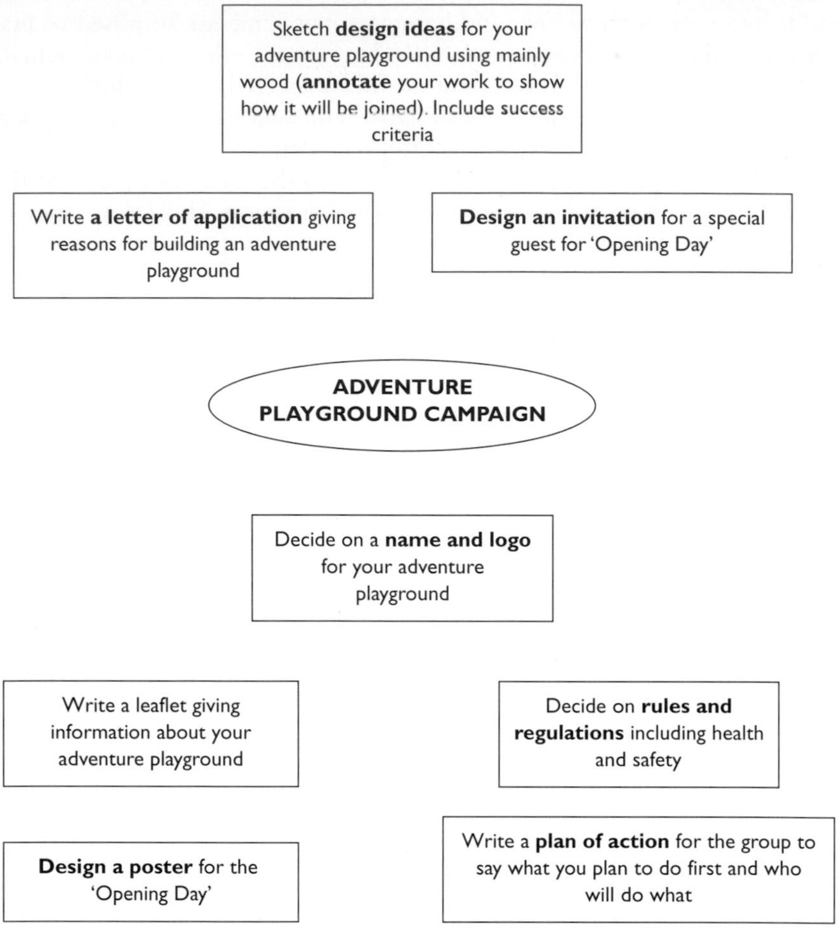

Sketch **design ideas** for your adventure playground using mainly wood (**annotate** your work to show how it will be joined). Include success criteria

Write **a letter of application** giving reasons for building an adventure playground

Design an invitation for a special guest for 'Opening Day'

ADVENTURE PLAYGROUND CAMPAIGN

Decide on a **name and logo** for your adventure playground

Write a leaflet giving information about your adventure playground

Decide on **rules and regulations** including health and safety

Design a poster for the 'Opening Day'

Write a **plan of action** for the group to say what you plan to do first and who will do what

Figure 11.1 Designing a model of an adventure playground.

Stage 1

First, the teacher carries out a task analysis and decides what skills, knowledge and understanding need to be explicitly taught; some may be identified and taught well in advance of the assignment as 'focused tasks'. Then the teacher decides on the timespan and format of the lessons and plans a careful balance of activities to deliver clear learning objectives to be shared with the pupils (Figure 11.3). Finally, consideration is given to the makeup and number of pupils in each of the teams (three or four pairs working within a team of six or eight works well for this project) and the skills needed for good team work (Figure 11.4).

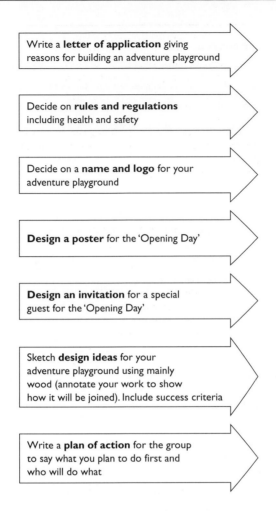

Write a **letter of application** giving reasons for building an adventure playground

Decide on **rules and regulations** including health and safety

Decide on a **name and logo** for your adventure playground

Design a poster for the 'Opening Day'

Design an invitation for a special guest for the 'Opening Day'

Sketch **design ideas** for your adventure playground using mainly wood (annotate your work to show how it will be joined). Include success criteria

Write a **plan of action** for the group to say what you plan to do first and who will do what

Figure 11.2 Adventure playground campaign 1.

Stage 2

- Pupils to investigate and research what makes a successful adventure playground (Figure 11.5). (Class discussion to share findings.)
- Working in teams, agree and write down five important things which make for a good adventure playground (timed activity). Teacher intervention at this stage focuses learning, makes it fun (Figure 11.6) and helps to provide the basis of the success criteria for pupils' designs. The writing activity is brought to life and given purpose because it is based on the initial active learning which boys particularly enjoy. Further

I will know that/be able to

I can design and plan an adventure playground and set my own success criteria

I can use a range of tools and techniques safely to join wood

I can work as part of a team including agreeing an action plan

I am able to evaluate my work against my success criteria

Figure 11.3 Main learning objectives.

Thinking of ideas	
Being able to change your ideas	
Drawing on your design sheet	
Writing on your planning sheet	
Persevering/not giving up	
Making your model	
Using the tools	

Figure 11.4 How good are you at teamwork?

Investigation/research

- Visit a local adventure playground
- Look for information in books, magazines and newspapers
- Talk to people about their favourite kind of playground activity
- Listen to what people tell you
- Use your own experience and imagination

Questions to ask

- What age group will our adventure playground be for?
- What kinds of activities/rides would be suitable?
- Can we make our activities/rides exciting, different, challenging, interesting?
- Consider how we travel and move on adventure playgrounds, e.g. up, over, under, round, between, through, balance, climb, swing

Figure 11.5 Adventure playground campaign 2.

Dear Campaign Member

I regret to inform you that the local community committee are not very happy about your plans to build an Adventure Playground in Dewsbury.

- They are worried that it may mean extra litter and noise (pollution committee).

- They are concerned about the safety of the children using the playground.

- They are worried that dogs may get in the way or cause accidents.

- They are concerned about the comfort of the adults waiting while their children are using the playground.

Please can you write back and let us know how you propose to deal with some of these problems.

Yours faithfully

Mr Colin Blundell

Figure 11.6 Sample letter to campaign member.

motivation can be gained by making this stage the 'gateway' to the rest of the assignment, i.e. 'the making'. This stage needs to be seen to be highly valued, for example, by displaying the completed success criteria (Figure 11.7) which will eventually become part of a design booklet to be displayed with the finished model.

Stage 3

- Each pair decide what they will make to contribute to their team's adventure playground.
- They individually sketch some design ideas (homework?).
- In pairs, they discuss each other's design ideas, taking positive features from both, and agree on one design idea – a composite of both. Pupils could use a pre-designed, computer-generated design sheet (Figure 11.8). Skilful teacher intervention is necessary here in order to find a balance between challenging design ideas and those that may lead to failure. We want pupils to be challenged but also to be successful as designers and makers.
- Using a structured writing framework (Figure 11.9) pupils plan what they are going to do and what they will need. Teachers should provide a 'print-rich' classroom environment that supports the various levels of literacy skills required, including technical vocabulary.

My playground .... will be/look/have/taste/

....

....

1. Will be designed for ....

.... ☐

2. Will have ....

.... activities ☐

3. Will be made of at least .... different materials. ☐

4. Will be finished by .... ☐

Figure 11.7 Design/success criteria.

Stage 4

- Any focused teaching of further skills and techniques needed.
- Skilful teacher intervention and questioning are essential in order to develop higher levels of thinking and problem-solving as the pupils embark on the making task.
- Pupils should frequently refer to their design ideas, success criteria and plans, evaluating and modifying where and when appropriate; the process is not a linear one.

Stage 5

The final evaluation should be against the original success criteria with any modifications and changes duly noted. If pupils are to value the learning involved, we must invest in the process by including evidence of the design process when we display, exhibit or discuss the outcomes. This has the valuable 'knock-on' effect of educating a wider audience such as other pupils and teachers and parents.

One thorough, rigorous and successful design-and-make assignment a year is worth far more than several half-baked attempts which produce many unfinished outcomes, often found in the stock cupboard hospital. We want *all* pupils in primary schools to develop confidence, skills and knowledge

---

DESIGN SHEET

DESIGNER   **DATE**

DESIGN TITLE

Figure 11.8 Design sheet.

and understanding at *all* stages of the process and to build on this during their secondary school experience.

Raising the achievement of secondary students in design and technology

Getting into good habits

The culture of the technology classroom in many ways captures the very best of education. Students are usually well behaved (health and safety issues have been successfully drummed into them); the atmosphere is informal with light conversation between students in a way which is often missing from general classrooms; there is occasional movement between benches without the teacher intervening and most students concentrate on their own work. Teachers are normally found helping individual students,

---

PLANNING SHEET

DESIGNER   **DATE**

DESIGN TITLE

TOP SECRET PLANS OF HOW TO MAKE MY DESIGN

MATERIALS I WILL NEED	**TOOLS I WILL NEED**

Figure 11.9 Planning sheet.

with occasional whole class teaching or demonstrating . So why don't boys do as well as girls?

In many schools, design and technology is taught in mixed ability groups in Key Stage 3. This is no bad thing for a number of reasons (see Chapter 6), but not least because low-achieving boys, and girls, often have the opportunity of seeing some of the academically more able struggle with the motor skills manipulations required. Their self-esteem, so often the root cause of poor achievement, can be given a fillip.

We have called this section 'getting into good habits', but we have not specified whose. It is just as important for the teacher to understand the preferred learning styles of boys, *and to act upon them*, as it is for boys to understand the main concepts and principles of the subject. In Chapter 3 we discussed the proposition that teachers, just like over-stressed people, often know the theory of what to do about their problem: they just never get round to doing it. The adoption of good habits helps this process immeasurably.

Awareness of language

We have discussed elsewhere in this book the central importance of language skills throughout the curriculum. We know that the starkest differences in gender achievement occur in English, and that this under-achievement of boys affects many other subjects. Design and technology would not, at first thought, qualify as a particularly language-based subject, but evidence suggests that it has a large part to play in boys' relative under-achievement. As an example of the power of language, one study found that more boys opted for food, and to some extent textiles, studies at GCSE level because it has become part of technology rather than home economics. The questions which departments should be asking about language are twofold: to what extent can design and technology help in raising literacy levels?; and what sort of literacy teaching will help to raise achievement in design and technology? Chapter 9 discussed Graham Frater's research that Year 7 students are introduced to whole new sets of jargonised English by the different departments, and asked to write in totally alien ways from that which they experienced in primary school. Do departments invest sufficient time in explaining how to set out the required formats? It would be an interesting exercise to ask the students how many new words they have come across in design and technology. There will be more than most teachers imagine – and many will not have been properly explained. One headteacher researched his school's Year 9 understanding of key words and phrases such as aesthetics and design brief. He found that it was negligible, despite their common usage by teachers in the faculty.

Some obvious examples of good practice are the display of key words and concepts on the wall or from the ceiling (the students could make a mobile) which may well change over time, project and according to progress. Developing writing frames *with* students (not giving them *to* students) to give them confidence in their skills of reporting, analysing and synthesising information may well help. The English department may be able to offer support in this field.

Do teachers in design and technology give sufficient emphasis to presenting written information, correcting spelling – particularly technical words – and the redrafting of work? Is the marking of the English – when it is chosen as a focus – in line with that used by the English department?

Design folders

Some teachers have suggested that the teaching styles in Key Stage 3 are often characterised by an over-reliance on the production of design folders. If this means a concentration on writing and copying, neatness, rewriting and presentation it is likely to demotivate boys. Girls, too, are not particularly inspired by such passive learning, but they are far more likely to produce what is asked and less likely to challenge and become distracted. Teachers, and probably the examination boards, need to be clear about what really has to be in the folder and to build on the skills which will assist good work (see below on marking and skills acquisition).

Ethos, display and anti-swotism

We have discussed display in Chapter 7 and countering the anti-swot culture in Chapter 4, and you may wish to go back to read the relevant sections in those chapters. However, both need to be re-emphasised in design and technology. Many GCSE-resistant materials groups are 'boy-heavy' and it is in such a setting where the anti-swot culture is particularly prone. Departments need to be clear that such attitudes will not be tolerated and negative references to 'swots' will be immediately challenged. Conversely, the department needs to give out all the messages it can that it supports the learning culture. Enthusing about new techniques, materials and equipment, magazines and journals in the workshops, pointing out new ideas in design in articles, discussing the outcomes of courses, conferences and research, urging the examination of interesting new buildings, restaurants, cars and household durables creates an air of learning and excitement. Some of this could be captured in display, as could posters giving positive messages about careers in design and technology, and photographs of last year's GCSE group with 'where are they now?' explanations.

Display of students' work is often done well. But could it be better? Could the content and nature of the display be discussed, or decided, with the whole group? If a finished product is to be displayed what should be learned from it? Are ideas and creativity celebrated as much as finish, quality and neatness?

Marking

Evidence suggests that students of all abilities do well when their work is marked by teachers as it progresses, using the assessment criteria detailed in the GCSE syllabuses. Two questions arise from this. First, are the level criteria displayed and discussed in student-friendly language and/or put into students' folders? Second, do teachers give *frequent and detailed* feedback by indicating to students what they have specifically to do in order to achieve higher marks for a particular part of their design folder? Marking folders at the end of a project does not help pupils to improve their work and can have a detrimental effect on the pace of learning and motivation. Similarly, is work marked before and after a redraft? This can help to inculcate good habits and a 'right-first-time' mentality.

Learning skills

One of the frustrations of teaching, particularly of secondary school teaching, is that the skills which students are taught, and learn, are not usually transferred by them between contexts. This is often the downfall of study-skills lessons, because students have not yet gained the maturity or development to apply the skills to specific contexts. They cannot particularise from the general. There are certain learning skills identified by inspectors which are highly applicable to the design and technology syllabus but which may not be specifically taught within the subject. The following, in particular, would help to raise the achievement levels of both boys and girls within design and technology:

- research skills
- writing questionnaires
- analysing information
- synthesising information and writing conclusions
- using evidence to influence designing
- developing graphic communication skills
- redrafting work
- evaluation techniques
- time and deadline management.

Benching/seating policy

We went into some detail about a seating policy in Chapter 8. Although the atmosphere and positioning of students is more informal and fluid in design and technology the same arguments apply. Each student will have a 'learning zone' for good or ill, and the nature of that zone should be largely under the teacher's control. Having the ambition that each student will have to work with everybody else during the year has to be tempered by a consideration of complementary personalities and learning strengths. Teachers who control student disposition in the room, with the criteria based on maximising learning rather than the squashing of unacceptable behaviour, generally report that time on task increases and better grades are obtained by the class as a whole.

Setting challenges and short-term goals

If boys like challenges and short-term tasks, it should be possible to design these into a unit of study. Let us take, for example, a typical D&T project such as designing a mouse for a computer, which has to be done over a four-week period. The teacher builds in several challenges throughout the lifetime of the project.

Week one: Look at the measurements and produce an orthographic drawing. This may entail going to the ICT room in twos or threes to look at the characteristics and dimensions of a mouse. Then draw it up and finish for homework. Challenge: check homework of partner and be prepared to criticise it constructively at the next lesson.

Week two: Feedback on homework. Class discussion on what makes a good design and what makes a good critic. Then examine the ergonomics and anthropometrics of the human hand. This means measuring each others' hands together with discussion from a book or leaflet. But remember the 'transforming' part of VEST (see Chapter 3). Ask the students, working in pairs (remember the 'social learning' part of VEST) to write down the five most important things about the hand, and then compare their answers to another pair or have whole class feedback. Who's got the best five? It's a challenge. Boys like challenges. They then have all the information they need to draw a mouse design of their own.

Week three: Finish drawing up the first ideas and then discuss their design, ensuring it is shaped by the original research. Ask pupils to debate their ideas in pairs, and then in fours by joining pairs together. Try to ensure that the fours have a gender balance, and that they feed back what they have learned from each other. ('Nothing' is not an acceptable answer.) Tell them that the point of the exercise is to learn from each other, to appreciate that everybody has a different perspective on the problem and that lots of answers could be right. There is very little writing involved. Boys like discussion. The challenge is to see how much you can learn from somebody else, so this requires skills of interrogation, active listening and winning trust. Girls should do very well at this, but boys will probably learn more from the exercise. Pupils begin to give shape to their ideas through the use of styrene. They have to cut, shape and sand it down. Homework is to design a logo for a mouse mat. The challenge is to see which teams of four produce the most original logo ready for the next lesson, a judgement they have to make as a whole class.

Week four: The end of the project, finishing off the model. At the end of the lesson, with models and mouse mats finished, each pair has to judge the work of every other pair and to give it marks based on criteria supplied by the teacher. This begins to put them in the role of assessor, and they begin to realise what their work will be marked on. Sloppiness and bad finishing are marked down. At the grand finale the teacher gives her or his judgement as well. Consider using some or all of the products for display.

Look carefully at curriculum coverage

There is some evidence that despite the potential and image of design and technology as a 'doing' subject, a number of schools tend to spend less time on the active parts of the curriculum, probably to the detriment of boys. The suggestions in the National Curriculum documents for brainstorming and role-play, for example, are seldom seen and the presentation of information is usually drawn or written rather than through displays, charts or diagrams. Are schools making the best use of ICT in technology? Is it only used for desk top publishing instead of producing 3D models and control systems within electronics, which are within reach? When assessing the processes and products of D&T, do students always have to write down their findings rather than evaluate orally, or record into audio-tape or video-tape? Do schools make the full use of group evaluations?

The project

> The only way to eat an elephant is one chunk at a time. Likewise, the only way to tackle a large project is to break it down into bite sized chunks.
>
> (Minton and Dupey, 1998)

In Chapter 2 we discussed six possible reasons why boys are now out-performed by girls. One reason was that the recent curriculum changes have been hostile to boys, and perhaps the upheavals in design and technology typify this more than in any other subject. Many boys view design and technology quite positively. They look forward to becoming more technical, using more complicated machinery and producing enviable products. What many do not really understand, despite having been told, is the nature and demands of the project they have to produce. The project, which typically accounts for 60 per cent of the total GCSE marks, is either started in the summer term of Year 10 or September of the autumn term and finished in the Easter of Year 11. They are often handed in late, the vast majority of the defaulters being boys. Two or three terms is far too long for boys to maintain interest and momentum in a project. Technology departments need to set shorter and more frequent deadlines, perhaps splitting the year into four-week modules, with a major review at the end of each module. The tasks to be completed within the four weeks will probably vary from student to student, so individual schedules will have to be negotiated. A teacher at the Ecclesbourne School in Derbyshire introduced a simple 'Major project process monitor' (Table 11.1).

Table 11.1 Major project progress monitor

Date	Week no	Proposed target	Actual progress

> At first [the students] were very sceptical about the system and some felt that it was an extra imposition, but gradually the majority of the group found it helped them to use their time more effectively, and some grudgingly admitted that it might even help them complete their projects on time.
>
> (Minton and Dupey, 1998)

The more detailed the project sheets, the more benefit was gleaned from the exercise. As discussed earlier in the book, it is the encouragement/coercion to reflect upon their work and the process of learning which really helps boys, as well as those girls who tend not to reflect.

Further research at the same school revealed what many teachers already strongly suspect: that the time given to pupils to undertake work has little or no effect on how much time they actually take to complete it. For many, an 'anxiety threshold' had to be breached before they began the work, a threshold determined by the proximity to the finish date, not the start date. This supports our argument about the preference for short-term goals. Small wonder that the school has adopted a list of fourteen 'bite-sized tasks' for writing up major projects.

The marks given for projects are based mainly on accuracy, neatness and quality as well as evaluation. Original ideas and creativity, sometimes seen as boys' strengths, are often not so well rewarded if they are let down by bad finishing or poor quality. Boys may understand this intellectually, but often they have not internalised the habits and protocols which eradicate poor presentation. This can be done both by the inculcation of good habits running through all the short-term tasks discussed above and through the teaching of design and technology at Key Stage 3, as discussed in a previous section.

Box 11.1 Raising attainment in design and technology

In primary schools

Obstacles to learning

Expectations

Learning to enjoy the journey

Stages 1–5

In secondary schools

Getting into good habits:

- awareness of language
- design folders
- ethos, display and anti-swotism
- marking
- learning skills
- benching/seating policy
- setting challenges and short-term tasks.

Curriculum coverage

The project

Chapter 12

Raising achievement in modern foreign languages

Introduction

An examination of recent national results at GCSE and A level confirms what most teachers feel they already know – that girls do far better in foreign languages than boys, and that this situation shows little sign of changing (Table 12.1).

The reasons why these differences occur are generally explored in Chapter 2. Many of the problems which boys have with English (see Chapter 9) are replicated in modern foreign languages (MFL), and to some extent the solutions are also similar. But there are different dimensions to be considered in MFL which make it worthy of an extra chapter.

Modern foreign languages are the least popular of all secondary school subjects (Economic and Social Research Council, 1998) and one which students would most like to drop in Key Stage 4 (along with RE and, for boys, music). Boys, in particular, report that MFL are irrelevant and too difficult. When a situation develops in which the male learner cannot see the point of trying, nor can he see the way to succeed, disaffection sets in:

> 'When I remember my first lessons teaching French I am appalled. The pupils, according to their degree of patience, either listened passively, switched off or misbehaved. One boy even built a bonfire between the desks and lit it.'
>
> (French teacher)

And it wasn't even 14 July.

By talking to students and teachers it is evident that motivation to learn comes from one or more of three sources:

1   It is a socially required norm, usually from parental attitudes and sometimes from peer groups.
2   Learning is seen to be useful in some way, either because it has an intrinsic purpose such as learning to drive or, more commonly, because

Table 12.1 National percentage of students gaining A*–C at GCSE, by gender

	1996		1997		1998	
	Boys	Girls	Boys	Girls	Boys	Girls
French	33.0	49.6	35.3	51.1	34.5	51.3
German	39.2	56.1	41.8	57.9	42.8	58.1

Source: DfEE (1998)

jumping the hurdles and collecting the certificates gives access to other opportunities.

3   The learning is interesting to the student.

These sources are not mutually exclusive, and an examination of any one student in any learning situation may reveal an overlap and entangling of different motivations. When all three are missing the teacher has a problem. In modern foreign languages (1) and (2) are perhaps less likely to be present than in other subjects, partly because most parents do not have a second language ('it didn't do me any harm; I can't see the point of it'), and partly because the cultural heritage of the United Kingdom is so Anglocentric that the case still has to be made for the intrinsic value of learning modern foreign languages. The use of modern forms of communication such as the English-dominant Internet, which boys use more than girls, tends to confirm this prejudice against French, Spanish, German and so on. Ironically, the Net can also be one of languages teachers' greatest modern tools, as it can give access to a wonderfully rich diet of documents and lifestyles in the target language. Some useful web-site addresses are given in Appendix 12.2 at the end of this chapter. Thus the major task for many teachers of modern foreign languages is to persuade the reluctant learner that the subject is both relevant and useful and that the lessons are interesting.

Motivating students

How do we convince students that learning a language is useful?

The Babel fish is small, yellow, leech-like – and probably the oddest thing in the Universe. It feeds on brain-wave energy, absorbing all unconscious frequencies and then excreting telepathically in a matrix format from the conscious signals and nerve patterns from the speech centre of the brain. The practical aspect is that if you stick one in your ear you can instantly understand anything said to you in any form of language.

(from *The Hitch-Hikers' Guide to the Galaxy* by Douglas Adams)

As in most countries we periodically worry about the attitudes and behaviour of young people. Why are they irreverent; why do they drink, smoke, take drugs; why don't they take enough exercise; why don't they care for the environment, work harder, relax more; and why, in Britain, don't they learn languages? The answer, of course, is that they are a reflection of the adult society in which they are growing up. To change young people we have to change ourselves.

Perhaps UK students are uniquely disadvantaged in Europe because historically there appears to have been no immediate *need* to learn a foreign language. In our 'sceptred isle set in the silver sea' there was no town or city just over the border which spoke entirely differently. In pre-Industrial Revolution Britain, with a largely sustainable economy, the vast majority of the population rarely needed to even know the existence of a foreign language. The past two hundred years have made some inroads into this bastion of ignorance, but not in any meaningful sense. The post-war mass travel revolution has not been sufficiently long in our psyche to persuade us of the need to learn a language, especially as most holidays are geared to keep us away from the need to speak anything but English. Moreover, the modern cultural imperialism of the USA tends to confirm this perception. When the world's most universal phrase is 'Coca-Cola' and every major city has a McDonald's, when the French habitually batten down the linguistic hatches to everybody's amusement, a very clear message is being delivered to the reluctant and struggling Year 9 student.

There are many ways through which a school can persuade its students of the usefulness of modern foreign languages. One obvious way is through exchange visits and the establishment of pen-friends' writing clubs. No matter what some boys may think about modern foreign languages, a great many of them would like to talk to the boys and girls of their own age when they meet them. Some schools link the two, and have strict rules about writing in French/Spanish/German rather than allowing the foreign partner to do all the hard work. We know that girls are currently more likely to maintain pen-friends than boys, so how can we make it more attractive to boys? By making it a condition of participating in the school visit or exchange that a set number of letters have been sent, but at the same time giving them support in preparing and checking the letters. By involving parents so that they can prepare linguistically for the return visit by the foreign students. By being very careful when asking for partners from abroad, so that football fans are paired, as are computer enthusiasts and so on. By introducing a reward system for the best or longest or most improved letter writers.

It is not always possible to maintain excitement about a foreign trip, but there is no reason why links cannot be maintained. Boys, in particular, often welcome the opportunity of using e-mail because of its intrinsic computer and hi-tech nature. Grants are available from the European Union via the Comenius scheme to set up European educational projects. Whole classes can work on joint projects with a foreign twin, comparing lifestyles, climate, diet, television programmes and, of course, language. If e-mail is not available, the fax or post are viable alternatives. Monkseaton Community School in Whitley Bay, Tyne and Wear, has witnessed a considerable improvement in its French GCSE results. Language students have access to multi-media and video-conferencing link-ups with schools in Germany and France. They are also given BT chargecards so that they can telephone fellow pupils in European schools from home, with Monkseaton bearing the cost. The performance of boys in French has improved even more than girls, and the headteacher believes that the use of hi-tech equipment has captured boys' imagination and commitment, with many putting in extra hours after school – because they enjoy it.

Elsewhere in the book we discuss the usefulness of industrial mentoring and role-models. It may be possible to strike up a partnership with local companies whose salesforce and other executives include speakers of foreign languages. You may not find enough people to mentor every under-achieving boy, but you could perhaps ask them to talk, and listen, to small groups. Hearing a man talk about his job, and the way another language is a passport to both his career and his success in it, could have a major impact on persuading boys that there is a point to it after all. If he can link this to tales of exotic foreign travel, so much the better. This theme of languages being useful for careers could be extended and helped by the careers department. Descriptions of the jobs (and salaries) where possessing an additional language is either an essential or desirable quality may increase the motivation as well as the possibilities for both genders.

Even those students who are obviously not going to succeed very well in modern foreign languages need to know that there is a positive benefit to them in succeeding at their level. They need to understand that using 'shopping French' is fun (particularly in France), and will make their visit more enjoyable; that they will meet more people and have a better time. Thus cross-channel trips for them is also a good idea.

How do we make the subject enjoyable?

Chapter 3 discusses the generally favoured learning style of boys, but makes the point that girls are not averse to boys' preferences either. It is the variety of learning styles, but with a distinct bias towards active learning, which will help boys to get the most out of modern foreign languages. A diet of listening and copying is perhaps harder to jettison in languages teaching than in other subjects, which may be one of the reasons why boys dislike it so much. It may be an idea to keep a record of the different kinds of teaching style used over half a term and to use the results as a baseline, determining to increase the amount of active learning. We know that in general the two favourite learning methods of both genders are group work and a practical activity (Sutcliffe, 1998) although a considerable percentage of girls also like to learn direct from the teacher. If this is what the students say:

> 'She just yabs on and on; it gets really boring ... you just get side-tracked and start writing on your pencil case or something'

rather than this:

> 'You take a lot more in, because they make it more, a lot more fun to be there, you know. ... Because it depends on the teacher and what the teacher's really like, and how well you get on with them'
>
> (from Clark and Trafford, 1995)

it's likely that the teacher enjoys the lessons no more than the students. Research suggests that students themselves perceive a link between enjoyment of the lesson and success in the subject: 'I think it's a circle. If you don't work, if you're no good at it, you're not going to enjoy it' (Male student).

Elsewhere in this book we discuss the use of the VEST acronym (see Chapter 3): giving students a Variety of learning styles; Engaging them on task by challenge, competition, short-term goals, production of a tangible or useful result; allowing them to learn Socially; and Transforming information, should result in a busy, learning classroom. Modern foreign languages are particularly well suited for the last two but arguably do not always offer a sufficient variety of learning styles, particularly active learning styles. If students do not see any usefulness in learning a second language they may not be easily engaged on task, and this is addressed below. The survey of favoured learning styles in Outwood Grange School, Wakefield (see Appendix 12.1, pp. 160–171) reinforced the idea of active learning being appealing to boys and so more of this was introduced.

How do we combat negative role models and negative stereotyping?

> In one of the schools where boys had performed above the national average, the Head of Department suggested tentatively that this was essentially attributable to the relationship between staff and pupils. The two higher sets had been taught by two male members of staff who were very interested in football and this interest was shared by a large number of the boys. Whether this common interest excluded and alienated the girls was not mentioned.
>
> (Clark and Trafford, 1995)

The obvious answer is to use positive role modelling. There are plenty of boys, albeit a minority, who enjoy and succeed in modern foreign languages. Schools can make better use of them, and embed their learning, by employing them as role models. In some cases, they may be able to help with younger classes and sometimes within their own class. If they have had a successful linguistic experience abroad, so much the better. They will need some careful instructions: showing off their prowess may alienate rather than excite. Their role would be to convince their tutees of the social benefits and to suggest to them that the same enjoyment is within their reach, if only they apply themselves a little more. They would have to concentrate on the existing strengths of the tutees and to help show them the next step forward, whether it be increased vocabulary, more confidence or clearer diction. All this could also be true of the industrial mentors discussed earlier. If it is not possible to have the tutors in the classroom it may be feasible to have a photographic display of students in the school, regularly updated, in conversation with foreign friends, shopkeepers, waiters, police officers, etc.

The use of a foreign teaching assistant can be a huge bonus to the teaching of modern foreign languages. Some secondary schools have discontinued their use in recent years, partly for financial reasons, and others do not use them as well as they could. In the context of the relative underachievement of boys it may be preferable to have a male assistant, but the gender is probably less important than the attitude and attributes. If the assistant can interest the students, be it about soccer, food, wine, beer, cars, beaches or the general lifestyle of their country. Schools can be clearer about the expectations they have of their assistant, who may be far more productive if they have an induction period in which they can understand the problem and what is expected of them. If they feel socially supported during their stay they may also be more likely to have an impact. Can they be invited to a football match with some under-achieving students? Go on a hike, bike ride, join the computer club? The more the students have access to the assistant, who may have a covert mission to introduce extra words into their vocabulary, the more effective he or she will be.

How do we create a supportive learning environment?

The learning environment, both physical and psychological, is obviously critical to how students can view the subject. Our comments (Chapter 8) about the teacher deciding where students sit – based upon learning rather than behavioural considerations – will have a major impact upon the learning environment. The use of colourful display, relevant to the students because it contains pictures of them or their friends in places they have visited or are intending to visit, combined with constant praise for what they can do and a constant repetition of high expectation will help to change negative perceptions. The use of neuro-linguistic programming is in its infancy in teaching, but the work of the Pacific Institute and its Investors In Excellence programme is being used in a growing number of schools. Students are well used to 'sehr gut' when the teacher is pleased, but what of 'muy bien, es tipico de lo que puedes hacer' or, when they under-perform, 'ce n'est pas très bien – tu es normalement beaucoup meilleur(e)!'.

To help the learning environment further, the teacher should also show that he or she is learning. This could take several forms, depending on appropriateness. It may be appropriate to show that the teacher also has problems with or is challenged by the language at times, as we all are with English. This helps the students to realise that a learning problem is normal, and that even fluent or native speakers can get it wrong. On another occasion teachers can share their own linguistic experiences with the class: what happened over the summer holiday, new words learned, new languages attempted, heroic failures, and social intercourse made possible by the use of a second language.

How do we know what pupils think of lessons?

If the modern foreign languages classroom really is a learning environment, then the teacher will constantly be learning about his or her teaching and what the students think about it. If the lesson has clear learning objectives, which it should, teachers should also be asking the class at the end of each lesson whether these have been met. It is obviously important to leave sufficient time for this. A consideration of the learning achieved is actually a critical part of that learning. It helps students to reflect upon their overall understanding, or it should do if the right questions are asked. This may mean getting students to consider, in pairs or groups, not just whether they have achieved the learning outcomes (for example, to understand how to ask for different types of food in French) but the extent to which they understand. A rough, five-point scoring system could be introduced with a quick class round in the target language. The students can also be asked how the lesson could have been improved and the parts they particularly liked or disliked. There will always be differences of opinion because there are different preferred learning styles, but patterns will emerge when a clear majority of the class strongly like or dislike particular ways of learning. This will, in time, give the teacher invaluable information about future planning parameters.

Modern foreign languages departments, as others, could use a questionnaire with students at the end of each term or year. This could initially provide a baseline for such issues as preferred learning styles, books, homework, perceived progress, as well as how useful languages are thought to be and the enjoyment of the lessons. This has obvious potential for staff uneasiness, and has to be viewed not as a beauty contest but as an invaluable guide to departmental planning. See Appendix 12.1 (p. 160) for an example of such a questionnaire.

Other issues for consideration

Setting

Teachers of modern foreign languages are often among the most vehement in championing setting by ability. They argue that, more than other subjects, MFL are linear in the acquisition of skills and understanding. This means that in a mixed ability situation they either have to slow the class to the speed of the least able, or that they are faced with the daunting prospect of producing multiple lesson plans every time they enter the classroom. Ergo, setting is the only reasonable answer to the situation – enabling students to be taught in groups of roughly equal ability.

The problem that this throws up is threefold. First, bottom sets tend to be over-represented by boys and, in some schools, by minority ethnic students. The bottom sets not only progress more slowly (with commensurately lower expectations by teachers and students of what they can achieve), but they often use different textbooks. Before very long the chances of moving out of a bottom set to a higher one are so negligible as to be non-existent. Modern languages are confirmed as the dwelling place of middle-class white girls, with a few of the generally more able boys providing an interesting variation from the norm. The rest are generally happy to have their views confirmed that French, German and the rest are feminine, and irrelevant to their present and future lives. The 'lower ability' sets are populated by students who see less need to learn a foreign language and have their views unchallenged by their classmates:

> 'Like maths, you can see a reason for doing maths, I know French, like if you go on holiday or if you want to work in France, you need a language, but if you don't want to do anything with it, it seems just a waste of time.'
>
> (Male student from lower set)

The second problem is that the information which informs strict setting, like the eleven-plus, is merely a snapshot of a point in time, and does not really tell departments much about the latent ability of the individual student. This does not matter so much if a fluid setting system is in operation, but this is not always the case.

The third and most damning problem is that strict setting does not do what it is intended to do. It does not raise achievement. Research in a number of schools (King James's, Huddersfield, for example) shows that those in the top languages groups generally achieve results which reflect their ability, as measured by NFER CATs scores, but those in the middle and bottom groups tend to under-achieve. It doesn't need a genius to hypothesise why this might be; teacher and student expectations tend to be lowered and to enter a cycle of self-fulfilling prophecies.

There are a number of strategies that can be considered by modern languages departments which employ a more flexible use of setting arrangements. One is to have more than one top set which will probably widen the ability grouping, but will give more chance to middle/high ability boys to learn from their peers and to maintain motivation. Another is to start with relatively small top sets, making it clear that there will be 'promotion' at regular intervals from the lower sets – although this will demand careful co-ordination of work between sets. There is no blueprint for success; it is up to each school to consider its particular needs and strategies. The question for each of them, however, is how to set pupils without demotivating the majority.

Setting by gender

A number of schools have been so concerned about the level of under-achievement by boys that they have split their languages cohorts into two, with parallel groups in single gender sets. The advantages of this are that boys are automatically in the top set and this will affect their level of motivation. Moreover, many would argue that girls are equally advantaged as their lessons are less prone to disruption and more of them are also in the top set. Research on the effect of single gender groups is yet to be properly undertaken. Reports from schools which have attempted it tend to be initially positive, although we have argued elsewhere that the nature of change to raise achievement is less important than the concentration upon achievement. There are a few aspects to consider before we all decide to jump on the bandwagon. One of the central theses of this book is that boys tolerate poor teaching less readily than girls. Moving the passengers around the deck is not in itself going to prevent the ship from going down, and other strategies will have to be employed as well. Many teachers also feel that boys and girls bring separate elements of learning to a lesson which the other gender needs to understand and use. Girls need to be more prepared to speculate, to volunteer answers, to take risks and to challenge the teacher and one another. Boys need to be more careful about their presentation, to reflect more on their work and to listen more carefully. Where are they going to learn this if they are surrounded by like-minded students? Some of the strategies we have described are unlikely to work as well in single gender groupings. On a more general point, co-education is usually accepted as being advantageous to the social and personal development of young people, and to society as a whole. Although girls do complain about boys' behaviour at times, the statistics suggest that they have not been held back in raising their attainment in recent years.

Systematic planning

Appendix 12.1 gives an example of a 'learning' modern foreign languages department. The department carried out many although not all of the above ideas in two Year 8 classes. Its results, after one year, were contradictory. The boys in the German class showed some signs of improvement, but some in the French class actually seemed to regress. However, the attitude of the students towards modern foreign languages was felt to have generally improved and the department is looking towards consolidating its strategy by amending the setting system, using more role models and arranging French visits and exchanges. Systematic planning ensures that all members of the faculty understand the strategy and their part in implementing it. It also means that other key figures – parents, students and other members of staff – can play a supporting role. The use of data enables the setting of success criteria within the objectives and so the department can measure its progress and plan more realistically for improvement. But perhaps more than anything else a modern foreign languages department needs to believe that boys' under-achievement in languages is not inevitable and that the process of change will raise the achievement of all.

> ### Box 12.1 Raising attainment in modern foreign languages
>
> Motivating students:
>
> - the usefulness of languages
> - getting to enjoy it
> - combating negative stereotypes and role models
> - creating a supportive learning environment
> - getting feedback.
>
> Setting
>
> Setting by gender
>
> Systematic planning

APPENDIX 12.1

Questionnaire for students at the end of the term

Consider these questions in pairs before the whole class discusses them.

1   To what extent have you enjoyed modern foreign languages this term?

- It's been fantastic
- It's been generally very good
- It's been okay
- I haven't enjoyed it very much
- I've hated it.

2   What sorts of activities in the lessons do you most enjoy? Give each activity below a number, with your favourite being 1, second favourite 2, etc.

- The teacher talking to you in the target language
- Copying from board
- Copying from book
- The teacher explaining on the board
- Dictation
- Watching videos
- Listening to tapes
- Working with a partner
- Whole class discussion in target language
- Whole class discussion in English
- Working on own from worksheet
- Working with partner from worksheet
- Playing a game
- Solving a problem
- Working on displays.

3   Do you think that your textbook is useful? Give reasons for your answer and examples of your work.

4   What progress do you think you've made in modern foreign languages over the past term? Pick one from the list below. Does your partner agree with you? Try to give reasons for your answers.

- I've made very good progress
- I've made good progress
- I've made satisfactory progress
- I've made poor progress
- I've made hardly any progress at all.

5   What do you think about the sort of homework you've been set in modern foreign languages over the past term? Has it helped you to learn, or to reinforce the learning you've done? How could homework be improved?

6   How useful do you think modern foreign languages will be to you in life?

•   Extremely useful
•   Very useful
•   Quite useful
•   Of little or no use
•   Not sure.

Raising boys' achievement

Background

It is well-documented that girls are currently out-performing boys at all key stages and at every level in the GCSE.[1] Moreover, with the exception of physics, the performance of girls in every major subject exceeds that of boys. This is particularly evident in languages, and is a trend which is reflected in French and German results at Outwood Grange. In 1997, 16.3 per cent of boys got A– C grades compared to 38.8 per cent of girls. In German, 21.25 per cent of boys got A– C grades compared to 42.75 per cent of girls. It is obvious therefore that as the languages department is committed to raising levels of attainment, the issue of improving the achievement of boys should be paramount in our planning.

Target group and evaluation

The project which we have agreed upon will target a group of Year 8 pupils in top/middle sets in both French and German. This group has been chosen since research suggests that it is at about this time that boys' performance begins to 'go off'. Key data received at the end of Year 7 about the boys involved will be compared with the corresponding data at the end of Year 8. We shall be trying to evaluate whether there will have been any significant improvement in standards. To enable a meaningful comparison to take place, we shall also look at the improvement made by boys from Year 7 to Year 8 during the academic year 1996/97 to assess whether our pilot group made greater improvements. Letters will be sent home to all parents concerned outlining our strategies and asking for their support.

The particular classes selected for the project are:

8.31   ERH/KRG French
8.22   NJH German.

Strategies

It is important to note that this project will be supplementing a number of initiatives already implemented by the department with the aim of raising boys' achievement. Of particular importance has been the change in the setting policy. By considering factors such as participation in lessons as a criterion by which pupils are setted, our groups have become much more balanced in terms of gender.

We intend to employ the following strategies within our target group:

- Change the seating arrangements once a term. There is evidence to support the claim that judicious pairings of boys and girls can lead to better outcomes

1 *The Gender Divide* (EOC/Ofsted, 1996).

since the boys and girls have skills which complement one another. Changing the arrangement every term ensures that pupils do not become disheartened by the thought of sitting next to their imposed partner for a year.

- Use more role-play and do more oral work in class, tasks at which boys generally succeed.
- Make use of competition, games and challenges in lessons, which traditionally appeal to boys.
- Use IT to a greater extent; once again this is an area which boys particularly enjoy.
- Use male role models. We shall try to invite male outside speakers to reinforce that learning languages is valuable. We shall use sixth formers in lessons in order to help the pupils and, where possible, encourage male members of the sixth form to participate.
- Make displays and worksheets 'boy friendly', e.g. by using male film and sports stars.
- Interview the boys in each of the targeted groups to get their views on language learning.
- Make use of praise, stickers, merits and complimentary letters home.
- Begin the lesson with tasks of short duration, with longer activities at the end to aid the boys, who, research implies, have a shorter concentration span than girls.

Raising Boys' Achievement project:
Examining key data

In order to see if there is any improvement in the performance of boys in Year 8 for 1997/98, it is important to have some form of comparison. The tables below detail the levels of attainment gained by boys in Year 8 in 1996/97 and chart the amount of improvement in terms of level made from the end of Year 7 to the end of Year 8.

It is our intention to examine the same information for our present Year 8 boys in July 1998. We hope that the improvement in level will be greater following the Raising Boys' Achievement project which we have undertaken.

Obviously, the data are flawed to some extent. They are based on teacher assessment which may not be totally objective. Some cohorts vary considerably from one year to another. Other variables may have affected the outcome, such as class size, time of day classes were taught, etc. It may also be the case that assessment tasks did not allow students to progress beyond a certain level, thus reducing the extent to which an improvement could be made. However, such a comparison may prove to be an indicator, albeit crude, of improvement.

Levels of attainment gained by boys in French at the end of Year 8

Level of attainment	Number of boys
4	29
3	25
2	2

Levels of attainment gained by boys in German at the end of Year 8

Level of attainment	Number of boys
4	10
3	25
2	1

Number of levels by which boys' performance in French improved from the end of Year 7 to the end of Year 8

Number of levels by which improved	Number of boys
3	3
2	22
1	29
0	2

Number of levels by which boys' performance in German improved from the end of Year 7 to the end of Year 8

Number of levels by which improved	Number of boys
2	2
1	17
0	17

OUTWOOD GRANGE

OUTWOOD GRANGE SCHOOL   POTOVENS LANE   OUTWOOD   WAKEFIELD   WF1 2PF

Headteacher: Telephone (01924) 303815
Mr Geoffrey A Smith MA   Fax   (01924) 303820

Date..
erh/sg/genlang/boys1

Dear Parents/Guardian

Raising Boys' Achievement Project

As you may be aware from recent articles in the press, it is a fact that nationally boys are performing less well than girls in nearly every area of the school curriculum. In particular, boys in British schools do considerably worse than girls in their foreign language studies.

Furthermore, research implies that it is at the age of twelve or thirteen that boys' performance begins to deteriorate and we are most concerned that this should not be the case with your son, and with the other boys in his year. Therefore, the Modern Languages Department has decided to target two classes in Year 8 in which a range of strategies will be introduced designed to improve the attainment of boys.

The measures we intend to implement will include changing the seating pattern in the classroom, using more role play, competition and information technology in lessons and making the study of languages appear more relevant to a career. Every boy in the class will fill in a questionnaire anonymously in which he will be asked to identify what he likes doing and what makes him learn best.

I would be grateful if you could support our project by taking an interest in your son's language work, asking him about the kinds of activities he is doing in his language lessons and by impressing on him wherever possible the need to work hard and to complete homework tasks thoroughly. Your support would be much appreciated. Should you wish to discuss this further with me, please do not hesitate to contact me at school.

Yours sincerely

Erica Hiorns
Head of Modern Languages

Deputy Heads: Mrs E A Brown (Personnel)   Ms M Healy (Curriculum)   Mrs P Hunter (Student Support)   Bursar: Mrs J Curtin

OUTWOOD GRANGE SCHOOL   POTOVENS LANE   OUTWOOD   WAKEFIELD   WF1 2PF

Headteacher: Telephone (01924) 303815
Mr Geoffrey A Smith MA   Fax   (01924) 303820

Date ....
erh/sg/genlang/girls1

Dear Parents/Guardian

Raising Boys' Achievement Project
As you may be aware from recent articles in the press, it is a fact that boys are performing
less well than girls in nearly every area of the school curriculum. In particular, boys do
considerably worse than girls in their foreign language studies.

Furthermore, research implies that it is at the age of twelve or thirteen that boys' performance
begins to deteriorate and we are most concerned that this should not be the case at Outwood
Grange. Therefore, the Modern Languages Department has decided to target two classes in
Year 8, one of which your daughter is in, where a range of strategies will be introduced
designed to improve the attainment of boys.

I am writing to you to assure you that this will in no way affect the attention given to your
daughter. Indeed, it is our aim to raise the attainment of all students. It is hoped that if the
performance of boys is improved this will have a beneficial effect on girls in that the pace and
attitude to learning will be better. Your support would be much appreciated.

Yours sincerely

Erica Horns
Head of Modern Languages

Deputy Heads: Mrs E A Brown (Personnel)   Ms M Healy (Curriculum)   Mrs P Hunter (Student Support)   Bursar: Mrs J Curtin

Reproduced with permission

Modern Languages Department

Raising Boys' Achievement: Questionnaire

You have been asked by your teacher to fill in this questionnaire. You do not have to put your name on it so we will not know that it is yours. However, we do ask that you take this seriously and think carefully about the answers you give.

I What is your favourite subject? Can you explain why you like it?

2 Which is your least favourite subject? Can you explain why you don't like it?

3 What are the things you enjoy most in your language lesson?

4 What things do you not enjoy doing in your language lesson?

5 Do you think that taking a language at school has any use?

6 Did you prefer languages in Year 7? If the answer is yes, can you explain why?

7 Do you do your homework regularly?

8 What is the classroom atmosphere like each lesson?

9 Are there any individuals or groups who are causing time to be wasted?

10 What grade do you expect to get in this subject at GCSE?

Modern Languages Department

Raising Boys' Achievement: Questionnaire

Thank you for asking the boys in your class to fill in this questionnaire. For your information, here is a summary of the results.

---

1 What is your favourite subject? Can you explain why you like it?
Overwhelmingly, the favourite subjects were games, D&T, drama and art. The reasons expressed for this were that they involved practical work and little or no writing. One pupil also mentioned there being an end product. Only one boy questioned had put that a language was his favourite subject.

---

2 Which is your least favourite subject? Can you explain why you don't like it?
Again, there were two subjects that were prominent here: music and maths. The reasons given for the first were mainly that pupils disliked singing or did not play an instrument; many stated that maths was difficult and boring. Quite a way behind, but disturbingly in third place, was languages. The reason given was that there was little point to studying a language. Some also mentioned a dislike of English due to having to write.

---

3 What are the things you enjoy most in your language lesson?
Easily the most popular answer here was IT work. Others did mention oral work and drawing pictures.

---

4 What things do you not enjoy doing in your language lesson?
This question gained a mixed response. Many boys identified that they hated learning new vocabulary and revising for tests. Quite a few said that they disliked doing listening work and others mentioned worksheets. Once again, some mentioned hating activities which involved writing.

---

5 Do you think that taking a language at school has any use?
The answers for this question were virtually half for 'yes' and the other half for 'no'.

---

6 Did you prefer languages in Year 7? If the answer is yes, can you explain why?
Here again the answers were roughly divided between 'yes' and 'no'. Those replying 'yes' said in the main that work in Year 7 was easier.

---

7 Do you do your homework regularly?
Virtually every pupil claimed that they did their homework regularly. Of the few who admitted that they didn't, the reason given was lack of understanding.

8 What is the classroom atmosphere like each lesson?
Happily for us, the answers to this question were very positive. Many referred to the classroom atmosphere as 'good', 'friendly' and sometimes 'noisy, but in a good way'.

9 Are there any individuals or groups who are causing time to be wasted?
Most thought that the answer was 'no'. On the few occasions that pupils were mentioned, they were always boys.

10 What grade do you expect to get in this subject at GCSE?
The answers ranged from A to C–. No boy thought he would fail. Most thought they would get a B or a C.

Raising Boys' Achievement project: Results 1998/99

In order to analyse whether our project was effective, we decided to compare the improvement in levels of attainment of boys in Year 8 in 1996/97 and boys in a specific French and German class in 1997/98. The 1996/97 results were as follows:

Number of levels by which boys' performance in French improved from the end of Year 7 to the end of Year 8

Number of levels by which improved	Number of boys
3	3
2	22
1	29
0	2

Number of levels by which boys' performance in German improved from the end of Year 7 to the end of Year 8

Number of levels by which improved	Number of boys
2	2
1	17
0	17

Let us now compare this with the results from 1997/98:

Number of levels by which boys' performance in French improved from the end of Year 7 to the end of Year 8

Number of levels by which improved	Number of boys
2	0
1	1
0	8
−1	3

Number of levels by which boys' performance in German improved from the end of Year 7 to the end of Year 8

Number of levels by which improved	Number of boys
2	2
1	11
4	4

These results make rather curious reading and it is difficult to know what reasonable conclusions can be drawn from them. Certainly, they do not indicate that the methods used have had a conclusive impact on boys' learning. The German results suggest some improvement while the French results actually suggest some regression. Teachers of these classes would probably draw attention to the fact that the German class contained a number of talented boys whereas the French teachers concerned feel that some of the pupils were misplaced in a top/middle ability set. The questions which arise are probably less to do with raising boys' achievement than with the subjective nature of awarding levels. The department is trying to address this by establishing assessment tests with clear marking criteria, and also by setting up profiles of students' work to give examples of different levels.

In terms of raising boys' achievement it is obvious that there is still considerable research to be done into what methods will work with languages in this school. The department for the academic year 1998/99 is trying a different setting system in Year 8. Sets will be more homogenous and it is hoped that this will raise the achievement of all.

A number of the strategies originally suggested have been tried out: the seating arrangements were altered and staff found that this did have beneficial effects on behaviour and achievement. IT was used to a greater effect and this was well liked by pupils. This is an area which has the potential to be expanded still further. Displays were created to be boy friendly. Boys were interviewed on their attitude towards language learning and the results of the survey were considered when preparing lessons.

However, we were unable to get any male outside speakers into school to promote languages and, although a number of male sixth formers have helped in lessons, there have been none in these specific classes. These are things that we could address during the forthcoming year.

The department also plans to set up a trip to France which will be targeted at Year 8 pupils. It is hoped that this will encourage and help pupils (and especially boys, many of whom reported in their questionnaires that they did not see the relevance of French or German) to recognise the value of learning a language.

APPENDIX 12.2

Some useful web-sites

(Note: this is a fast-moving medium. There may be other, even better, web-sites by the time you read this list, which is derived from an Internet Skills for the Modern Foreign Languages Teacher Course at Trinity and All Saints College, Leeds)

Turpsoft

Good links to Spanish sites, search engines and resources.
   http://dspace.dial.pipex.com/turpsoft/

Webservers in Europe

A useful gateway to all the webservers in Europe. http://www.tue.nl/europe/

Resources for Spanish teachers on the Web

http://www.bus.bton.ac.uk/Staff/Shade/recursos.html

CILT: Centre for Information on Language Training

Good for resources and good for links.
   http://www.bt/Campus World/pub/CILT/index.html

BBC Languages Education

http://www.bbc.co.uk/education/languages

CTI Centre for Modern Languages: University of Hull

Very good for computer-based language learning materials.
   http://www.hull.ac.uk/cti

Lingua @Net

The on-line virtual language centre.
   http://www.ncet.org.uk/projects/linguanet/index.html

School on-line

Excellent site.
   http://SOL.ultralab.anglia.ac.uk/pages/schools_online

Chapter 13

Raising achievement in the humanities

Introduction: performance in the humanities

Table 13.1 National percentage of students gaining A*– C at GCSE, by gender

	1996		1997		1998	
	Girls	Boys	Girls	Boys	Girls	Boys
History	54.8	44.7	56.9	48.3	57.6	50.2
Geography	54.8	44.2	56.9	47.0	57.6	48.5
Religious Education	54.0	37.4	56.4	40.6	57.6	40.5

Source: DfEE (1998)

There is probably no other subject area more conducive to, and in more need of, the application of the VEST principles discussed in Chapter 3 than the humanities. The use of VEST would do much to arrest the decline in popularity of the humanities in schools. Recent research (see Lomas, 1998) suggests that the major factor governing popularity of history is the quality of teaching, followed by the status afforded to the subject. The other subjects within humanities are likely to be similar. The humanities have long been viewed as very literary subjects, with the written word playing a predominant role in both teaching and assessment. They are probably more open than others to being labelled 'Applied English', and many humanities teachers find themselves marking more English than geography or history. In that light it is perhaps more understandable to find that boys achieve less than girls. If the humanities are Applied English and boys are so much worse than girls in English, it stands to reason that boys will under-achieve in humanities as well – an expectation borne out by the figures in Table 13.1 above.

However, we feel that it is not acceptable to hide behind the skirts of the English department. One of the themes, indeed the implication of the title of this book, is that both boys and girls sometimes receive less than appropriate teaching – and that the difference in achievement is partially explained by the fact that girls will usually accept it and plough through a diet of tedium and confusion, while boys are more likely to rebel. There is plenty that the humanities can do to raise the achievement of both boys and girls.

Teaching and learning styles

> 'Another damned, thick square book! Always scribble, scribble, scribble! Eh! Mr Gibbon?'
>
>   (Duke of Gloucester to Edward Gibbon the historian)

Mr Gibbon was also a young history teacher at a South London grammar school in the 1970s whose sole teaching method was to dictate notes from his files. He nearly killed the subject for one of the authors. Scribble, scribble, scribble is possibly no longer the main activity of humanities lessons. The five essays in a two-and-a-half hour O level paper is no longer with us, but there is still a great deal of writing to be done by today's students.

Pupils, when asked, do not refer to the intrinsic difficulty of the humanities, but many question the amount of writing that has to be done, especially if they cannot see the point to it (Lomas, 1998). They are much more likely to accept the need to write if:

* it has purpose
* it has logic
* it has structure in leading pupils towards more complex, analytical work
* it has discussion and sharing of ideas built in.

There is possibly no typical humanities lesson, but if we were to characterise one it would look something like this:

* a brief recapitulation of work done earlier, often through questions to the whole class. Many of these questions will be closed (we are dealing with facts, after all), and there will be little need for the boys to reflect on their answers (see Chapter 8, 'Hands up in class')
* teacher talks about a new area
* some reading
* pupil work, usually working as individuals and using worksheet or textbook
* a summarising session, with homework from a worksheet or completing work.

This could be viewed as an entirely reasonable formula. It reflects the ways in which most history and geography teachers were taught, and what most parents – and pupils – expect a lesson to look like. Unfortunately, it does not conspire to maximise enjoyment, understanding and achievement. A vigorous, engaging teacher – exuding enthusiasm and bonhomie – can cajole the class along. At the other extreme the classroom is reduced to a battle of wills with bored and rebellious boys, and teaching has metamorphosed to classroom management. The methods used not only miss all four elements of VEST; they also use the least effective methods of retaining information. The learning pyramid (Figure 13.1) is applicable to all subjects in the curriculum, but none more so than the humanities. It may well come as a shock to university graduates – victors of the lecture and book-learning methods – when they reflect that they have been using the two most inefficient pedagogies at their disposal. Their only comfort is that there is a 90 per cent chance that they will have forgotten this uncomfortable fact before long.

What is useful to teachers about the learning pyramid is that the more efficient teaching methods (in terms of retention) coincide with boys' (and most girls') preferred learning styles. Most teachers are not making use of it, however. Research at GCSE (Lomas, 1998) suggests that the top six most common teaching and learning strategies at this level are, in order of teacher popularity:

1   pupils working at individual exercises
2   teacher presentation

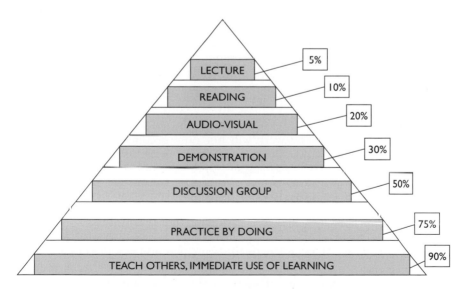

Figure 13.1 Average retention rates by method of learning.
Source: George (1995, p. 71)

3   teacher dictation (although this position may be skewed by the work
     of one South London history teacher)
4   pupils given individual help by the teacher
5   answering past questions
6   pupils taking lesson notes.

It is not a diet to keep pupils or teachers enthralled. One of the reasons
given for following such a torpid regime is that the content of the curriculum
is so large that 'efficient' methods of information-giving have to be employed.
We know that these methods are not particularly efficient.

An alternative lesson plan

Let us take a possible humanities topic and examine how a lesson plan
could differ if the methods used were more varied, more engaging, more
social and more transforming, i.e. if a little more VEST were used. The
topic in question is the historiography of the London Blitz, a topic which
is commonly taught in both Year 6 and Year 9. On the left of Table 13.2
is the traditional lesson; on the right is the one which is (1) much more
likely to appeal to boys, (2) more likely to appeal to girls, and (3) to be
more successful in meeting its aims. Each activity may be annotated V, E,
S or T to signify that it is designed to give a variety, engage the students,
be social or involve transforming information.

It can be easily seen that the alternative lesson has far more VEST than
the traditional lesson. Although the latter could be more engaging if the
teacher is lively the pupil is still involved in passive learning, and is therefore less likely to retain what has been taught or read. The alternative
lesson offers less marking, fewer discipline problems and more successful
teaching. There is more preparation involved in the alternative lesson, but
only in the first year. It is much better to invest more initially for greater
rewards than to put in lower initial investment for continually depressing
results. If the whole faculty is engaged in producing the resources and ideas
for lessons with VEST the work will not only become much lighter, but
positively enjoyable.

Other factors to consider

Seating policy and preferred learning styles

Chapter 8 discusses at some length the principles and practices of a seating
policy. The teaching of humanities would benefit as much as any other
subject from the application of such a policy. Not only does it carry the
benefits discussed in Chapter 8 – such as maximising learning, cutting down
on bullying and teasing, giving pupils access to a wider variety of learning

Table 13.2 An alternative lesson plan: The London Blitz

Traditional lesson plan	More engaging lesson plan
• A brief resumé of last week's work through questions to the whole class. Boys put up their hands more than girls, and are frequently wrong. Girls tend to say little. (**E**)	• Teacher moves class to his/her seating plan for the half term (see Chapter 8). (**S, V**)
• Teacher talks about the Blitz, refers to last week's video and gives talk on 'Was there a Blitz spirit?' Introduces the idea of the traditional history of the Blitz, the revisionists' claims and the view of the counter-revisionists.	• In groups of three or four they have one minute to recall the five main points from previous lesson. It's a challenge; boys reflect. Each group has to answer. Girls have to answer as much as boys. (**V, E, S**)
• Some silent reading about different witnesses' accounts and feelings about the Blitz from textbook or handout.	• Teacher points out the objectives of the lesson on the board. Gives out fifteen cards to each group, each with evidence from a witness, a song or a photograph about the Blitz. The group has to discuss them and place them into one of three piles: traditionalist, revisionist and counter-revisionist. (**V, E, S, T**)
• Pupils write in files individually on work entitled 'Historiography of the Blitz'. Teacher moves around the classroom helping individual students. Those with poorer reading or writing need most help.	• Students then have to write a short report using the evidence, no more than three-quarters of a side of A4 paper, about the historiography of the Blitz – to a writing frame introduced and explained by the teacher. (**E, T**)
• Quick discussion about how they have got on. (**E**) Finish for homework.	• Re-form into groups of six which debate which interpretation is right. A pair in each group has to argue a particular corner. (**V, E, S**)
	• Homework is to collect evidence and artefacts about the Blitz from grandparents and neighbours. (**V, E, S, T**)

styles – but it brings a culture of flexibility and adaptability which complements the preferred learning styles reported by lower achievers, i.e. those whose motivation and interest have to be engaged if overall achievement is to be raised. These styles are:

• brief, snappy teacher talk
• brief question-and-answer sessions (although see Chapter 8, 'Hands up in class')

- most non-written activities
- the teacher reading aloud
- problem-solving activities
- fieldwork
- local history
- worksheets with a *wide variety* of activities and information
- producing work for wall displays
- structured simulations and role-play (although not so much that it becomes expected in most lessons).

(Adapted from Lomas, 1998)

The last six of these activities lend themselves to careful teacher planning about who is sitting and doing what with whom. How can the different learning strengths of each individual be complemented, reinforced, exposed or transferred by seating them with another, or within a selected group? It is an issue of which the students themselves should be aware. Thus the verbally confident but poorly organised boy could both give and take by working with the shy but thoughtful girl in role-play and wall display. This will succeed far better if both fully understand why they have been put together. And the old caveat still applies. The goal is to raise the achievement of both, not to penalise one for the benefit of the other.

Setting

Chapter 6 deals extensively with setting, and it may be worthwhile reading or re-reading it with the humanities specifically in mind. The main points to bear in mind are:

1   There is no research evidence that setting in itself raises achievement, but there is a strong school of thought that tight setting penalises boys and some ethnic minorities, i.e. those very students whose achievement is in most need of being raised.
2   Whatever system a department or school decides to use, it will have intrinsic weaknesses. The most successful departments fully believe in the system they have chosen, but at the same time recognise the weaknesses and take steps to address them.
3   Any setting system needs to be carefully discussed and imaginative solutions found to particular situations, for example, two top sets, two middle sets; make it a policy only to move upwards, and plan modular work so that it is possible to move up without feeling left behind. Alternatively, some departments differentiate by syllabus with the 'top' set following one and the rest following another. This obviously makes transfer impossible, but it may better sustain the interest of the less able. There is no 'right answer' to setting, but departments need to

recognise the issue and come up with the most suitable answer for their students.

Support for and from literacy

The humanities are literacy-rich subjects. The written, read and spoken word shape and define all that goes on within them. This chapter started by postulating that the humanities are Applied English. In that context, the two questions which all departments should be asking of themselves – how can literacy raise achievement in my subject?, and how can we raise literacy through the subject? – are especially pertinent. The answers are not very complex, but they are not always in evidence. The following are some suggestions which have come from a number of schools:

1   Display in the classroom key words or concepts which the students need to learn. 'Anschluss', 'drumlin', 'monotheism', 'eccentric', 'pact', 'Divali', 'marginal propensity' and a legion of others make the subject incomprehensible to many students. By entering the jargon of the language the students are entering a club which may not seem very exclusive to those already in it, but which appears inaccessible to those outside. Teachers invariably assume too much about students' language experiences (Jones, 1988). This is not the same as having low expectations of students, but rather trying to become more student-focused, and starting from where they are. The displays, if hung in a mobile, could have an explanation of the word on the reverse. The students themselves could design and make such a display, which would obviously have to be changed regularly.

2   Explore the extent to which the school library supports the subject, and keep a handy reference to such books and magazines. There is a range of historical fiction, some of which will be popular with both boys and girls. The general disappearance of war and adventure stories, some believe, has penalised boys' reading, but there will be accounts, some biographical, which boys typically will find interesting. The use of geographical journals, often kept in the library, with their fantastic photographs and topical research is something which can bring the subject to life. Historical, geographical and religious trails and challenges can be established in the library with the help of the librarian.

3   Introduce a peer mentoring system, more fully explained in Chapter 7, in which pairs have to check each other's written work before completion. This should take a variety of focuses such as spelling, grammar, vocabulary, structure.

4   Explore the possibility of working in a more complementary fashion with the English department. How and when do they teach particular skills of writing and reading? Can these be exemplified and reinforced

in the humanities? Can the English marking scheme be adapted within humanities when you are marking for correct use of English? Are there any historical, geographical and religious concepts which could be explored within English and drama? If so, is such teaching synchronised?

5   Introduce and develop with the students the idea of writing frames. It is less productive to merely *give* them the frames, as this will often lose the purpose and the students will see the frame less as a tool and more as just another meaningless hurdle that has to be overcome.

6   Consider the potential of oral history and other forms of oral investigation in Religious Education and sociology. This type of work often allows pupils to start from the solid base of what they know – their family, environment, churches, mosques, etc. – and to work towards abstract concepts. It gives plenty of scope for social learning, transforming information, variety of learning experiences and engagement on task. You can introduce key phrases and words which you need them to work with or from, and these will be far more meaningful and memorable than if taught from a book.

The humanities and minority ethnic pupils

The humanities, because they are essentially about people, their environment and their history, are very well placed to make the curriculum more relevant to pupils from minority ethnic groups. In *Making the Difference*, Blair and Bourne (1998) noted that a feature of successful multi-cultural schools was the 'attention given to curriculum enrichment, partially to give a voice to the languages and cultures ignored by the National Curriculum', and they concluded that schools should be designing:

> an inclusive curriculum, e.g. artistic experiences, music, college partnerships, homeless people's project, local history research, own experiences, i.e. using the experiences, culture and traditions of the children themselves. The availability of heritage language teaching and accreditation is also considered important.

These views of effective practice are supported by Fleming (1998) in his work in Bradford and Ilkley College with Asian girls. Interestingly, Lomas (1998), in researching the most popular historical topics in Key Stage 3, found that:

Pupils often spoke with some affection about:

*   aspects of medieval life
*   aspects of the twentieth century

- the non-European theme, but this depended on the theme chosen. Indigenous Americans and black peoples often proved popular.

Thus it seems that the study of the history and cultures of ethnic minority groups could prove effective with pupils both from such groups and also the white pupil population. Religious Education departments are already doing much in this field with comparative studies of Islam, Sikhism and Hinduism.

Working with parents

Working with parents is universally viewed as 'a good thing' by educationalists. There is often less advice about what that actually means, especially in the secondary school, where parents are often left behind by the content of the subject. Target-setting (see Chapter 7), option-choosing and the expression of concern are the main reasons why most secondary schools communicate with parents. More could be done, especially in the humanities which is more person-centred than other subjects. All students live in a rich historical and geographical context, and some within a religious context. Departments should be capable of producing literature/leaflets which could help parents to explore important concepts with their children through the medium of the local environment. Causality, the evolution of architecture, geological landforms, settlement patterns, place names, river systems, churchyards and a host of other ideas and artefacts are all there waiting to be used. Parents themselves will learn much from the exercise, and some may be in a position to contribute a great deal of information, design and printing. The exercise may be more appropriate for Key Stages 2 and 3, but the important thing is to help parents realise that their potential is far more than encouraging homework, revision and neatness.

Parents could also be advised which books, tapes and CD-ROMs have interesting, humanities-based games and information (see the *Times Educational Supplement* for regular reviews). These will make better birthday and Christmas presents than those often received.

Challenge

'For some of our students, the field trips to Malham Cove and Skipton are the highlights of the year, and finally bring the subject to life. I'm always impressed by their responsibility in getting on with the challenge of the investigative work, even though it can be no joke when you're at the top of the Cove in the pouring rain with only a shawaz kameez for protection.'

(Geography teacher from multi-cultural school)

One of the themes we have dealt with in this book is the need for challenge, and how boys will often be motivated by it when all else has failed. A field trip to another town or county is generally very exciting for many pupils. In the age of the car and foreign holidays it is easy to forget that there are still hundreds of thousands of pupils whose life experiences have been confined to home, school and local shops. The field trip – be it for history, geography or Religious Education – can be a challenge for all students (and all teachers) if planned appropriately. It can be differentiated by ability, size or time of task. It can involve questioning the local population and putting quite advanced concepts to the test, as well as fun treasure/date trails. For many the responsibility of being on one's own in a strange place and trusted to behave and perform is challenging enough. Field trips could also reflect what we have written about timespans. A geography department in a northern school has deliberately decided to adopt two, smaller scale GCSE field trips rather than one large one. The head of department feels that locally based, very structured and time-limited trips are more likely to elicit a positive response from those pupils (mainly boys) who have difficulty in dealing with all the data they acquire on a long trip.

Humanities has plenty of scope in working as a whole faculty, or with other departments such as art, design or modern foreign languages, when planning field trips. The history visits to the battlefields of the two World Wars could easily be combined with a study of physical geography, a look at the social stratification in Paris and a 'grand tour' of the art galleries and modern architecture.

One of the aspects often missing from field trips is a detailed explanation to pupils about what they will be expected to have learned by the time they return, including personal and social skills development. Our experience of taking field trips, especially residential ones, is that reflection on personal development can be very valuable. In addition, few schools appear to consider the question of seating plans on the coach or train. Students can quite often see field trips as a pleasurable time away from school, with no parental control, a fairly loose leash exercised by teachers and plenty of free time with friends. We would not want to jeopardise the enjoyment, but field trips are usually in school time and they have educational purposes. When so much time is spent travelling, it seems a pity not to make better use of it. Being asked to consider their learning, feelings, experiences from the last museum, trench, tidal power station or temple with a partner can be as valuable on a coach as it can be in the classroom. Where the pupils sit will have a considerable bearing on how they reflect and if they will be subject to a different interpretation from their own.

Challenge can take many forms, and should not be seen merely as a 'boys' thing'. Girls can respond equally enthusiastically to appropriate challenges. Appendix 13.1 at the end of this chapter has a summer challenge issued by an RE department which has the additional merit of involving parents. The other humanities subjects, with a wealth of artefacts all around, could do something similar. The logical consequence would be a humanities challenge which deals with the holistic nature of the environment experienced by the pupils.

Information and communication technology, etc.

Both geography and history are excellent subjects for exploration via the worldwide web as so many countries, regions, towns and villages have built their own web-sites to promote themselves, giving the sort of information that pupils may find interesting and relevant. This type of evidence-gathering encourages skills of discrimination and rewards perseverance. Boys are particularly attracted to ICT and many will take pleasure from finding something quirky on the web, of which you as the teacher were perhaps unaware. It is a little disappointing that, at the time of writing, the History and Geography Associations have fairly uninspiring web-sites which offer very little to enquiring pupils.

In addition, the well-considered use of video- and audio-tapes can bring meaning and explanation to the humanities, although it is even better if the students can make their own programme or report. Some schools have made programmes about their locality and history, and sent them to their twin schools in other parts of Europe. The 'Down The Line' project organised by Channel 4 and Oxfam to mark the millennium is the sort of curriculum-enriching initiative which both gives an international perspective to students and obliges them to consider their own environment.

Box 13.1 Raising attainment in the humanities

Teaching and learning styles

An alternative lesson plan

Seating policy

Setting

Support for and from literacy

Humanities and minority ethnic pupils

Challenge

Information and communication technology

APPENDIX 13.1

Fulford School

FULFORDGATE, HESLINGTON LANE, FULFORD, YORK YO10 4FY
Telephone York (01904) 633300 Facsimile York (01904) 626899
Email: fulford.secondary@york.gov.uk

Headmaster: E. K. HAYTON, M. A. Cantab

JM/CG/Ext/RE/REfest   July 1998

Dear Parent,

My colleagues and I in the RE Department are promoting an RE Challenge for our future Year 7 pupils this summer. The Summer Challenge is for pupils and parents to visit a place of worship at home or abroad, and to collate information and resources for a display or pamphlet/brochure based on that visit. It can relate to any of the recognised world religions and must be ready for display by the Open Evening on 21st October. There will be prizes awarded in each year group for those pupils whose work indicates that positive effort has been made. We will be allowing time in school and some homework allocation prior to the Open Evening in support of this task, together with provision of resources and materials. Further information is provided overleaf.

The RE Department is particularly keen that parents and pupils should be aware of the changing role and nature of RE and its contribution to a better understanding of the world. We will be displaying the completed projects together with a wide range of resources and pupils' work in the RE rooms and elsewhere in the school during the Open Evening of Wednesday 21st October. If you are planning to attend the Open Evening you are invited to visit the RE Faculty in Rooms T1, T2, T3 and T5 to share in some free refreshments and see for yourselves the work we do.

Yours sincerely,

J. Molyneux
Head of RE

Fulford School Summer Challenge 1998 – Places of worship
Pupil information sheet

The challenge is for you and your parents to visit a place of worship of any religion either at home or abroad. You are then to gather information and resources which will enable you to produce either a display or a pamphlet/brochure about the place of worship visited. In order for your work to be considered for a prize and/or an award, it must be completed for, and be ready for display by the Open Evening on Wednesday 21 October 1998.

Set out below is a chart of issues and information you might like to consider during your visit.

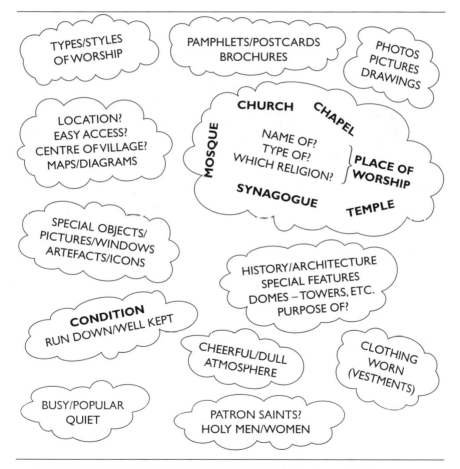

ALWAYS ASK PERMISSION BEFORE TAKING PHOTOGRAPHS INSIDE THE PLACE OF WORSHIP – TAKE CARE TO RESPECT THE TRADITIONS AND CUSTOMS OF THE RELIGIONS CONCERNED – ENJOY YOUR VISIT!

Welcome to GCSE Religious Studies

You have opted for the new GCSE course in Religious Studies. We hope that you are going to enjoy the course. If you have any questions, please do not hesitate to ask either Mr Molyneux or Mrs Prud'homme. The following is intended as a brief outline to what we will be studying, i.e. the syllabus, together with some general guidelines.

Aims of the course

- Stimulate interests in and enthusiasm for a study of religion;
- develop knowledge and understanding of two living religions;
- identify and promote exploration of, and reflection upon, questions about the meaning and purpose of life;
- consider religious and, where appropriate, other responses to moral issues;
- develop skills relevant to the study of religion.

The course is divided into two parts – Religion and Ethics. We are required to study two religions. After taking a survey of what you wanted to take, the vote came out as Christianity and Judaism. Mr Molyneux will be teaching Christianity and Mrs Prud'homme will be teaching Judaism. The first two terms will largely be spent on learning about the religions themselves. There may be an occasional ethics topic put in to liven things up though. The rest of the time will be spent looking at ethical issues and preparing for coursework.

The syllabus comprises the following:

The *Religion* part of the course concentrates on the following issues and is detailed on further sheets: the principal teachings and/or beliefs of each faith; sources of authority; ceremony – how religious commitment is demonstrated.

The *Ethics* part of the course concentrates on personal and social ethics. The three areas of ethical concern in the light of two world religions are:

> marriage and the family
> peace and conflict
> humankind and nature

The details of this part of the course are provided on the following sheets.

You will need to be familiar with the texts as mentioned on the following sheets (the examiners like it if you can produce quotes as evidence for what you are saying). We will also be studying the Universal Declaration of Human Rights as a modern statement of ethical belief. You will be expected to know the differences and similarities between customary, legal, moral and religious values and be able to use the language of ethical discourse. We will be looking particularly at the Assisi Declarations, which express the religious view on ethical issues.

Assessment

The coursework carries 20 per cent of the total marks. The written paper carries 80 per cent of the total marks.

Coursework: you will do two written assignments, each of about 1500–2000 words. Each of these assignments must be related to one of your two chosen options, so that both options are covered by coursework.

Exam: the one and only paper is of two hours' duration and consists of three sections. You must answer questions from the two sections relating to your options. Each section comprises six questions. The first question in each section is compulsory and consists of between ten and fifteen sub-questions requiring a fairly brief response. The other five are structured questions designed to be answered in longer written essay form. Pupils must answer two of these five questions.

Five per cent of the total assessment will be for spelling, punctuation and grammar.

Details of how work will be graded will be provided later on in the course.

Resources

You will be provided with paper to write your notes on and you are asked to keep these in order in the file provided. It will be helpful to you to keep an index where for every piece of written work completed (including notes) you write down the title and page number. An exercise book will be provided so that you can keep a 'dictionary' of any unusual or difficult words.

You will each be provided with a textbook. There will be one on Judaism and another on Christianity. There are other sources in the Resource Centre and it is always good to consolidate your notes with further research. This is often what makes a piece of work rather special – or so the examiners tell me.

We would like all pupils to collect newspaper articles, which are relevant to any issues on the syllabus, to put into a Religious Studies Library of articles. This way, we will all be able to work together and share resources and ideas. Articles of interest will be about the religion itself, religious people, religious events, ethics and morality. So, let's all work together on sharing any snippets of information that we might discover!

Trips we hope to arrange

We are looking into arranging trips to the following places which might be relevant to the course: Walsingham, London, Synagogue in Leeds, the Jewish Museum in Manchester, Inter-Faith Centre at Bradford, possibly a trip to Rome if the cost proves feasible. We'll keep you posted about developments.

So now on with the course, we hope that you find it rewarding and enjoyable! Good luck!

SEG GCSE syllabuses 2000: Religious Studies B

The issues

Candidates need to know the background of each issue and then study the different moral stances that are held by adherents of different beliefs.

Judaism

Candidates should be familiar with the following extracts from the TeNaKh, the Jewish Scriptures:

1 *Marriage and the Family*

   (a) Partner selection, monogamy, polygamy, wedding promises

   (b) Parenthood, implications of modern medical research and practice, abortion

   (c) Divorce, remarriage

   (d) Death – euthanasia

Genesis 1:27; 2:18–25
Exodus 20:13, 14, 17

Deuteronomy 24:1–4
Isaiah 49:5, 15
Psalm 139:13
Proverbs 31:10–31

Jeremiah 1:5
Hosea 3:1

2 *Peace and Conflict*

   (a) Punishment – corporal, capital

   (b) Majority and minority rights

   (c) Sacred and secular authority, obedience to the law

   (d) War – just war, holy war, pacifism, conscientious objection, non-violent protest

Exodus 20:13
Leviticus 19:33–34
Deuteronomy 16:18–20
Isaiah 10:1–4
Micah 4:1–7; 5:2–5a
Psalms 34:15; 146:7–9

3 *Humankind and Nature*

   (a) Attitudes to the environment

   (b) Health – drug abuse

   (c) Animal rights

Genesis 1–3; 8:22–9:17
Exodus 23:10–11
Deuteronomy 20:19–20; 22:6
Psalm 24:1
Proverbs 12:10; 23:20–21
Job 38–39
The Assisi Declarations

Chapter 14

Raising achievement in the arts[1]

The 'arts' offer a rich avenue in which both boys and girls can find enjoyment, enhance their personal and social skills, discover creative and motor skills and improve their self-esteem. Skilfully taught arts courses not only raise achievement in the arts; they improve pupil performance across the curriculum.

The arts

For the purpose of this book the arts constitute art and design, dance, drama, music and PE. These subjects are often difficult for managers and educationalists to pigeon-hole either in neat management structures or philosophically. For example, in some secondary schools many of these subject areas may be lodged in the same faculty but it may be the case that art is to be found in a technology faculty, drama might be located in an English department, and dance could be found in PE. Further compounding the problem is the inherent nature of these individual subjects. Set aside for a second the thought that these are all arts subjects and ask what could be more different than music and visual arts; not only in the nature of the end product but also in terms of the activity and skills needed in order to realise that end product. Compare the philosophy of sport and its underlying principles with the philosophy of dance as an artform. Complicating the picture still further are large numbers of multi-arts courses such as performing arts and expressive arts.

The relative health of these subjects in both primary and secondary schools varies enormously too. Where some schools may have a thriving provision in one particular area others may not teach it as a discrete subject at all. In some schools there may not be a specialist, or anyone who feels vaguely comfortable with these subjects (especially true in some small rural

1 This chapter has been written by Paul Brennan, Inspector for the Arts for Kirklees Local Education Authority, and is based on his research for a Master of Science degree.

primary schools). Indeed in some classrooms some of these subjects are being taught by teachers who have been told from an early age (and what's more they believe it) that they are outright failures in that subject. Of course the opposite is also true, and it may be that in PE, for example, the subject is being taught by a member of a national squad.

It has long been the case that arts and sports teachers have been subjected to many an INSET focused on improving schools, target-setting, raising achievement and so on where the whole thrust of the course has at best made scant reference to the idiosyncrasies of teaching on a playing field, in a gym or in a studio, or indeed teaching any of the arts in a general purpose classroom or school hall. We aim here to try to unravel some of the basic lessons from recent research undertaken in schools – in particular that done in Kirklees and Salford schools which looked at raising boys' achievement in the arts.

The arts are learning

'Art in under an hour, it's impossible but . . .!'

'By the time they've changed and warmed up what time are you left with?'

Arts and sports teachers – whether specialist or untrained – are dedicated to the rights of their children to a full entitlement to the arts and sport. This is quite a challenge in an age where there are ever-increasing demands on the time available. A common response is to try to make the best of the situation by cramming as much practical activity as possible into lessons.

This can mitigate against a structured lesson, which means that some of the vital reflective elements of learning are often ignored. Allowing pupils to come in and just get on with it, with an emphasis on as much practical activity as possible, is often failing them with kindness in the long run: it is sending out all the wrong signals about the place of the arts and sport in the curriculum.

All individual arts and sport should be a right for every pupil. But they are not an entitlement to an hour's relaxation, letting their hair down, getting some exercise, blowing away a few cobwebs. This may seem obvious, but in our attempts to fit as much activity into our all-too-short lesson there is a tendency to forget some of the basic principles that underpin sound learning in all disciplines.

Boys and the arts

Elsewhere in this book we have discussed the idea that boys, more than girls, often need to have a reason for doing something – a reason which satisfies them as well as their teacher. As boys develop, the need for the arts and sport in their lives may disappear. Just as they have outgrown the need for milk, an afternoon nap or playtime at break, so many find that they lose interest in painting and drawing, playing games, singing, improvising and composing, etc. By maintaining a tangible link with the need for the arts *as a form of learning*, this particular obstacle can be eradicated.

This is not a bid to remove any sense of fun from arts lessons or to add prescription or rigidity, but rather an explanation of the philosophy that all teachers and children should focus on the real reason for the place of the arts and sport in the curriculum: to facilitate the development of many of the key life skills necessary to succeed and which can be learned effectively in and through the arts.

Many young artists fail as artists

The art class is not there to allow the pupil to be a mini-artist. It is there to allow pupils to learn about themselves, the world they inhabit and to develop the skills to operate successfully within that world. It may be that the process of being a young musician is the best way of doing that, but whatever teaching and learning style is chosen the teacher must acknowledge that it is a means to an end and not the end in itself.

Most youngsters come to recognise their shortcomings, in fact to overestimate them, and the vast majority of children carry around in their heads league tables that accurately place them in context with their friends. They will discuss these league tables openly and regularly, updating them with each new piece of data. Who is the cleverest in the class, who is the tallest, the best fighter, etc. And who is the best artist, footballer, runner, singer, etc. These children will see themselves as successes or failures and, they believe, just as it is difficult to do much about one's height, so it is difficult to do much about one's arts skills. This is true of girls as well as boys. It is another reason why the arts must be strenuously delivered as a form of learning. Sadly it is something that most of society does not believe because the phrase 'You're either born with it or you're not!' can be heard as much in staff rooms as in the street and at home.

School should be seen as a place where students *learn* to be artists, but not a place where they *are* artists. This may seem a subtle difference, but many boys do not access the arts at a later age in schooling because their macho coolness will not allow them to and, as previously discussed, because boys cannot engage with activities that they do not see a reason for. Boys are often criticised for being lazy, but what is emerging from research is the principle that boys try to achieve success with the minimum of effort. If there appears to be no purpose to an activity their psyche will not allow them to put effort into it. If boys see no reason for dance because they are not going to be a dancer when they grow up, they will not be able to put effort into that activity. If, however, the activity is seen for its aims and objectives (for example, we are going to learn X, Y and Z over the next few weeks and the best way to learn this is through a dance project, by-products of which are fitness, etc.), they are far more likely to participate.

Homophobia and enhanced stereotypes

Many of the stereotypes that boys hold are created and/or fuelled in school by well-intentioned teachers. In primary schools there are major problems in getting specialist staff, so it is not uncommon for sports development officers to undertake sessions, or peripatetic music teachers to come in, or a parent or member of the community to run an art class. The possible problem with this is that it separates the arts from mainstream learning. The image of the arts as being 'not quite serious' education is reinforced in the minds of parents, teachers and pupils. If there are also regular visitors who teach mathematics, English and humanities this problem would not exist.

Many of the stereotypes that we all accept come from teachers: How many male PE teachers run dance clubs? How many teachers would make amusing asides if boys were to take part in dance clubs? If boys assume that dancing is a female or homosexual activity, there is no way that they can engage with it. The phrase 'cannot engage' is used purposely because for the boys concerned it is not a matter of choice. As far as they are concerned the whole of society is against them doing this activity. The same may be said of any of the other arts or parts of arts subjects (e.g. textiles, stringed instruments, netball, etc.).

Chapter 4 highlighted the need to eradicate the anti-swot culture in the same way that racism is being dealt with. We all know how racist our society can be, yet it was not so long ago that *Love thy Neighbour* was shown on British television, and it is only the hardened racist who cannot watch a clip from that programme without wincing at the content. But in schools today, teachers will be indulging in homophobic banter that isn't intended to slight in any way but which is having an enormously detrimental effect on the life choices of young men.

'Many boys especially in this school succeed in the arts and sport and we don't really have a problem here'

In some arts departments boys do indeed succeed but in the vast majority of departments there are major problems that are polarised in the arts, more so than in any other subject on the curriculum. In some arts subjects in many schools boys not only fail to achieve to the same standard as girls but do not access and cannot engage with the subject at all. The problem facing the arts and sport is quite different. All the subjects have varying problems, with PE exhibiting the greatest polarity especially where dance is a part of the PE curriculum. It is common for boys to out-perform or have comparable performance levels with girls at sport and in GCSE PE (national figures suggest that girls have only recently overtaken boys with regard to numbers achieving A*– C grades at GCSE), yet in the same curriculum area with the same team of teachers boys may well not opt for dance at all. In drama, art and music it is often the case that the gender of the teacher can determine the perceived gender of the subject, and this might determine participation levels among boys and girls. Nevertheless there is on average a 20 per cent shortfall in boys' achievements in these subjects across the UK. Even in PE where boys are traditionally successful there is evidence that they are not only under-achieving but they invariably create many more problems than their female counterparts. It is common for boys to balk at uniform regulations in PE and to express anti-social behaviour. There are suggestions by some authors that the PE lesson can often fuel the anti-swot culture and that schools can unwittingly strengthen the boys' resolve that the only acceptable school success is a sporting one. Again this is often the case whereby the culture of sport in school is divorced from the mainstream school.

Women artists

The historical domination of the high arts by men has led to attempts to redress the balance by focusing on 'women artists', 'women musicians', etc. We believe that schools must continue to do this but they should be careful about the way it is done. It would be very strange to see a display entitled 'Men artists'. It would also be strange to refer to Michelangelo as a 'man artist'.

What does a boy think when he looks at a display entitled 'Women artists' picturing perhaps a dozen contemporary and historical women artists and their work, none of whom he recognises? What do *you* think about it? You might have had your eyes open to the fact that there are some women artists, you may even like their work, but you would also know that women are not in the big league and have only really made the second grade. A boy looking at a display of this nature will, especially if he is from a chauvinist background, rapidly assimilate the information to fuel his chauvinism. If, on the other hand, the class is introduced to the work of a group of artists who happen to be women and they study their work as a part of the course, there will be no attempt to write off the 'women artists' as a piece of 'equal opps' evangelism. The issue of women as artists, sports people and musicians must be done in such a way that it does not create the opportunity for boys to see another area of endeavour with which to beat women. It also does not allow them to accept that they are by nature better at sport, art, music, etc. and therefore they have no need to try too hard because it comes naturally. Another interesting exercise is to examine the school or department library. Look for books about great artists/musicians/sportsmen, etc. It is likely that what you will find are listings of great, white, dead, European men. Posters around the school, textbooks and assemblies may all help to perpetuate this message. Your response can use the same channels to open students' eyes to a different reality.

Assessment

All Michelangelo's paintings must have got an 'A*'

Children, like many adults, like to know how much things are worth. Sadly for the arts we teach our youngsters to be 'mini-valuers' when looking at works of art and this is also true of adults in school. If it's a painting by Van Gogh everyone will wonder how much it is worth. If it is a painting by a Year 10 or Year 11 pupil everyone will wonder what grade it will get at GCSE. (Interestingly, some GCSE work transcends GCSE marks to monetary valuation, and comments such as 'You could sell that' can be heard, along with other less flattering comparative comments listing its superior merits to that of the Van Gogh).

It is vital that we teach children to value the arts and sport and not to link everything to monetary or numerical value. Assessment must be an aid to the teacher to facilitate planning, and it must inform the pupils in what ways they need to work in order to improve. In the arts, pupils do not need to know where they stand in relation to National Curriculum levels: knowing that will neither help them nor their parents. The end of Key Stage level descriptors were kind, but many schools (and now the Qualifications and Curriculum Authority) have unilaterally broken them down into levels which is wholly inappropriate. In all the arts, feedback to pupils is vital and must form practical advice to enable improvement. It must be based on evidence which should be shared and it must not be numerical. Pupils must be involved in the assessment and helped by a description of the work that is non-judgemental in itself, but can facilitate a positive judgement by the pupils themselves. Most boys will welcome this approach and it will avoid the problems caused by boys becoming complacent because they can play football, draw or dance well already – and it helps weaker boys to improve. Further, assessment must focus upon what children have achieved and what they are able to achieve. Too often, assessment focuses upon shortcomings, mistakes and failures – with the end result that students begin to define themselves in the subject by these shortcomings. In assessing work, no matter how good, how often do you search for the weaknesses: in a ten-minute performance of a personal composition how much feedback would focus on the achievements of the piece, and their further development, and how much would focus on the weakest sections?

Scaffolds

Boys will not do two compositions if they are quite happy with the first one. Boys will not keep a diary or log if they cannot see themselves using it or if it is never going to be seen by anybody. It is difficult to persuade boys to move away from the more obvious prescriptive motif and to develop their creative skills. Earlier in the book there is the recommended use of 'scaffolds' to enable boys to complete their work (see p. 135). The same method can be used in the arts. In art, for example, it can be useful to provide ready-drawn frames that restrict the size of the boys' work so that they don't finish while ignoring attention to detail. These can be quite sophisticated and might further encourage the students by trying different approaches in terms of mood, media, colour, style, etc. The same can be done in music and drama and dance, with the class being instructed to work to create five five-bar phrases, five two-minute sequences, etc.

In terms of keeping journals, logs and sketchbooks, boys need first to be given clear reasons for keeping them, ideally listed in the inside front cover of the books, and they need to be regularly monitored by teachers, and if possible parents. Reasons for keeping the books must be backed up by an adequate reward system that does not simply favour the best one or two in the group but which recognises that with effort all can succeed. In addition, and most importantly, the usefulness of the books must be made explicit early on; for example, by referencing them in project work.

Words are all-important

Many schools have thriving choirs, bands, orchestras and dance groups, but all too many are dominated by girls. It is often not cool to be in the band, choir, etc., so it is important for teachers to do some basic research. Is it that the activity is seen as boring, or a girls' thing, or swotty? Whatever the reason there will be a way round it, and getting boys involved in extra-curricular activities will enable them to raise achievement across the board.

Where there is an insurmountable block to boys accessing an artform, alter the description. It allows a face-saving explanation to be offered to sceptical peers. A boy who can say that he is part of the 'Year 9 Singing Team' (in one school they dubbed themselves 'The Really Hard Choir') will feel better when telling friends at home that he's in the choir. The boys will come up with the 'street cred' names, but it is important when recruiting that consideration be given to targeting influential opinion-formers in the year group; the rest will then follow. Consider also all-boy choirs, dance groups, recorder groups and bands perhaps with a challenge to the girls' existing supremacy.

Nothing will be gained by simply standing at the front of an assembly and asking for more boys to come forward. The boys will need good reasons for joining up, so make sure that you have your battery of benefits ready to hand. Once it becomes acceptable, you can start introducing the correct terminology, but that may be some years down the line.

Planning

'What will you need to know to be able to . . .?'

Allow boys to take ownership of their own learning by involving them in the planning of their experience; for example, 'What will you need to know to undertake an expedition to the Peak District?' This will enable them to see for themselves the greater picture and it will give them a deeper understanding of where they are going and why. As a teacher you will be there to guide by asking about the things they have forgotten, and this exercise will also be of enormous value in discovering the group's conceptual knowledge of the topic. This can be done in groups but it is also useful for individuals to record what they personally hope to achieve and what they need to do in order to attain their goal. This information can then form part of their sketchbook, log or journal and can be used for assessment purposes at the end of the project.

Delivery

Once you have decided the basic skills and concepts that you wish to teach, try to teach these skills in a variety of styles. Plan for and allow pupils to use their preferred learning style. To do this you will need to know what these are, and you may be able to adapt the teaching and learning questionnaire discussed in Chapter 3. Teaching in a variety of styles which the pupils have discussed and agree most suits them is a very liberating experience. They will also accept that, given the constraints of time and the curriculum, there may be occasions when you have to impose their less favoured learning style.

It may be useful to discuss with other colleagues in the arts 'family' their different teaching strategies. For example, art and drama teachers might well explore and exchange expertise in the use of display and improvisation.

Group work

Be explicit from the start that the group is here to learn, not for a social hour. Be clear that you expect the class to learn from each other and from their own endeavours as well as from you. To that end give explicit examples of where different people have to work together and the importance of being able to do so. Then regularly set up projects that rely on groups working co-operatively. In many art rooms pupils often adopt a space to themselves, and this has many benefits, but there are times when you should be considering projects that rely on groups of pupils with different skills working together. Consider groups that have different strengths for different activities; for example, one pupil to act as a researcher, one pupil to present and one to act as a recorder. Ensure that the group records how it worked as a team as well as where it was successful.

Art

Older boys can often be seduced by larger scale works, perhaps on canvas if a painting or by modelling heavily grogged clay into large forms. This monumentality and making one's mark appeals to some boys, but strangely the opposite seems to be true for others who delight in detail. Whatever, it is very tempting – if not even beholden upon us – as art educators to free up our charges from the prescriptive adolescent images. It is a constant struggle to get boys to look at the form of what they are doing beyond the realism and also to move beyond the importance of the content and imagery. A way forward is to challenge the image through media or scale; for example, by developing an elaborate pen and ink drawing in oil or charcoal. ICT can be an invaluable source of abstraction and can provide the levels of development that could only previously have been undertaken over hours of effort.

Music

At age 13, boys spend the majority of their pocket-money on CDs, much more so than girls, and the level of interest that boys have in music is much higher. Yet the numbers of boys involved in playing musical instruments is much lower than girls. What seems to have worked for many schools has been the concentration on more popular instruments such as the guitar, drums and steel band as well as instruments from the boys' own culture such as the Indian harmonium and talba. High-technology, electronic instruments are also favoured by boys.

There is nothing more harmful to a boy's 'street cred' than being heard to play simple nursery rhymes badly. Many boys drop their instruments in the early years at high school, but this should not be accepted as an inevitability. Research why it is happening and try to take appropriate remedial action. It may mean encouraging peripatetic instrument teachers and music services to invest in 'Indi' sheet music. Another approach is to look at issues-based composition where pupils write and perform about those things which matter to them.

Dance

The essential element in successful access to dance is the provision of an acceptable male dance culture. This needs the input of male role models: older boys, external visitors or staff – but it must be accepted across a whole school pyramid that dance is an acceptable activity for boys and there can be no tolerance of homophobic humour. Dance can benefit from the challenge aspect. Can you be that fit? Can you keep going for fifteen minutes? Reference to sportsmen who dance, especially footballers, can be helpful. At all levels it is always useful to be able to use macho imagery such as the Maori 'Hakka' or 'Men in Black' to enable boys to take a full and enthusiastic part.

Drama

Drama varies enormously from school to school, but it is at its best where pupils have moved away from the prescriptive macho imagery and where they are able to look at the form of their work. However, it may be useful to work with pupils in developing skills through a variety of genres that would not otherwise have been chosen. If this is backed up by the collation of a journal that is constantly reflecting on learning, boys will make more rapid progress. Reflection at the end of lessons and projects is essential, especially where it enables pupils to distil those new skills that have been developed and employed. Most drama studios lend themselves to being print-rich environments where new terminology and vocabulary can be displayed.

PE

In 1997 girls overtook boys for the first time in gaining more A*– C grades at GCSE level. It is therefore useful to inculcate earlier in school life some of the skills that boys will need in order to pass GCSE. Many boys who are good at sport choose the subject, but are disappointed by the amount of written work that is required. Many of the suggestions in the other chapters would be helpful here together with making the gymnasium and changing rooms much more 'print-rich environments'. If boys and girls are seeing much of the specialist vocabulary displayed in the changing rooms from Year 7 (or Key Stages 1 and 2 if possible) it will be easy to digest at Year 10 and 11, especially if it forms a part of plenary sessions after changing.

Conclusion

Our aim at the end of all this is to provide a generation of young men who are learners in the arts, not a generation of musicians, actors, directors, artists or sportsmen and women (or worse, failed musicians, artists . . .). We want the very best for all youngsters, and if we can help boys to access the arts then we will be helping both boys and girls by giving them all a richer life experience.

Box 14.1 Raising achievement in the arts

Make the arts part of the mainstream learning activity

Extra curricular activities help to raise achievement through the arts

Importance of stressing the need for learning in the arts and the development of the basic skills that learning in the arts can bring about

Boys learn best when they have a valid reason for learning. Give them that reason

Assessment needs to be very carefully considered at all levels and appropriate planning implemented

Consider all-boy teams of singers, performers, etc.

Consider more contemporary artforms, media, etc.

Build in plenty of reward

Use journals, logs, etc. to encourage reflection

Use scaffolds to develop creativity and development

Consider learning styles by consulting the pupils and adopt appropriate teaching styles

Develop a considered and intelligent approach to equal opportunities in terms of gender and multi-cultural issues

Develop print-rich environments in all teaching spaces

Use as many male role models as possible

Involve pupils in curriculum planning

Chapter 15

Getting it right in the secondary school library[1]

'I like to spend time in the library because it's warmer than the rest of the school, and it has comfy chairs.'

(Luke, Year 8)

Boys are seldom interested in the traditional school library – often perceived as a silent, orderly collection of boring classics. However, many schools now have accessible, modern libraries integrated within the school with relevant books, computers with CD-ROM and Internet, magazines, videos, etc. . . . and comfy chairs! These libraries can make a significant contribution to raising boys' achievement by providing a unique environment which boys may use – away from the pressures of their peer group.

The crucial role of the librarian as handler and manager of information and as trainer of others is recognised in *Focus on the Child* (Elkin and Lonsdale, 1996). Frater (1997) also observed that the school library is important in supporting the development of literacy in general and among boys in particular. He identified five common strengths in effective school libraries:

- an energetic librarian
- close liaison between the English department, the special needs team and the librarian (I would also include the language development team)
- a library training programme for pupils that involves study skills and research skills
- well-judged stocks
- the involvement of the library in school-wide curriculum developments.

While there is a great disparity of provision between secondary school libraries, most librarians can contribute to raising boys' – and girls' –

1 This chapter has been written by Kathryn Sheard, Librarian at Salendine Nook High School, Huddersfield.

achievement. One of the more recent initiatives is Launchpad (1999), which encourages school and children's librarians to get involved in community reading promotions in venues as diverse as record shops and sports centres: this is a new opportunity for most librarians.

Over one-third of secondary school libraries are staffed by chartered librarians, whose expertise centres on information-handling. These skills complement those of teachers, and many librarians welcome the opportunity of working in partnership with teachers (NCET, 1996). Librarians are not subject specialists, but if they have the confidence to admit gaps in their knowledge they may create unique opportunities to work with boys to discover answers to their questions.

Investors In Information

The Library Association's Investors In Information scheme is perhaps the most significant recent challenge for school libraries. It aims to help organisations recognise the importance of acquiring, organising and sharing information. Many schools contain a wealth of under-utilised, departmentalised, fragmented information. Pupils have the right to benefit from the expertise trapped inside your school. By encouraging your school to take part in Investors In Information, you will be taking the first step towards the development of an information-sharing culture (Library Association, 1998). This helps to reinforce the school as a learning organisation, an image discussed in Chapter 4, which plays a powerful, pro-active part in countering the anti-swot culture so favoured by boys.

Transition from Year 6 to Year 7: libraries . . . a quiet life?

If contact is to be made with Year 6 pupils, many boys will make use of the library during their first term in a secondary school. Year 6 boys may especially value the chance to 'order' a reading book, to be waiting for them in the library, on arrival in Year 7 at their new school (Clark and Millard, 1998). Encourage future pupils to look upon the library as a source of help and information, as well as computers and books. Some boys need a haven where they can spend time and adjust to the larger number of pupils, increased size of school and the altered delivery of subjects. Year 7 boys are especially likely to take advantage of the library if they receive induction about the facilities during the first half of the term. Libraries which afford this opportunity for boys to integrate and develop will be busier, livelier and noisier. When planning and developing facilities, remember the gender split (Adler, 1997) – boys like more computers in libraries, whereas girls prefer more fiction and quiet corners.

Reading is the key: SEN, low reading ages, able pupils and dyslexics

'I like the library because I can get help to choose a book, and I can use the computers.'

(Shanwaz, Year 9)

The library may be the perfect setting for schemes focusing on reading development. Language development departments may target small groups of Year 7 pupils (mainly boys) with low reading ages. Such pupils can 'kid-test' a selection of carefully chosen, new, entertaining fiction during school hours or after school. This intensive support aims to develop reading fluency and inculcate the 'library habit', often helping pupils with English as a second language.

Schemes pairing reluctant readers with pupils from Years 10, 11 or the sixth form provide boys with important role models, as discussed in Chapter 9. Similarly, schemes where Year 7 or Year 8 boys act as 'reading buddies' with pupils from a nearby primary school can benefit both groups. In some areas schemes have been developed using the National Year of Reading as a focus.

In *Able Children in Ordinary Schools*, Eyre (1998) highlighted the contribution that school libraries can make towards supporting able pupils. The role of the library should be included in a school policy for able pupils. As well as encouraging pupils to contribute to making choices, become independent and organise their own work, the policy should emphasise the role of the library to provide a resource for private study, research and extension activities. Where departments (for example, science) are keen to deposit extension materials in the library (such as more 'advanced' texts, Royal Society magazines, lists of web-sites, etc.), able pupils may be directed to these at suitable times within lessons.

Writing about the librarian's ability to support dyslexic students, Pottage (1999) realised that the 'happy to help' attitude of the librarian and an acceptance that each 'customer' is an individual are more important than anything else. This maxim applies equally to all boys, whether gifted, disaffected, with learning difficulties, or with dyslexia. Try to project yourself as a helpful, approachable person who can listen to questions and help to solve problems.

Reading is the key: all pupils

'I like to use the library because you can read books without buying them.'

(Simon, Year 8)

Boys benefit from more varied reading tasks, short-term reading targets and opportunities to discuss reading preferences. These strategies have been found to improve the scope and quantity of materials read by Year 9 boys (Penny, 1998). The library is the perfect venue for activities of this type. However, 'silent' reading for long periods seldom inspires boys to continue reading their books outside school. Simple strategies can transform this type of library-based lesson; for example, fifteen minutes spent choosing a book, fifteen minutes spent in silent reading and fifteen minutes when a pupil, teacher or librarian reads from 'their' book. One teacher was encouraged to discover that a significant number of boys desperately wanted to share their book with the class: in previous lessons these same boys had shown little or no interest in reading.

Listening to fiction

'At first I just came to eat my lunch, but now I like listening to Mr Hodgson reading.'

(James, Year 9)

Literary lunches are hugely popular in some schools. Pupils eat a packed lunch in the library while listening to a teacher reading an instalment from a work of fiction. In this way pupils can be introduced to a wider range of fiction than they might otherwise tackle. In one scheme we found that three-quarters of the 'regulars' for our literary lunches were boys: these included disaffected as well as able and statemented boys. This makes severe demands on the reader and also on the book choice. *Fire, Bed and Bone* by Henrietta Brandford (viewed through the eyes of an old hunting dog and set during the Peasants' Revolt) was universally popular. Many boys enjoy listening to fiction on audio-tape, and, where this is accompanied by exactly matching text, this assists and reinforces reading skills.

Boys appreciate being involved in the choice of book stock, both fiction and non-fiction, and magazines (*Shoot, Film Review*, etc.). It is a good idea to take boys to the local bookshop to choose materials. If this is difficult, try to buy in a collection of new books and then allow pupils to 'select' one for the library. This book could then bear their name; for example, 'Chosen by . . .'. This scheme could be used as an extra 'reward' for boys who have taken part in reading activities such as Readathon.

Access

'There's a friendly atmosphere and somewhere quiet to work.'

(Imran, Year 10)

If the library is open before school, at break time, lunchtime and after school, it may attract boys through the 'back door'. Some boys take advantage of the facilities away from tutor group, peer pressure, subject teachers, etc. Boys may benefit greatly from library-based holiday club activities. Try to produce library 'publicity' (i.e. guides to finding books, tasters for genres of fiction, using the Internet, etc.) on tape or computerised Powerpoint programmes. Most boys will make far more use of these than printed leaflets.

Place signs and posters featuring the library around the school. Inside the library, signs should clearly indicate the major areas. Consider colour-coding the non-fiction: this will develop the confidence of boys in using the Dewey system.

Visiting authors

Charismatic visiting authors may prove a real incentive to some disaffected boys. Removed from the 'normal' lesson routine, some boys relish the opportunity to question and learn from an adult who has had interesting experiences outside of the classroom. However, visiting authors, reviewers, poets, etc. must be chosen with care: an articulate, polished radio reviewer may not be the person to inspire a group of difficult Year 9 teenagers. An ideal author profile might be inspirational, effervescent, flexible, a born communicator – preferably a former teacher. At Salendine Nook High School several authors have worked brilliantly with boys. Robin Jarvis captivated all pupils who were involved in his sessions; Tim Bowler shocked some boys by his honesty and sympathy for victims of bullying; and Sue Mayfield touched a nerve when she read from one of her books which follows the story of a teenage boy whose mother is dying. Sometimes visiting authors prompt boys to participate in these sessions in a new and very positive way.

Information handling

'It's a fun research centre.'

(Michael, Year 7)

The National Curriculum requires pupils to select, reject and handle information in a competent way. Within most subjects there is no specification when or how pupils are to acquire these skills. Lack of information-handling skills appears to be a key factor in boys' inability to effectively organise their work. Most pupils would benefit from a cross-curricular, sequential programme to acquire and practise these skills, which are readily transferable from books to computerised sources. These programmes could capitalise on investigative Year 6 projects, consolidate progress in Key Stage 3 and prepare boys for the 'research' required in many subjects at Key Stage 4. Such courses will be most effective if endorsed by senior management, incorporated in the school development plan, and delivered across the curriculum.

The Library Association (1998) recommends that the role of the school library should be firmly identified in this process. Some schools encourage library-based programmes across whole years; for example, *Places of pilgrimage* (religious studies), *The Earth and beyond* (science), *crusades* (history), etc. Pupils need a brief introduction to library facilities: this aims to bring pupils to a shared level of competence and compensate for pupils' varying levels of confidence in using a library system. If this induction is delivered principally through subjects other than English (for example, science, ICT, history), then boys are less likely to see the library as an extension of English. Emphasise the aspects of the service with maximum impact – Internet, CD-ROMs, computerised presentations and catalogues, charismatic visiting authors, etc.

Library-based 'research' learning programmes can improve the achievement levels of low ability pupils (Streatfield and Markless, 1994). Some boys at all levels of ability respond well to a programme of library-based work where they have the opportunity to practise locating, retrieving, processing and evaluating information. These programmes should be carefully structured to allow for sufficient practice and progression towards independence. Programmes are most successful if they cover a specific curriculum theme and are prepared and delivered by a partnership of teacher and librarian. Time for reflection, assimilation and sharing of information is needed. Pupils may take part in individual or group presentations, incorporating the information they have retrieved, while others may produce displays/posters to share the newly acquired knowledge with the whole class. Some boys who normally contribute little within lessons can sometimes excel at this type of activity.

Independent learning

GNVQ courses require pupils to move towards independent use of libraries if they are to achieve a merit or distinction. Librarians, especially those who have undertaken GNVQ assessor training, can contribute to boys' GNVQ achievement, especially communications and IT key skills. Some boys (not always the ones you would expect!) respond well to the required action planning and take responsibility for their own learning.

Libraries are ideal locations for skills cards; for example, tips on basic skills such as use of capital letters, percentages and fractions. If these are laminated and on open access in the library, many pupils will make active use of them.

Ownership

> 'I came mainly to the library in Year 7 as I'd nothing better to do. Now I've read a lot of the books I like and I help with the computers.'
>
> (Mark, Year 9)

Encourage boys to feel involved in running the library. Ask year councils for suggestions for library developments and organise questionnaires to assess boys' – and girls' – opinions. Ask the school television crew (often boys) to feature the library. Organise exciting events to celebrate World Book Day, National Year of Reading, and so on. Teams of boys (of all abilities) may undertake practical tasks in the library; others may enjoy teaching younger pupils how to make best use of the facilities.

School library services

These services may make an enormous contribution; for example:

*   Books, materials, artefacts to support information-handling programmes. For example, Books + (Kirklees Schools Library Service) provides extra books, audio, slides and artefacts to support a Year 8 English project where pupils extract information as a prelude to writing a diary of a person during the Second World War. The artefacts – ration books, garments – often capture boys' imaginations and integrate them into the activity.
*   Boxes of 'books for boys' may be available.
*   Fiction to extend able pupils and support those with low reading ages.
*   Differentiated non-fiction books.

The library environment

Aim to make the library a bright, interesting, welcoming environment. Posters promoting reading, writing and maths skills are readily available from the Library Association and others. These have more impact if you can arrange to locate them in areas other than the library; for example, science laboratories or PE changing rooms. Make the most of opportunities for displays incorporating boys' work. Give boys responsibility for a display area, for example, of Internet images of today's weather, or sport in the news.

ICT

> 'I use the library to check my e-mail and surf the net for information.'
>
> (Year 10 boy)

A 1997 national poll (Gordon and Griffiths, 1997) asked 'What would encourage you to visit the library?' Two-thirds of children said, 'access to the Internet and CD-ROMs'. A computerised (networked) catalogue will be used by most boys; take advantage of this technology to key word fiction and non-fiction to make most effective use of stock. Invite boys to produce computerised presentations (for example, Powerpoint) on aspects of the library service; for instance, a favourite CD-ROM. Boys will make more use of these than printed leaflets.

Many boys will be only too willing to share their knowledge of Internet addresses and build a 'Web Wall' of favourite sites. Be prepared to tutor girls separately from boys; many girls possess information-handling skills but may need more reassurance and building of confidence using CD-ROM and computerised sources. Most boys are fascinated by the Internet, but many need extra help to make sensible, efficient use of the information acquired. They often do not recognise that they need help to manage computerised information, but one way to demonstrate this need is to give pupils a free choice of medium when looking for answers to a set of questions. Invariably, most boys choose to use the computers, while most girls choose to use the books. It is salutary for boys to realise after thirty minutes that the 'book users' have found most/all of the answers and the 'computer group' has found few/none. This usually makes boys more receptive to guidance on searching methods. It often helps to write a list of questions/key words before starting a search.

Be prepared to investigate the worth of buying into specialist educational Internet/online providers; for example, Internet for Learning or KnowUK. These provide limited access, but more worthwhile results. Many boys will have used computers since 'birth', and librarians should be prepared to admire their expertise and capitalise on this skill. The Kurzweil 3000 scheme affords wonderful opportunities for those libraries with a computer, a scanner and some available funds. Boys will relish the 'reading machine' which enables a page from a book or worksheet to be easily transferred to a computer screen. The computer then 'reads out' the text, highlighting the words as it progresses. This system, originally designed to help the visually impaired, may be of great benefit to a large number of boys.

Conclusion

These are just a few ideas which school librarians may wish to bear in mind when considering optimising the use and impact of the library. By working with students, and researching their individual needs, each librarian will discover many more, and those that are more relevant to their school. These librarians and teachers have a unique opportunity to maximise the contribution which libraries can make to raising boys' and girls' achievement levels.

APPENDIX 15.1

Salendine Nook High School library provision for raising boys' achievement

Library-based learning programme
e.g. Year 8 science astronomy project. Information skills project. Research by NFER shows that library-based 'research' learning can make a dramatic improvement to achievement levels of low ability pupils.

INFOMATCH information handling skills
Inset for whole departments – history, then RE – to facilitate transfer of information handling skills across the curriculum. Differentiated to 3 levels. To formalise practice in locating, retrieving, processing and evaluating information. Opportunity for targeting boys identified as under-achieving.

Through the back door
At break, lunchtimes and after school. Boys (prefect and boy helpers) help boys, especially, with developing ICT skills – !Libsearch, word processing, CD-ROM Interact. *Ad hoc.*

To support Development Plan/Operational Plan. Dept. strategies for improving GCSE results with an emphasis on boys' under-achievement

Literacy Year 7 kid-tested reading
Language Support Department targets small groups of pupils with low reading ages. Intensive support during tutorial session. Uses boxes of books from local library service, produced with the help of English advisers.

Internet and ICT
Access to 'Successmaker' and 'Ginn Impact' – both integrated learning systems aimed at improving basic skills levels and reading ages of boys.

GNVQ engineering foundation and intermediate
Involved with key skills, especially communication. To develop towards merit or distinction boys must move towards independent use of the library. Help on an individual basis with action planning, information handling, assessment and feedback.

Support English Department objectives
Library-based lessons. Sponsored reading. Visiting authors to inspire boys, e.g. Sue Mayfield, Robin Jarvis. Microlibrarian – library management system allows analysis of reading habits by gender.

Support cross-phase links
Library provides a haven for some boys to adjust, integrate, then develop.

Structured library induction
Attempts to bring Year 7 pupils to shared level of competence. Attempts to lessen disadvantages of home backgrounds. Delivered via English, history and ICT.

APPENDIX 15.2

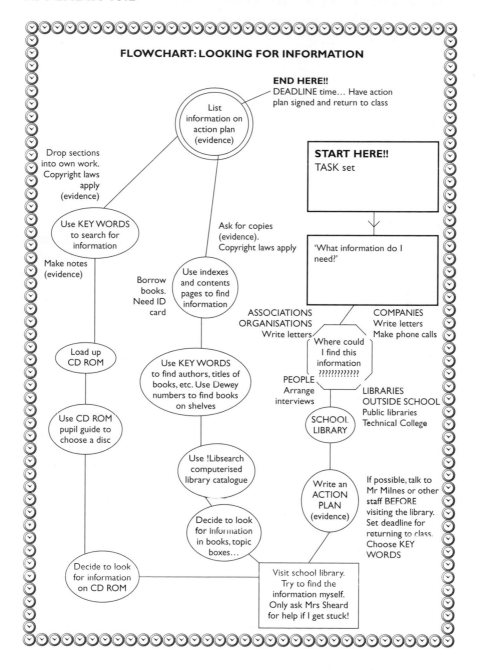

FLOWCHART: LOOKING FOR INFORMATION

END HERE!!
DEADLINE time... Have action plan signed and return to class

List information on action plan (evidence)

Drop sections into own work. Copyright laws apply (evidence)

START HERE!!
TASK set

Use KEY WORDS to search for information

Ask for copies (evidence). Copyright laws apply

'What information do I need?'

Make notes (evidence)

Borrow books. Need ID card

Use indexes and contents pages to find information

ASSOCIATIONS ORGANISATIONS
Write letters

COMPANIES
Write letters
Make phone calls

Where could I find this information ????????????

Load up CD ROM

Use KEY WORDS to find authors, titles of books, etc. Use Dewey numbers to find books on shelves

PEOPLE
Arrange interviews

LIBRARIES OUTSIDE SCHOOL
Public libraries
Technical College

Use CD ROM pupil guide to choose a disc

SCHOOL LIBRARY

Use !Libsearch computerised library catalogue

Write an ACTION PLAN (evidence)

If possible, talk to Mr Milnes or other staff BEFORE visiting the library. Set deadline for returning to class. Choose KEY WORDS

Decide to look for information in books, topic boxes...

Decide to look for information on CD ROM

Visit school library. Try to find the information myself. Only ask Mrs Sheard for help if I get stuck!

Chapter 16

Raising boys' achievement across the pyramid[1]

The Newsome Pyramid Gender and Achievement Working Party

The Newsome High School Gender and Achievement Working Party was formed in December 1993. This followed an Ofsted inspection at the high school where one of the points raised was the fact that there existed a significant difference between the number of boys and the number of girls achieving good GCSE results. At Newsome, as was the case in almost every high school in the country, girls were doing considerably better than boys.

The group began to study the national picture which showed very clearly that right across the country, in almost every test sat by 7-year-olds, 11-year-olds, 14-year-olds and 16-year-olds, girls were improving at such a rate that boys were finding it almost impossible to keep up. Indeed, girls were now getting better results in every single subject at GCSE level. While on the one hand this was very pleasing (for the girls), it was very worrying as far as the boys were concerned. For the next two years the group did extensive research at the high school into differences in reading ability, attitudes to school, behaviour, homework, SATs results, GCSE results and so on. At the same time the group also did as much as it could to raise teachers' and pupils' awareness about the issue. Training sessions were run for the teachers and various groups of boys were interviewed to discover their points of view.

At the high school it was decided to begin to tackle the problem by supporting those boys in Years 10 and 11 who were identified as under-achieving and give them individual attention through a process called 'mentoring'. In addition, a system of 'befrienders' was set up which used older pupils to support younger pupils who might be having problems. The school also started to hold a series of assemblies about the subject and introduce work to do with gender into its weekly PSE (personal and social

---

1 The following is taken from a report by Gary Wilson, Head of English at Newsome High School, Huddersfield, based on work undertaken for the Teacher Training Agency.

education) lessons. Believing that many of the causes of under-achievement among boys were to do with behaviour, the group also worked on a bullying policy and a sexual harassment policy.

Knowing that a lot of boys' problems were caused by difficulties with reading and writing, the high school also introduced two initiatives – an early morning literacy club and 'shared reading' (a system whereby more confident, although not necessarily more able, boys helped those with reading difficulties).

In 1996 the working party decided that here was an issue that clearly merited being worked on with the full family of schools, using intimate knowledge of the same children, from the same families in the same community. The group then took the issue of boys and achievement to a meeting of all the heads of the Newsome Pyramid. The handout for the meeting read:

WHY WORK WITH THE PYRAMID?
- You share the same children
- You share considerable knowledge of the same communities
- You have colleagues you can bounce ideas off
- What one school does will directly affect others
- You can gain instant access to information about an individual child's or group's progress
- You can track children
- You can raise the profile of literacy, of homework, of anything (!) as a whole pyramid
- The issue of what happens to boys at the time of transition is of vital importance
- There is great strength in numbers.

It was decided at this point that a working party would be formed using a representative from each school. The teachers organised a conference where awareness was raised by sharing each others' experiences and observations. The conference, which was attended by over fifty teachers from the pyramid of schools, was a significant occasion and a real success. The first item at the conference was an account from a representative of each phase of the way they perceived boys in their classes, with particular reference to their behaviour and attitude. In addition, each phase highlighted significant statistics related to assessment. The picture was a sobering one. The conference also included a series of extremely lively discussions at which many important areas for further investigation and action were raised. These included:

- The need to inform parents about the differences in attitude and behaviour. (This was followed up in part by a brief presentation at the new Year 7 induction evening a few months later.)

- The need to explore pupil groupings and their effect on work.
- The need to identify practical classroom strategies to help overcome the problem.
- The need to raise the self-esteem of boys.
- The need to investigate how boys and girls see themselves.
- The need to raise awareness of lunchtime supervisors and dining-room staff.
- The need to monitor performance, behaviour and attitude.
- The need to look carefully at construction and IT.
- The need to consider whether the materials used in the classroom are more attractive to girls than they are to boys.
- The need to look carefully at the different ways in which we speak to boys and girls.
- The need to look carefully at the presentation of work.

The list was endless. It was clear that there was a need to raise awareness generally among teachers, pupils and parents alike. It was also clear that there was a need to look at many other things including how we grouped pupils, how we planned work and what we expected of boys and what we expected of girls. Each school featured the issue as a single item on their next staff meeting agenda. One junior school minute read:

> After discussion, consensus of opinion is that low self-esteem seems to be at the core of most under-achievement in our school. Language development and inappropriate behaviour were noted as particular areas of concern in under-achieving boys.

All issues raised were then discussed and worked upon in greater detail by the working party over the next twelve months, with each school initially agreeing to conduct one investigation and implement one initiative. The investigations ranged from research into the relative attractiveness of certain classroom materials for boys to the use of playground space. They also included an investigation into the school experiences of high-achieving boys in Year 11 and a series of interviews with Year 6 boys about their attitudes to work. There were several 'shared reading' projects and experiments with pupil grouping. In the high school we began group mentoring of Year 8 boys to track through what was beginning to be identified nationally as the year at which boys were beginning to orientate away from school in general.

Since the conference, the pyramid's working party, declaring its dual purpose to 'make a difference' and 'to help create a more caring masculinity', has met on a regular basis, continuing to discuss a range of ideas which have then been tried out in school. In addition, the group, ever mindful of the need to keep all staff well informed, has produced a regular newsletter containing minutes of meetings and news of all the latest developments.

At the end of the first year of the working party's existence we decided to invite parents to participate in a conference with teachers where they would discuss the issues and become involved in raising awareness among other parents. The conference itself and the outcomes are cited here as an example of good practice in developing in boys a more positive attitude towards learning, using, in this instance, parents working in close partnership with their child's school.

Strategies: junior schools

Executives

After discussion, consensus of staff opinion was that low self-esteem seemed to be at the core of most under-achievement within the school, and that this seemed to be most evident among the boys. The issue of boys' expectations of themselves became a senior management team agenda item on several occasions. A questionnaire was created in an attempt to gain an accurate picture. This was given to at least one class from each year group.

It was eventually decided that a new system of monitors would be introduced. Boys, sixteen in total, were chosen because staff felt that they were under-achieving largely as a result of low self-esteem. They were given the title of 'Executive'. A certificate and badge were presented in assembly to enhance their status and a photograph of each 'Executive' was displayed on the children's notice-board, mounted in the same way as were staff photographs in the entrance hall. Executives were given responsibilities in classrooms, the dining-hall, main hall, library and in the office at lunchtimes. The initiative has been running for exactly a year at the time of writing and the feedback from staff, children and particularly parents has been very positive. The executive contract lasts for half a term. The scheme has gradually incorporated girls, but the criterion of under-achievement due to low self-esteem still applies.

Choosing time

This initiative was introduced to 'raise the profile of a caring school ethos'. The philosophy behind the scheme was to encourage pupils to demonstrate a more caring approach to all aspects of school life by rewarding them for doing so. Children were given a block of time on Fridays when they were allowed to choose an activity from a selection of high-quality games, puzzles, art and craft activities, etc. If a child, during the course of the preceding week, was to transgress from the generally accepted codes of behaviour, the punishment would be to lose minutes from their choosing time, although opportunities were given to 'earn' back those minutes.

This initiative did take time and money to establish. Moreover, the full involvement of all staff and children was necessary from the outset.

After one year the scheme is widely held to be a great success. The head-teacher wanders from classroom to classroom on Friday afternoons examining the lists and seeking explanations from those who have failed to 'win back' any time lost during the course of the week.

Action against bullying

This initiative stemmed from a questionnaire used in both lower and upper school. Year 6 were involved in producing a short play, *Sticks and stones*, to present to the rest of the school. Although clearly not a 'boys only' issue, the project was directly aimed at effecting a change in one of the least appealing aspects of 'boy culture'. Techniques such as allowing victims to take the role of perpetrator proved most successful.

Tray exercise

The headteacher of one school selects one child a week to bring their tray of work to the office. Together they go through the work and discuss it. Typically, the child will be suffering low self-esteem and the exercise will be a positive one.

Peer partnering

This is used in all manner of ways; for example, to support younger pupils with statements for behaviour, newcomers to the school and so on. The support is provided at breaks and lunchtimes as and when required.

Monitoring/mentoring

Common across the pyramid, one school commented on their approach which was fairly typical:

> 'In September we identified fourteen children we believed to be under-achieving. Ten were boys and four were girls. A meeting was arranged with their parents at which the school's plans for how to help the pupils were outlined. Plans were also agreed as to how the parents might contribute. By Christmas the group was down to ten. By Easter only three remained.'

Strategies: infant and nursery schools

Pupil grouping

Several experiments have taken place with pupil grouping within this phase in the pyramid. The following are teachers' accounts of their experiences:

'A small boys only group was formed consisting of five boys who have been difficult in some way. None were without ability, but all were under-achieving. Although difficult to assess how much it might have been due to the grouping, four showed a marked improvement. Two made major strides in their reading. Those among the group who are happy to be moved are going to be moved on and the appropriate number of boys will be slotted in to replace them. The group received a limited amount of extra help from a classroom support assistant consisting of fifteen minutes two or three times a week. It was interesting to note that the boys never perceived their group as being different from any of the others (which were all mixed).'

'Pupil grouping has been specifically engineered to help tackle disruptive boys by placing them in groups with more positive role models. This has succeeded in calming the boys down and increasing their rate of progress. The major spin-off has been that the whole atmosphere of the class has become far more positive. Moves are afoot to begin to look at reception children.'

'Another experiment involving a boys only group has resulted in four out of five of the pupils involved making major strides with their reading – although concerns remain about their writing. Work is now taking place on peer tutoring whereby a pupil who needs assistance chooses another pupil to help them with their own writing.'

Developing a home/school partnership in literacy

Mindful of the need to not only raise awareness of the importance of literacy as a key factor in achieving success but also to actively involve the home in attaching the required high status, one infant and nursery school in the pyramid now proudly claims to be raising the profile of literacy from day one. It is using a variety of initiatives including the simple but 'massively effective' technique of sending 5-year-olds home with a blank piece of paper, headed 'Please will you help me write a story?' Pupils, parents and staff were 'equally thrilled' by the idea and the results. The school describes its work as 'moving towards a home/school partnership in literacy'.

Lunchtime council

One infant and nursery school, mindful of the potential for rowdy behaviour at lunchtime and its potential for spillage over into school time, established a lunchtime council made up of representatives from each class. The group monitors and reflects upon behaviour in the playground and puts forward its own recommendations for improvement.

Strategies: junior, infant and nursery schools

Shared reading

Adopted by most schools within the pyramid, with some slight variations, the aim of this long-term project was not only to raise levels of literacy but also to raise the self-esteem of those boys involved. Typical of the organisation of the scheme across the pyramid was the selection of older boys who possessed low self-esteem but who were reasonably competent readers. These boys were then asked to work with boys of lesser ability. Training sessions were then planned and run by the headteacher in order to give the whole process as high a profile as possible. This was done over a period of four days, one hour per day. It included the use of a video produced by the local authority and a considerable amount of discussion on their feelings about reading. Typically, the boys chosen, while not being avid readers themselves, clearly recognised the importance of reading. On the fifth day the 'trainers' were given a certificate in assembly by the headteacher, giving them designated trainer status.

The trainers then commenced their work on a daily basis, first of all spending considerable time selecting a book to share, discussing their choice, looking at the cover, pictures, presentation, layout of chapters, index, and predicting the story. After some time had been spent in this process, during which emphasis would be placed on the expression of feelings, the process of reading the book together would begin. The reader and trainer, having previously worked out a signal to show when help was required, would work their way through the book with the trainer 'clicking in' to help on the given signal or when the reader faltered, 'clicking out' again at the given signal.

One school offered the following account of the scheme:

> 'This initiative has continued successfully. We have a male student in the reception unit and he has made himself responsible for collecting the Year 2 reading buddies from the classroom after playtime in the afternoon. The two reading partners come to reception and spend twenty minutes reading with their partner. The Key Stage 1 children have continued to be enthusiastic about the task even though they have limited reading abilities themselves. We have continued to try and target boys who could be described as "one of the lads". It has

helped raise their self-esteem as well as showing others that boys can and do want to spend time reading. The younger boys from reception have been selected because they have little access to literature outside school and because they tend to be those involved in more boisterous, over-enthusiastic play outside in the playground. The next stage will be to discuss the project with the two groups of children to get some feedback. The initiative will be continuing with any alterations suggested by the children and hopefully with the collection of some simple data on attitudes to books before and after the involvement.'

Corrective speech tally sheets

These are employed by several schools within the pyramid to raise teachers' own awareness of their interactions with pupils. Typical of reports after their implementation was: 'Teachers now comment more encouragingly on boys not doing so well and have become increasingly aware of the need for the positive reinforcement of good behaviour and work.'

PSE

Several schools within the pyramid are developing PSE programmes that include a significant strand of work on gender issues. Typical is one junior school where a group of boys were chosen to demonstrate through drama the negative side of using bad language as part of the school's anti-swearing campaign.

Breaking down stereotypes

Many of the schools are, through their PSE work and policy statements, continuously striving to break down stereotypes. One junior school is particularly concerned that this should take place in sport. A girls' football team has been created and is receiving coaching from high school pupils.

Resource bias

Several schools have carefully evaluated their resources for gender bias. The results have often had far-reaching consequences for both planning and budgets. Typical outcomes have been the realisation that book purchases are needed to make libraries more 'boy-friendly', and that considerations of gender need to be applied when planning topic work, ensuring a balance. With regard to planning, one headteacher stated:

'When I review medium term planning I raise questions with staff that encourage them to be constantly critical and reflective of their practice. A focus when I am reviewing is teacher expectations, especially for under-achieving boys.'

Display policies in some schools also now carry statements about the need to avoid gender stereotyping in display materials and the need to ensure a healthy gender mix in the display of pupils' work around the school.

Raising the profile of literacy across the pyramid

Considerable amounts of cross-phase work take place within the pyramid in the area of literacy, the most notable of these being the WoW day established during 1997. The high school hosted a full day of activities including theatre workshops, writers' workshops with real authors, newspapers in education, 'storystarts', library trails, and computerised book reviews for all Year 6 pupils. They worked together with teachers, high school pupils and parents. One outcome of the event was a published book of book reviews for the pyramid to share. Even more significant was that as a result of its declared 'major success' status, the whole process has been extended to incorporate all seven schools who in turn will be hosting pupils from another phase.

Conclusion

In terms of what has been discovered in the process of this small piece of research into the issue of boys' attitudes towards their learning, a number of distinct patterns have emerged that reverberate through the literature and echo in far more meaningful terms in the words of a sizeable group of highly committed professionals. A picture emerges of half a school population that in many ways begin school at a disadvantage, for the most part less independent than their female counterparts and often significantly less well disposed to involve themselves in the type of activities that are vital for their intellectual development. For many, it is difficult to see any value at all in certain activities. Such behaviours that they subsequently exhibit in both the playground and the classroom are regarded as inappropriate by their teachers and highly desirable by their peers. For many, the rejection of some or all elements of their schooling takes place on the basis that education is seen as a female preserve. The absence of male teachers, the absence of a father as a partner in their education and the pressures to simply be 'one of the lads' is often just too much. For some, the feeling that everything will turn out fine without any effort significantly reduces their motivation, as might deferred gratification or, perhaps most worryingly, the potential for rejection by their peers should they, as they approach adolescence, show an aptitude for work.

Admittedly, such a dramatic portrait can, and often does, turn teachers spinning on their heels or joining in the general despair that characterises the tabloid presentation of 'the boys' issue'. Not so with the teachers engaged in the work described here. The committed professionals, whose work is documented here, have moved way beyond the 'ah well, boys will be boys' position and way past the 'but what about the girls?' opt-out clause (aware as they are that boys' attitudes, behaviour and demands in the classroom are hugely detrimental to the work of *all pupils*). Instead, they are in the realms of having considered the issues presented here, and in the business of trying out and adapting a range of strategies in an attempt to 'make a difference'.

Chapter 17

Exercises for continuous professional development

Introduction

In the following pages you will find a number of exercises for continuous professional development. All have the overall aim of getting school education right for both boys and girls – the main thrust of this book. You will see that they have differing objectives. Some are mainly concerned with raising the awareness of staff; some with encouraging personal reflection on existing classroom practice; and others with working towards a whole school policy and action plan.

Ever since the introduction of the so-called 'Baker Days', some whole school in-service training has been unpopular or ineffective, to the point that disaggregation is commonplace in many schools. Much of the scepticism has been borne of poor training provision, an unwelcome imposition from outside the school, a feeling that whatever the training nothing fundamentally changes, and a lack of follow-up – but often the root cause has been the isolated nature of the training experience. In an attempt to counter this we have prepared some exercises with the implication or suggestion that initial action is followed up later after a trial period, time for reflection, etc.

Great care should be taken to ensure that:

- The training provided is of a high quality, whether you are providing your own facilitators or using an outside agency.
- The staff feel it is *their* issue. Do they think that boys are under-achieving? A whole staff discussion about results may help.
- The staff feel that they control the outcomes, that their professional expertise will be recognised and that they will have ownership (ugh!) of any initiatives.
- Whatever is decided is not viewed as a 'bolt-on', but a better way of doing things holding out the prospect of a less stressful working life.
- The senior management team consider very carefully how it will go about managing change, and embedding any changes into the culture of the school.

EXERCISE 1: HAVE WE GOT A PROBLEM?

Aim

To get school education right for boys and girls.

Objective

To determine whether the school has a significant problem regarding the achievement of boys and girls.

Note: This exercise is intended to be undertaken by senior management teams, not by the whole staff.

Method

1   What we are suggesting here is what the vast majority of schools are already doing: poring over their SATs and GCSE results to see what meaning, if any, they can pick from the runes. It may be insulting to some readers that this exercise is even included. However, we are astonished to find that many schools are still oblivious to the gender gap in achievement, particularly in the primary sector. A sort of gender blindness is often in evidence.

2   Look at the pro forma to this exercise (Tables 17.1 and 17.2) and consider adopting or adapting it for use in your school. It can be complemented by data which the school will receive from sources such as the PANDA, from bench-marking with similar schools, from baseline assessment, from SATs results and from CATs scores.

3   It may be advisable to adopt a three-year rolling average rather than be over-worried by a rogue cohort, particularly if you are dealing with small numbers.

4   The questions that may be asked when looking at the data, either gathered on the pro forma or information sent by the government or LEA, are:

(i)   Are there any differences in achievement between the genders:

- at certain key stages?
- in certain subjects?
- in certain aspects (e.g. writing) within subjects?

(ii)   If so, do we know why?

(iii)   Are there any differences in achievement between ethnic groups:

- at certain key stages?
- in certain subjects?
- in certain aspects (e.g. writing) within subjects?

(iv) If so, do we know why?

(v) If there are no discernible gaps in achievement between the genders or ethnic groups, can we be sure that they aren't all under-achieving equally:

- at certain key stages?
- in certain subjects?
- in certain aspects (e.g. writing) within subjects?

(These three questions will mean a recourse to bench-marking etc.)

(vi) How can we support our data based evidence with other evidence, e.g. observation, questionnaire, pupil discussion, staff discussion?

(vii) Could/should we add other, process-based questions to the pro forma such as attendance rates, suspensions and whether top/bottom sets are dominated by boys/girls/ethnic groups? If they are, what are the implications for the school, equality of opportunity and achieving our targets?

Table 17.1 What is the pattern of gender and ethnic achievement in our school? Results showing percentage achieving national expectation

Percentage	Key Stage 1 – Level 2 or above			Key Stage 2 – Level 4 or above			Key Stage 3 – Level 5 or above		
	English	Maths	Science	English	Maths	Science	English	Maths	Science
All									
UK white boys									
UK white girls									
Afro-Caribbean boys									
Afro-Caribbean girls									
Pakistani boys									
Pakistani girls									
Bangladeshi boys									
Bangladeshi girls									
Indian boys									
Indian girls									
Mixed race boys									
Mixed race girls									

Note: This table can be adapted in all sorts of ways, and to include racial groups that have been omitted here because of space. For example, it could provide a snapshot in time for the school, or it could be used to trace the achievement of a whole cohort as they grow up.

Table 17.2 What is the pattern of gender and ethnic achievement in our school? Results showing percentage achieving A*–C at GCSE

	English	Maths	Science	Design and technology	History	Geography	Business studies	MFL	Art	RE	Music
All											
UK white boys											
UK white girls											
Afro-Caribbean boys											
Afro-Caribbean girls											
Pakistani boys											
Pakistani girls											
Bangladeshi boys											
Bangladeshi girls											
Indian boys											
Indian girls											
Mixed race boys											
Mixed race girls											

Note: This table can be adapted in all sorts of ways, and to include racial groups and subjects that have been omitted here because of space.

EXERCISE 2: FINDING YOUR VEST

Aim

To get school education right for boys and girls.

Objectives

1 To introduce the concept of VEST (see Chapter 3) in lesson plans.
2 To enable staff to reflect upon the use of VEST in making learning enjoyable and relevant.

Method

1 Explain to staff the objectives of the session, that it is an opportunity to discuss good professional practice, and that any changes that may accrue as a result of today's session will need a great deal more discussion – and agreement by all staff.
2 Ask staff to spend a maximum of five minutes in writing out a simple, typical lesson plan – perhaps one which they have taught during the week. They should include objectives, main activities and rough timings. It is not a beauty contest: nobody is going to judge them on it, but they will be asked to share it with one other member of staff.
3 Introduce the idea of VEST as described in Chapter 3. You may need to put this on the board/flip chart/OHT and to leave it there. Alternatively, you could distribute an information sheet. It may need a period of discussion before everybody is confident about what it means. You should give examples of its different characteristics.
4 Ask staff to swap plans with a partner. (It is a matter of professional judgement whether you ask them to keep within departments/year groups/key stages or to swap with somebody with whom they do not normally work. They will probably learn more from the latter.) The partners should examine the lesson plans and change them, if necessary, to reflect as much VEST as possible – placing a 'V', 'E', 'S' and 'T' at the appropriate parts of the new lesson plan.
5 Ask the partners to discuss their respective, new plans. Has any improvement been made? Would they work? If not, why not? If they would, how well? What are the implications for time, resources, personal preference, professionalism?
6 Bring the staff back together for a whole group discussion. What do they think about the idea of VEST? Would they be willing to discuss it, or their own amended version, in departmental meetings?
7 Did they enjoy the exercise and/or learn anything from it? Point out that the way they have learned used VEST itself. They had a variety

of things to do; they were engaged upon a short-term, finite task; they learned socially; and they had to transform information. If their partner was someone they do not normally work with, did they learn more about them and their subject? What are the implications of this for seating arrangements in the classroom?

Conclusion

This exercise will not change teaching styles overnight. The follow-up is at least as important as the exercise. A head of department/year group/key stage discussion will need to take place later in order to harness the learning and cement change. If whatever is agreed could be incorporated into the school's policy for monitoring the quality of teaching and learning, so much the better.

EXERCISE 3: LET'S HEAR IT FROM THE BOYS – AND GIRLS

This exercise is one which can be started on a training day/evening but will need constant revisiting and good planning. If it is done well the rewards should be high, and to attempt it is indicative of a learning school.

Aim

To get school education right for boys and girls.

Objectives

1   To introduce to staff a method of finding out from the pupils what they think about school.
2   To incorporate pupils' suggestions into school policy.

Method

Either:

1   Show the Kirklees LEA video *Let's hear it from the boys* (available from Kirklees LEA) to staff, and discuss the views of the boys which are expressed in it. To what extent do the staff feel that some boys at their school would echo the feelings?

Or, better:

2   Ask staff to produce a list of questions which would be suitable to ask the pupils. Here are some ideas:

- what do you like about school?
- what do you think about homework?
- what are boys (or girls) not doing as well as girls (or boys)?
- do you think boys work as hard as girls?
- why do some boys misbehave in lessons?
- have you ever felt under pressure from other boys/girls not to work?
- people say that girls are better readers than boys – what do you think? how important is reading?
- do you think that boys are treated any differently from girls in school? why?
- is it cool to be seen to do well in school?
- is it OK to be seen to carry a school bag to and from school?

The answers to these questions, or your amended versions, will give the school an agenda for discussion and action. They should tell you the extent to which the anti-swot culture is flourishing and the areas of school life that could be made more supportive of learning. Are there any trends/differences between subjects and year groups?

3   The questions can be put, or the video shown to stimulate discussion, to each class in the school by the class/form tutor or in PSE. One popular way of doing this is to ask groups of three pupils to respond to different questions while the rest of the class listens and later comments. The answers from the school as a whole can be collated and discussed by the staff.

4   The school will need to be clear from the start what it intends to do with the pupils' observations. To do nothing is an unwise option and makes it a pointless exercise. A meaningful school council may well help the process. In some cases you will be presented with what reads like a list of complaints. It may be possible to set up a staff working party or even staff/pupil working party to suggest ways forward. This book will hopefully have provided some ideas.

EXERCISE 4: EXCELLENT TEACHING AND LEARNING

Aim

To get school education right for boys and girls.

Objectives

1　To enable the school to decide what excellent teaching and learning are.
2　To enable staff to come up with their own ideas about how to bring about excellent teaching and learning.

Method

1　Introduce staff to the objectives of the day, and explain that they can forget what Ofsted may have told them about teaching and learning. Today, it is their chance to use their professional expertise and reflection to set an agenda for the school and for their department/year group/key stage.
2　Ask staff to sit together in departments/year groups/key stages (depending on school). Then, individually – without any discussion – ask them to write down five things which they would hope pupils would say about their subject (or key stage) by the time they leave school. When this is done they can share what they have, amend, reject and incorporate the different ideas so that they end up with a minimum of five and a maximum of seven key statements about their subject/key stage. Ask for feedback from the different groups.
3　Explain to staff that they now have the beginnings of a vision of the essence of their subject/teaching, but that they now have to give greater clarity to the vision. With their five to seven agreed statements they must now spend some time (five minutes) in silence and imagine in a series of pictures just what sort of teaching is going on in order to achieve the statements of what you want the students to say. Emphasise the need to think in a series of static pictures, which they will be able to describe later on.
4　After the five minutes, ask staff to record the sort of teaching which was going on.
5　Having got the vision of high-quality/excellent teaching ask staff to consider how it can be brought about. The following may be helpful to assist discussion:

- teacher-controlled seating plan
- the use of VEST
- encouraging reflection

- review of setting arrangements
- more active learning
- parental involvement.

All these issues are discussed in the book.

Each department/year group/key stage now has a common view of what their subject, etc. should be all about, the vision of what sort of teaching is required to achieve that common view and the beginnings of an action plan to introduce or enhance the teaching.

6   Ask heads of department/year, etc. to draw up action plans which describe high-quality teaching and learning and at the same time describe how they will be embedded into departmental practice.

Conclusion

This exercise will need to be very carefully followed up to achieve maximum impact.

EXERCISE 5: HOW WOULD YOU EAT *YOUR* ELEPHANT?

Aim

To get school education right for boys and girls.

Objectives

1   To enable teaching staff to consider the usefulness of cutting the curriculum into bite-sized chunks.
2   To reduce the curriculum to a series of discernible teaching modules and plan appropriate ways of celebrating achievement.

Method

1   Ask the whole staff if they ever have problems getting work in on time. Are project deadlines often missed, or at least threatened? Do pupils make full use of the time allocated to tasks in a positive and effective way? (*Note:* These exercises may be of less relevance in primary school.)
2   Explain that there is a growing view among educationalists that many pupils, and especially boys, find it hard to remain focused and enthusiastic about long-term project work – even medium-term project work. The task for departmental or year teams is to cut down the syllabus

into two- or three-week modules. This may elicit howls of protest. 'You *can't* do that in X subject: its integrity will be compromised!' Explain that the purpose is not to truncate natural learning spans, but to erect a number of milestones which pupils will feel are always within reach and which gives them a chance to reflect on where they are in the syllabus, what they have learned and to celebrate it.

3   The other task for the different teams is to think of different ways of appropriately celebrating the completion of the module. Some can be fun and others are more serious (a pound of apples and a plastic cow is on offer for the best efforts made in studying the Agricultural Revolution; a certificate after the volleyball course; a businesswoman will come in and talk to the business studies class; the best pupils at the end of the Vikings will get a longboat badge, etc.).

4   Arrange with the year or key stage leaders/heads of department for a feedback meeting where they can report what has been agreed.

5   Plan a series of visits to different celebrations to take photographs. These can later form the basis of a rolling exhibition, in which you would aim to include all pupils.

Conclusion

You need to ensure that the different, agreed ways of eating the elephant are maintained and that staff do not slip back into old, familiar ways. The best way of doing this is to value the exercise and its outcomes as much as possible, and to get other members of staff to do so publicly as well. It could form part of your schedule for monitoring the quality of teaching and learning.

A further exercise is to monitor the views of both pupils and teachers in those departments/year groups which are doing it well. If it makes a difference to concentration, excitement, interest and motivation – as it should – you have the evidence to persuade other colleagues.

EXERCISE 6: ESTABLISHING MACRO AND MICRO STRATEGIES

Aim

To get school education right for boys and girls.

Objectives

1   To establish departmental/year group strategies to raise boys'/girls' achievement.

2   To establish whole school strategies which the staff will support.

Method

1 Introduce gender under-achievement as an issue for the school. You may wish to refer to the latest or three-year rolling average for boys' and girls' achievements at Key Stage 1/2/3 SATs and/or GCSEs, and possibly use NFER/CATs scores or baseline assessment to show that there is very little difference in overall ability between the sexes.

2 Refer to the three-part plan discussed in Chapter 4, and explain the difference between micro and macro strategies.

3 Use a board or OHT to display the following list and explain its relevance to raising the achievement of boys and girls (all issues are described in detail in this book):

- seating
- group work
- move away from tight settings
- praise
- role modelling
- shared work/reading
- parental involvement
- pyramid working
- the importance of reflection, including hands up in class
- short-term goals and rewards
- monitoring
- mentoring
- literacy across the curriculum
- challenge the anti-swot culture/reinforce the school as a learning organisation
- display
- target Year 8/8-year-olds.

Ask each year group or department to come up with three things they would like to support as a whole school policy and two or three things they would like to attempt within their department or year group. Give them between forty-five and seventy-five minutes, depending on the size of the groups.

4 After sufficient time, bring the groups together and ask for their whole school (macro) suggested strategies. Record these and have a whole staff discussion about which three (or maximum four) they would like to adopt.

5 Having established the macros, ask departments/year groups to describe their two or three micro policies. Distribute action plan pro formas based on the one in the Appendix of Chapter 4 (p. 46) and ask year leaders/heads of departments to complete them within a specified time.

Conclusion

The school now has the bare bones of a strategy to tackle gender under-achievement, but don't forget the first part of the three-part plan – raising awareness. The teaching staff may now be fully aware of the issues, but what about the rest of the staff, governors, parents and the pupils themselves?

EXERCISE 7: HUNT THE GENDER MESSAGE

Aim

To get school education right for boys and girls.

Objectives

1 To carry out an audit of the whole curriculum about the gender messages the school is giving to pupils.
2 To enable staff to become more aware of gender stereotypes and how to avoid them.

Note of caution: This exercise has the potential to upset or threaten staff, as well as having high rewards. It should be used only in the right atmosphere of genuine enquiry and with the intention of moving forward as a learning organisation. If in doubt, leave it out. The atmosphere can be lightened by having a cross-section of staff investigating the work of the senior management team.

Method

1 Each department or year group is twinned with another of a similar size. Each will 'investigate' the other. The intention is to examine aspects of the other's work with the foremost question: What does this say to me as a boy/girl learner? It may be an idea to divide the teams into pairs and to each tackle a couple of aspects. The suggested aspects are:

  • Display in classrooms and corridors around their area: what do they tell me, as a learner, about the usefulness/applicability of the subject?
  • The gender messages in textbooks and other printed resources.
  • The marking/assessment scheme.
  • The gender messages in curriculum content/schemes of work.

You will probably be able to think of others.

2   This audit should not take up more than half a day at the most. The rest of the day can be spent in writing up a brief report and then discussing it with the partner department/year group concerned. The report may be amended as the investigators receive clarification. What can both learn from their reports? They may find messages for themselves in the report they prepare for their colleagues.
3   Ask heads of department/year to prepare a short action plan to address points made in their report.

Conclusion

One outcome from this activity may be requests for extra capitation to replace outdated stock, or to buy in commercial posters. The governors or PTA may be able to help – another reason for beginning the work by raising the awareness of all.

EXERCISE 8: INTRODUCING THE BENEFITS OF A SEATING POLICY

Aim

To get school education right for boys and girls.

Objectives

1   To introduce to staff the possible benefits of a seating policy.
2   To enable staff to get to know each other better professionally.
3   To discuss differences in learning styles between the genders.

Note: This exercise should take only ninety minutes maximum, and is suitable for an after-school session.

Method

1   Ask staff to sit outside their normal comfort zones, i.e. not in departmental/year teams or within friendship groups. A variation on this theme for 'fun' staff rooms is to use a game to split them randomly.
2   Ask them to sit in threes and to take a few minutes each to describe to each other a time/lesson when the education they provided went particularly well for boys, for girls, and for both. They will be asked for feedback of what they hear.

3   After ten or twelve minutes, stop them and ask them to provide feed-back of what has been said to them, not by them, and record it on the board. You will have an interesting collection of teaching experi-ences which may inform practice. (*Note:* In a large staff room this could take so long that it could become tedious; an alternative is for each trio to record their thoughts on flip-chart paper, attach these to the wall and so establish a 'market-place' where everyone can read what has been written. You will, however, achieve better discussion and learning from verbal feedback.)

4   Process the whole experience. Have they learned anything about the other people in their group and the subject/year they teach which they did not know before? Do they feel professionally closer to the people they worked with? Have they learned anything they would otherwise not have learned? *What are the implications for using seating plans in classrooms?* Should pupils be taken outside their comfort zones? If so, how often? How should they be grouped? Randomly? By teacher diktat? How could you work with a group who themselves came to recognise the value of working with different people on a regular basis?

EXERCISE 9: PARENTAL INVOLVEMENT

Aim

To get school education right for boys and girls.

Objectives

1   To produce subject or year group specific leaflets for parents on the issue of raising achievement.
2   To enable staff to think about how best to involve parents in supporting the learning of their children.

Method

1   Explain to staff that in order to achieve a coherent strategy to tackle gender under-achievement, the school has taken steps to raise the awareness of the whole community about the issue. However, you feel that there is scope for taking it further. Parents need to know how they can encourage and support learning in specific subjects other than in English. Parents, particularly in the secondary curriculum, often feel disempowered by their lack of knowledge and are left with only 'Do your homework', 'Try harder' and 'Don't worry about it'.

2   The school wants to provide parents with a series of leaflets which will
     not make them quasi-teachers, but will help them to bring out the
     usefulness and skills of different subjects in everyday living. This may
     be easier in some subjects than others; for example, business studies
     should have ample scope, but all subjects will have skills or concepts
     which are difficult to grasp for some students, but are echoed in everyday
     life.
3   In drawing up their leaflet, departments or year teams may wish to refer
     to their programmes of study for each year. What are the main learning
     outcomes for the year? Can the parents be told these easily? How can
     they be seen in the local environment? It may be appropriate to produce
     a leaflet for each year in the subject. Parents may then receive up to
     ten leaflets for the year, but that should not matter. Most will be very
     glad to be better informed about what their child(ren) are meant to
     be learning, and how they can help exemplify it and bring it to life.
4   Departments/year teams may find it beneficial to split into smaller groups
     to work on specific leaflets.
5   In some schools it may be possible to involve the parents and pupils
     in the discussions, and for older pupils to design and produce the leaflets.

Epilogue

As we firmly believe in the power of teachers to bring about change and improvement in their schools and classrooms, it may be appropriate to end this book by reflecting on a small number of representative views of some teachers and pupils who have tried out some of the strategies suggested. We have grouped the comments by initiative.

Seating patterns

'The kids understand it was to get the boys working and stop the girls chatting. They sussed it. I think it has worked. It's certainly developed the boys. They speak more, rather than just shouting out any inane answer and then giving up. Now they haven't got their mates guffawing beside them. It has developed the boys and stopped the girls gabbing to their partners. The girls were quiet, but off-task in subtle ways, 'nice' ways, not disruptive but certainly not on task. Now they are all learning from other people, and not cloning off their mates.'

(Senior teacher, northern high school)

'It's amazing. People say "There's this group of lads and they never do any work." So you say "Why is there this group of lads? Why don't you split them up?" "Well, they don't like being split up." We were part way through the year, but we started by explaining why we were introducing it. Once they saw that it wasn't just because the wind blew that way, or because the teacher was feeling particularly awkward it wasn't a problem. When people tried it they said "Yes, it works".'

(Lead teacher, northern comprehensive)

'I felt a bit nervous about it, but it just wasn't an issue. The children here like the idea that things are organised. They can see that the teacher is thinking about how they are going to learn, and is structuring things so that they can learn well.'

(Head of English)

'It was almost as if they were wanting the teachers to take charge of seating in the classroom. They know they can't coast. They have to be on their mettle all the time and are expected to work.'

(History teacher)

Literacy

'There are still things we want to do in English, and there will be fluctuations from year to year. But I'm fascinated by this Year 7 and how our work with them is progressing. The Scrabble tournament was full of boys.'

(Head of English)

'I really think we need to encourage parents to be more involved, especially dads, especially with reading. I think we need to encourage more male role models into the school as well. Education is very female oriented right up to high school.'

(Year 1 teacher)

'Stage 3 and 4 pupils should sit next to English proficient students who do not speak their heritage language, so that they are intended to stretch their English. . . . Stage 1 and 2 pupils should sit next to somebody who speaks the same heritage language as they do, but is at a higher (English Language) stage.'

(Language policy, multi-cultural high schools)

The process of change: the role of heads and middle managers

'At the end of the day, it's down to the Head. The Head has got to drive it through and say "I'm expecting to see this." The middle manager has got so many priorities and most of them are listed in order of "Well, who is going to cause the most fuss if I don't do it?" If the Head is ambivalent it will slip down the middle manager's priority list.'

(LEA link officer)

Setting

'Our observation of outcome data showed that this pattern of girls in higher sets and boys in lower sets becomes fixed quite early in children's learning experiences at high school, and is incapable of much change thereafter. We developed the sense that setting at an early stage was harmful to boys and that there was a crucial period between Years

7 and 8 when boys might become trapped in lower sets. . . . I think
we were moving away from a position where a significant section of
the school population was quite openly deprived of the full range of
educational experiences, to which you might say they were entitled,
by the structure of the curriculum and the attitudes which had led to
the creation of that structure.'

(Headteacher, northern high school)

Celebrating achievement

'There's some good teachers. Mr . . . . . . he gives you lots of merits.
[Good teachers] should give more merits out; they don't give a lot out.'

(Year 7 boy)

'Most boys just need encouragement to make them work harder in
lessons and also in homework.'

(Year 10 girl)

Group work and discussion

'I like it when you can work together in a group of four and help each
other.'

(Year 7 boy)

'I think there should be more class discussions which would involve
boys more.'

(Year 10 boy)

'Teachers should use more group work and discussions. Boys prefer to
work in pairs or groups and discuss work whereas the majority of girls
prefer to work quietly as individuals.'

(Year 10 boy)

Parents

'Our socks were knocked off as 500 people turned up to watch [the
Year 10 Achievement Evening]. We just couldn't stop them coming
through the door. For the first time in all my time here we had got a
truly cultural mix of parents and a true class mix. They came off the
local estates and they drove up in their Bentleys from the other places,
and I thought goodness we really have appealed to everyone here.
We made the press and parents said it was the best night they had
ever been to at this school.'

(Head of Year 10)

'We need to change parents' expectations and teachers' expectations
... the number of times I've heard "boys will be boys" and the boys
are hearing that and thinking "oh right, I'm a boy; I'm expected to
behave this way".'

(Reception teacher)

'A change of attitude and approach to boys and girls would be needed.
This change of attitude would have to be from society as a whole –
parents, friends, etc. Schools cannot do anything on their own; it has
to be everybody.'

(Year 10 girl)

Target-setting

'I think we should be doing a lot more on target-setting and, particularly for boys, short-term goal-setting. I think this is part of the reason
they like maths: they see things getting done very quickly ... they
reach one answer then move on to the next.'

(Year 3 teacher)

Teacher confidence

'I think it's all down to the confidence it's given me to try things out
and to know that some of the things we've tried have made a difference. It's confidence to do something rather than just going on about
how boys are.'

(English teacher)

And finally:

'It seemed that good practice, and practice that enabled children to
show their skills and to achieve skills, wasn't simply a boys' under-
achievement issue at all.'

(Head of English)

References and further reading

Adams, E. and Burgess, T. (1989) *Teachers' own records. A system promoting professional quality*. NFER/Nelson.

Adelman, C. (1989) 'The practical ethic takes priority over methodology' in Carr, W. (ed.) *Quality in teaching: arguments for a reflective profession*. The Falmer Press.

Adelman, C. (1993) 'Kurt Lewin and the origins of action research', *Educational Action Research*, Vol. 1, No. 1, pp. 7–24.

Adler, S. (1997) 'Gender and the school library resource centres', *School Libraries Review*, Autumn, pp. 15–16.

Allison, B. (1997) *The student's guide to preparing dissertations and theses*. Kogan Page.

All Saints' RC High School and Ginnis, G. (1995) *Towards a wider range of teaching styles: help! What shall I do with 9K?* All Saints' High School, Huddersfield.

Altrichter, H. (1993) *Teachers investigate their work. An introduction to the methods of action research*. Routledge.

Angus, L. (1993) 'The sociology of school effectiveness', *British Journal of Sociology of Education*, Vol. 14. No. 3, pp. 333–345.

APU (1988) *Attitudes and gender differences. Mathematics at age 11 and 15*. NFER/Nelson.

Arnold, R. (1995) *The improvement of schools through partnership: school, LEA and university*. NFER/EMIE.

Arnold, R. (1997) *Raising levels of achievement in boys*. NFER/EMIE.

Arnot, M. and Weiner, G. (1987) *Gender and the politics of schooling*. Oxford University Press.

Arnot, M. *et al.* (1996) *Educational reforms and gender equality in schools*. Equal Opportunities Commission.

Arnot, M. *et al.* (1998) *Recent research on gender and educational performance*. Ofsted.

ASE (Association for Science Education) (1999) *Science education 2000+*. ASE.

Askew, S. and Ross, C. (1988) *Boys don't cry. Boys and sexism in education*. Open University Press.

Atkinson, P. and Delamont, S. (1985) 'Bread and dreams or bread and circuses: a critique of case study research in education' in Shipman, M. (ed.) *Educational research, principles, policies, and practices*. The Falmer Press.

Atkinson, S. (1994) 'Rethinking the principles and practice of action research: the tensions for the teacher-researcher', *Educational Action Research*, Vol. 2, No. 3, pp. 383–401.

Babbie, E. and Halley, F. (1995) *Adventures in social research. Data analysis using SPSS for Windows*. Pine Forge Press, California.

Barber, M. (1994) *Young people and their attitudes to school. An interim report*. University of Keele.

Barber, M. (1996) *The learning game. Arguments for an education revolution*. Gollancz.

Barber, M. and Graham, J. (1994) 'That critical first year', *Times Educational Supplement*, 29 September, p. 7.

Barker, B. (1997) 'Girls' world or anxious times: what's really happening at school in the gender war?', *Educational Review*, Vol. 49, No. 3, pp. 221–227.

Barnes, M. and Coupland, M. (1990) 'Humanising Calculus: a case study in curriculum development' in Burton, L. (ed.) *Gender and mathematics: an international perspective*. Cassell.

Bell, J. (1987) *Doing your research project. A guide for first-time researchers in Education and Social Science*. Open University Press.

Bell, J. (ed.) (1995) *Teachers talk about teaching. Coping with change in turbulent times*. Open University Press.

Bell, N.J. and Bell, R.W. (1993) *Adolescent risk-taking*. Sage.

Bell, J. et al. (1994) *Conducting small-scale investigations in educational management*. PCP Ltd.

Bingham, W.C. (1983) 'Problems in the assessment of self-esteem', *International Journal for Advanced Counselling*, Vol. 6, pp. 17–22.

Birmingham LEA (1995) *Quality development*.

Blair, M. and Bourne, J. (1998) *Making the difference: teaching and learning strategies in successful multi-ethnic schools*. Open University Press/DfEE.

Bleach, K. (ed.) (1998) *Raising boys' achievement in schools*. Trentham Books.

Bleach, K. et al. (1996) *What difference does it make? An investigation of factors influencing the motivation and performance of Year 8 boys in a West Midlands comprehensive school*. University of Wolverhampton Educational Research Unit.

Bloom, B.S. (ed.) (1985) *Developing talent in young people*. Ballantine Books, New York.

Boaler, J. (1996) *Setting, social class and survival of the quickest*. King's College, London.

Boaler, J. (1997) *Experiencing school mathematics: teaching styles, sex and setting*. Open University Press.

Bondi, L. (1991) 'Towards a non-essentialist feminist pedagogy', *Gender and Education*, Vol. 3, No. 1, pp. 87–90.

Boustead, M.W. (1989) 'Who talks? The position of girls in mixed-sex classrooms', *English in Education*, Vol. 3, No. 3, pp. 42–51.

Bradford, W.A. (1995) 'The progress of boys in secondary school'. Dissertation for M.Ed., University of Huddersfield.

Bradford, W.A. (1996) *Raising boys' achievement*. Kirklees Local Education Authority.

Brandes, D. and Ginnis, P. (1986) *A guide to student-centred learning*. Simon & Schuster.

Bray, R. et al. (1997) *Can boys do better?* SHA.

Brennan, P. (1999) 'Raising boys' achievement in the arts'. Unpublished M.Sc. thesis, Manchester Metropolitan University.

Brighouse, T. (1991) *What makes a good school?* Network Educational Press.

Brown, S. and McIntyre, D. (1993) *Making sense of teaching*. Open University Press.

Bryman, A. and Cramer, D. (1990) *Quantitative data analysis for social scientists*. Routledge.

Bunyan, P. (1998) 'Comparing pupil performance in Key Stages 2 and 3 science SATs', *School Science Review*, June, Vol. 79, No. 289.

Burn, P. (1989) 'A comparison of the self-concepts of boys and girls of secondary school age'. Dissertation for M.Sc., University of Manchester.

Burroughs, G.E.R. (1975) *Design and analysis in educational research* (2nd edn). University of Birmingham School of Education.

Bush, T. (1986) *Theories of educational management*. Harper & Row.

Bush, T. (1988) *Action and theory in school management*. Open University Press.

Bush, T. and West-Burnham, J. (1994) *The principles of educational management*. Longman.

Caffyn, R.E. (1987) 'Attitudes of British secondary school teachers and pupils to rewards and punishments', *Educational Research*, Vol. 31, No. 3, pp. 210–220.

Caruthers, L. (1996) *Classroom interactions and achievement*. Webmaster@mcrel.org.tjs

Charlton, T. and Hunt, J. (1993) 'Towards pupils' self-image enhancement: the EASI teaching programme', *Support for Learning*, Vol. 8, No. 3, pp. 107–111.

Clark, A. and Millard, E. (eds) (1998) *Gender in the secondary curriculum*. Routledge.

Clark, A. and Trafford, J. (1995) 'Boys into modern languages', *Gender and Education*, Vol. 7, No. 3, pp. 315–325.

Cohen, L. (1976) *Educational research in classrooms and schools: a manual of materials and methods*. Harper & Row.

Cohen, L. and Holliday, M. (1982) *Statistics for social scientists: an introductory text with computer programmes in Basic*. Harper & Row.

Cohen, L. and Manion, L. (1985) *Research methods in education* (2nd edn). Croom Helm.

Colley, A. (1997) 'IT and music education: what happens to boys and girls in co-educational and single sex schools?', *British Journal of Music Education*, Vol. 14, No. 2, pp. 119–127.

Connell, R.W. (1989) 'Cool guys, swots and wimps: the interplay of masculinity and education', *Oxford Review of Education*, Vol. 1, No. 3, pp. 291–303.

Cooper, P. and McIntyre, D.C. (1996) *Effective teaching and learning. Teachers' and students' perspectives*. Open University Press.

Coultas, V. (1989) 'Black girls and self-esteem', *Gender and Education*, Vol. 1, No. 3, pp. 283–294.

Cullingford, C. (1993) 'Children's views on gender issues in school', *British Educational Research Journal*, Vol. 19, No. 5, pp. 555–563.

Davies, B. (1990) *Education management for the 1990s*. Pitman Publishing.

Davies, L. (1984) *Pupil power. Deviance and gender in school*. The Falmer Press.

Day, C. (1993) 'Reflection ... A necessary but not sufficient condition for professional development', *British Educational Research Journal*, Vol. 19, No. 1, pp. 83–93.

Dean, C. (1998) 'The problem of failing boys', *Times Educational Supplement*, 27 November, p. 1.

Delap, M.R. (1994) 'An investigation into the accuracy of 'A'-level predicted grades', *Educational Research*, Vol. 36, No. 2, pp. 37–39.

Denning, K., Gough, G. and Johnson, M. (1998) *An evaluation of middle school effectiveness*. Keele University Department of Education.

Denscombe, M. and Aubrook, L. (1992) 'It's just another piece of school work. The ethics of questionnaire research on pupils in schools', *British Educational Research Journal*, Vol. 18, No. 2, pp. 113–131.

Denzin, N.K. and Lincoln, Y.S. (eds) (1994) *Handbook of qualitative research*. Sage.

De Gauna, P.R. *et al.* (1995) 'Teachers' professional development as a process of critical action research', *Educational Action Research*, Vol. 3, No. 2, pp. 183–194.

De Vaus, D.A. (1990) *Surveys in social research* (2nd edn). Unwin Hyman.

DfEE (1989) *'Discipline in schools'. Report of the committee of enquiry chaired by Lord Elton*. HMSO.

DfEE (1997) *Excellence in schools. A white paper*. HMSO.

DfEE (1998) *The autumn package. Results at Key Stages 1, 2, 3 and 4*. HMSO.

Downes, P. (1994) 'The gender effect', *Managing Schools Today*, Vol. 3, No. 5, pp. 7–8.

Drew, D. and Gray, J. (1990) 'The fifth-year examination achievements of black young people in England and Wales', *Educational Research*, Vol. 32, No. 2, pp. 107–117.

Duff, R. (1997) *The lost boys*. Childwise.

Eames, K.J. (1996) 'Action research, dialectics and an epistemology of practically-based professional knowledge for education'. Ph.D., University of Bath.

Ebbutt, D. (1985) 'Educational action research: some general concerns and specific quibbles' in Burgess, R.G. (ed.) *Issues in educational research*. The Falmer Press.

Eckhard, T. (1997) 'Dare to dance', *Ninety Five Percent*, autumn.

Eisner, E. (1993) 'Forms of understanding and the future of educational research', *Educational Researcher*, Vol. 22, No. 7, pp. 5–11.

Elkin, J. and Lonsdale, R. (eds) (1996) *Focus on the child*. The Library Association.

Elliott, J. (1978) 'What is action research in schools?', *Journal of Curriculum Studies*, Vol. 10, No. 4, pp. 355–357.

Elliott, J. (1991) *Action research for educational change*. Open University Press.

Elliott, J. (1993) 'What have we learned from action research in school-based evaluation?', *Educational Action Research*, Vol. 1, No. 1, pp. 175–186.

English, T. and Harris, A. (1992) *An evaluation toolbox for schools – a practical guide to the design and implementation of school-based evaluation*. Longman.

EOC/Ofsted (1996) *The gender divide. Performance differences between girls and boys at school*. HMSO.

Epstein, D. *et al.* (1998) *Failing boys? Issues in gender and achievement*. Open University Press.

Evans, M. (1997) 'An action research enquiry into reflection in action as part of my role as a Deputy Headteacher'. Ph.D., Kingston University

Eyre, D. (1998) *Able children in ordinary schools*. David Fulton.

Fairbairn, G.J. and Winch, C. (1996) *Reading, writing and reasoning. A guide for students* (2nd edn). Open University Press.

Fitz-Gibbon, C.T. (1990) *Performance indicators*. BERA Dialogues 2. Multilingual Matters Ltd.

Fitz-Gibbon, C.T. (1996) *Monitoring education. Indicators, quality and effectiveness*. Cassell.

Fleming, P. (1998) 'Asian girls' needs. Is your school doing enough?', *Managing Schools Today*, March.

Foot, H.C. (1990) *Children helping children*. John Wiley & Sons.

Frater, G. (1997) *Improving boys' literacy*. The Basic Skills Agency.

Freeman, J.G. (1996) 'An exploratory study of a gender equity program for secondary school students', *Gender and Education*, Vol. 8, No. 3, pp. 289–300.

Frith, R. and Mahony, P. (1994) *Promoting quality and equality in schools. Empowering teachers through change*. David Fulton.

Fullan, M. and Hargreaves, A. (1992) *What's worth fighting for in your school?* Cassell.

George, B. (1995) *Gifted education: identification and process*. David Fulton.

Ghouri, N. (1998) 'Finding the mission', *Times Educational Supplement*, 27 November, p. 4.

Gill, J. and Johnson, P. (1991) *Research methods for managers*. PCP Ltd.

Glatter, R. *et al.* (eds) (1988) *Understanding school management*. Open University Press.

Glissov, P. (1992) 'Social and motivational aspects of secondary school pupils' computer use, with particular reference to the gender issue'. Thesis for Ph.D., Glasgow Polytechnic.

Gold, K. (1995) 'Hard times for Britain's lost boys', *New Scientist*, 4 February.

Goldstein, H. and Sammons, P. (1997) 'The influence of secondary and junior schools on sixteen year old examination performance', *School Effectiveness and School Improvement*, Vol. 8, pp. 219–230.

Goleman, M. (1996) *Emotional intelligence: why it can matter more than IQ*. Bloomsbury.

Gordon, J. and Griffiths, V. (1997) 'A national poll for children', *Library Association Record*, July, Vol. 99, No. 7, pp. 372–374.

Gordon, T. and Lahelma, E. (1996) '"School is like an ant's nest": spatiality and embodiment in schools', *Gender and Education*, Vol. 8, No. 3, pp. 301–310.

Goulding, S. *et al.* (1984) *Case studies in educational management*. PCP Ltd.

Graham, J. (1994) *Gender differences and GCSE results*. Centre For Successful Schools, Keele University.

Grant, L. (1994) 'First amongst equals', *Guardian*, 22 October.

Gray, J. (1994) 'Building for achievement'. A discussion at the Curriculum Development Centre, Dewsbury, 30 November.

Gray, J. and Jesson, D. (1990) 'The negotiation and construction of performance indicators: some principles, proposals and problems', *Evaluation and Research in Education*, Vol. 4, No. 2, pp. 93–108.

Gray, J. *et al.* (1983) *Reconstruction of secondary education*. Routledge & Kegan Paul.

Gray, J. *et al.* (1990) 'Estimating differences in the examination performances of secondary schools in 6 LEAs: a multi-level approach to school effectiveness', *Oxford Review of Education*, Vol. 16, No. 2, pp. 137–158.

Green, A. (1995) 'Equal opportunities: has technology helped?', *Modus*, Vol. 13, No. 3, pp. 79–83.

Green, H. (1994) 'Motivating pupils', *Croner's Headteacher's Bulletin*, November, pp. 3–16.

Green, H. (1995) 'Issues in staff development', *Croner's Headteacher's Bulletin*, July, pp. 3–24.

Gregorc, A. (1982) *An adult's guide to style*. , Gabriel Systems, Massachusetts.

Griffiths, M. (1993) 'Educational change and the self', *British Journal of Educational Studies*, Vol. 41, 2 June.

Grima, G. and Smith, A.B. (1993) 'The participation of boys and girls in home economics', *Gender and Education*, Vol. 5, No. 3, pp. 251–268.

Grundy, S. (1994) 'Action research at the school level: possibilities and problems', *Educational Action Research*, Vol. 2, No. 1, pp. 23–37.

Gurney, P.W. (1988) *Self-esteem in children with special educational needs*. Routledge.

Haggarty, L. and Postlethwaite, K. (1995) 'Working as consultants on school-based teacher-identified problems', *Educational Action Research*, Vol. 3, No. 2, pp. 169–181.

Hallam, S. (1996) 'Grouping pupils by ability. Selection, streaming, banding and setting'. Institute of Education, London.

Hallam, S. and Toutounji, I. (1996) 'What do we know about the grouping of pupils by ability?' Institute of Education, London.

Hammersley, M. (1993) 'On the teacher as researcher', *Educational Action Research*, Vol. 1, No. 3, pp. 425–446.

Handy, C. and Aitken, A. (1986) *Understanding schools as organisations*. Penguin.

Hannan, G. (1997) *The Gender Game and how to win it*. Published by the author.

Hargreaves, D. (1967) *Social relations in a secondary school*. Routledge & Kegan Paul.

Hargreaves, D.H. and Hopkins, D. (1991) *The empowered school. The management and practice of development planning*. Cassell.

Hargreaves, D.H. and Hopkins, D. (1994) *Development planning for school improvement*. Cassell.

Harris, A. and Russ, J. (1994) 'Pointers for prizes', *Times Educational Supplement*, 29 September, p. 5.

Harris, S. *et al.* (1993) 'School work, homework and gender', *Gender and Education*, Vol. 5, No. 1, pp. 3–15.

Harris, S. *et al.* (1995) '"It's not that I haven't learnt much. It's just that I don't really understand what I'm doing": metacognition and secondary school students', *Research Papers in Education*, Vol. 10, No. 2, pp. 253–271.

Harter, S. (1982) 'The perceived competence scale for children', *Child Development*, No. 53, pp. 87–97.

Harter, S. (1985) *Manual for the self-perception profile for children*. University of Denver.

Hartley, J. (1991) 'Sex differences in handwriting: a comment on Spear', *British Educational Research Journal*, Vol. 17, No. 2, pp. 142–145.

Hill, J. (1994) 'The paradox of gender: sex stereotyping within statementing procedure', *British Educational Research Journal*, Vol. 20, No. 3, pp. 345–355.

Hill, N. (1996) *Value added and school performance: recent LEA initiatives*. NFER/EMIE.

HMI (1978) *Mixed ability work in comprehensive schools*. HMSO.

HMI/Ofsted (1993) *Boys and English*. HMSO.

Hofkins, D. (1995) 'Girls out-perform boys at school-age entry', *Times Educational Supplement*, 24 March, p. 3.

Hofkins, D. (1995) 'Why teenage boys think success is sad', *Times Educational Supplement*, 18 August, p. 5.

Hoinville, G. *et al.* (1978) *Survey research practice*. Heinemann.

Holden, C. (1993) 'Giving girls a chance: patterns of talk in co-operative group work', *Gender and Education*, Vol. 5, No. 2, pp. 179–189.

Holley, E.C. (1997) 'How do I as a teacher-researcher contribute to the development of a living educational theory through an exploration of my values in my professional practice?' M.Phil., University of Bath.

Hopkins, D. (1993) A teacher's guide to classroom research (2nd edn). Open University Press.

House, E.R. (1981) 'Three perspectives on innovation' in Lehming, R. and Kane, M. (eds) Improving schools: using what we know. Sage.

Howard, K. and Sharp, J.A. (1983) The management of a student research project. Gower Press.

Howe, C. (1997) Gender and classroom interaction. A research review. The Scottish Council for Research in Education.

Hoyle, E. and John, P.D. (1995) Professional knowledge and professional practice. Cassell.

Hutchinson, B. and Whitehouse, P. (1986) 'Action research, professional competence and school organisation', British Educational Research Journal, Vol. 12, No. 1, pp. 85–94.

Hutchinson, T. and Neal, T. (1998) Managing targets. Secondary Heads Association.

Hymas, C. and Cohen, J. (1994) 'The trouble with boys', The Sunday Times, 19 June, p. 14.

Iles, M. (1995) Boys and reading – some thoughts. National Literacy Trust.

Imich, A.J. (1994) 'Exclusions from school: current trends and issues', Educational Research, Vol. 36, No. 1, pp. 3–11.

Institute of Education (1992) Report on analysis of 1991 examination results. University of London, for the AMA.

Investors In Information, Library Association Scheme. Details on http://www. la-hq.org.uk

Jackson, B. (1964) Streaming: an education system in miniature. Routledge & Kegan Paul.

Jesson, D. (1992) 'Beyond the league tables', Education, 28 February, pp. 179–180.

Jesson, D. and Gray, J. (1991) 'Slants on slopes. Using multi-level models to investigate differential school effectiveness and its impact on pupils' examination results', School Effectiveness and School Improvement, Vol. 2, No. 3, pp. 230–247.

Jones, L.P. and Jones L.G. (1989) 'Context, confidence and the able girl', Educational Research, Vol. 31, No. 3, pp. 189–194.

Jones, P.R.R. (1988) Lipservice: the story of talk in schools. Open University Press.

Kelly, J. (1998) 'Let creativity shape the future', Times Educational Supplement, 27 February.

Kemmis, S. and Carr, W. (1983) Becoming critical. The Falmer Press.

Kemmis, S. and McTaggart, R. (1981) The action research planner. Deakin University Press, Victoria.

Keys, W. and Fernandes, C. (1993) What do students think about school? Research into the factors associated with positive and negative attitudes towards school and education. A report for the National Commission on Education. NFER.

Kincheloe, J.L. (1991) Teachers as researchers: qualitative inquiry as a path to empowerment. The Falmer Press.

Kirklees LEA (1995) Teaching Key Stage Two through a menu system. Kirklees LEA.

Kirklees LEA (1996) Raising boys' achievement. Kirklees School Effectiveness Service.

Klein, R. (1995) 'Tales of snips and snails', *Times Educational Supplement*, 9 June, English supplement, p. 4.

Kozeki, B. and Entwistle, N.J. 'Identifying dimensions of school motivation in Britain and Hungary', *British Journal of Educational Psychology*, No. 54, pp. 306–319.

Kress, G. (1998) 'The future still belongs to boys', *The Independent*, 11 June, pp. 4–5.

Kruse, A.-M. (1992) 'We have learnt not just to sit back, twiddle our thumbs and let them take over', *Gender and Education*, Vol. 4, No. 1/2, pp. 81–103.

Kurzweil. Details on http://www.kurzweiledu.com

Langeveld, M.J. (1965) 'In search of research', in course file for EP851, p. 4. (1984), Open University.

Lawrence, D. (1987) *Enhancing self-esteem in the classroom*. PCP Ltd.

Leeds LEA (1996) *Discussion papers in literacy. A kindness about it: improving perform-ance at GCSE. A study of English results at Temple Moor High School*. Leeds LEA.

Leicester, M. (1991) *Equal opportunities in school: social class, sexuality, race, gender and special needs*. Longman.

Lemon, N. (1973) *Attitudes and their measurement*. Batsford.

Levine, T. and Geldman-Caspar, Z. (1996) 'Informal science writing produced by boys and girls: writing preference and quality', *British Educational Research Journal*, Vol. 22, No. 4, pp. 421–439.

Lewin, K. (1946) 'Action research and minority problems', *Journal of Social Issues*, No. 2, pp. 34–36.

Linchevski, L. (1995) 'Tell me who your classmates are and I will tell you what you have learned: mixed ability versus ability-grouping in mathematics classes'. Paper presented at King's College, London.

Lloyd, D.P. (1989) 'Self-perception and self-worth in secondary school children. Implications for health education.' Dissertation for M.Sc., University of Manchester.

Lofthouse *et al.* (1994) *Managing the curriculum*. Pitman Publishing.

Lomas, T. (1998) 'Secondary school history: pupils' likes and dislikes and planning for more positive attitudes towards the subject'. Paper given at History Conference, Trinity and All Saints College, Leeds.

Mac an Ghaill, M. (1994) *The making of men. Masculinities, sexualities and schooling*. Open University Press.

Macintosh, H.G. (ed.) (1974) *Techniques and problems of assessment*. Edward Arnold.

McCourt, F. (1997) *Angela's ashes*. Flamingo.

McNiff, J. (1988) *Action research. Principles and practice*. Macmillan.

McNiff, J. (1993) *Teaching as learning. An action research approach*. Routledge.

Marland, M. (ed.) (1983) *Sex differentiation and schooling*. Heinemann.

Martinson, J. (1994) 'Keen at seven, lost by eleven', *Times Educational Supplement*, 18 March, p. 14.

Matheson, T. (1988) in O'Sullivan, F., Jones, K. and Reid, K. *Staff development in secondary schools*. Hodder & Stoughton.

Measor, L. *et al.* (1996) 'Gender and sex education: a study of adolescent responses', *Gender and Education*, Vol. 8, No. 3, pp. 275–278.

Merrett, F. and Wheldall, K. (1992) 'Teacher's use of praise and reprimands to boys and girls', *Educational Review*, Vol. 44, No. 1, pp. 73–79.

Merriam, S.B. (1988) *Case study research in education. A qualitative approach*. Jossey-Bass, USA.

Merton, B. (1998) *Finding the missing* – a report for the National Youth Agency. Youth Work Press.

Meyer Reimer, K. and Bruce, B. (1994) 'Building teacher–researcher collaboration: dilemmas and strategies', *Educational Action Research*, Vol. 2, No. 2, pp. 211–221.

Mifsud, C. (1993) 'Gender differentials in the classroom', *Research in Education*, No. 49, pp. 11–22.

Millard, E. (1996) *Some thoughts on why boys don't choose to read at school*. Sheffield University.

Millard, E. (1997) *Differently literate: boys, girls and the schooling of literacy*. The Falmer Press.

Mills, M. and Lingard, B. (1997) 'Masculinity politics, myths and boys' schooling: a review essay', *British Journal of Educational Studies*, September, pp. 276–292.

Minton, J. and Dupey, R. (1998) 'Project management for pupils', *Managing Schools Today*, March, pp. 37–39.

Morris, E. (1996) *Boys will be boys? Closing the gender gap*. The Labour Party.

Moser, C.A. and Kalton, G. (1971) *Survey methods in social investigation* (2nd edn). Heinemann.

Murphy, R. and Torrance, H. (eds) (1987) *Evaluating education: issues and methods*. Harper & Row/Open University Press.

NCET (1996) *Alternative resourcing: making the most of support staff in developing the use of IT in schools*. NCET.

Nisbet, J. and Watt, J. (1978) *Case study*. Nottingham University School of Education.

Nixon, J. (ed.) (1981) *A teacher's guide to action research. Evaluation, enquiry and development in the classroom*. Grant McIntyre.

Norfolk Inspection Advice and Training Service (1997) *Underachievement of boys in secondary school*. Norfolk LEA.

Nuttall, D.L. *et al.* (1989) 'Differential school effectiveness', *The International Journal of Educational Research*, Vol. 13, No. 7, pp. 769–776.

Nuttall, D.L. *et al.* (1992) 'AMA project on putting exam. results in context', Centre for Educational Research, London School of Economics and Political Science and the Institute of Education, University of London.

Ofsted (1998) *Standards in secondary schools*. Ofsted.

Oliver, P. (ed.) (1996) *The management of educational change. A case-study approach*. Arena.

Oppenheim, A.N. (1992) *Questionnaire design, interviewing and attitude measurement. New edition*. Pinter Publishers.

Pacific Institute (1997) *Investment in excellence*. Pacific Institute Inc.

Parker, A. (1996) 'The construction of masculinity within boys' physical education', *Gender and Education*, Vol. 8, No. 2, pp. 141–157.

Parry, O. (1997) 'Schooling is fooling: why do Jamaican boys under-achieve in schools?', *Gender and Education*, Vol. 9, No. 2.

Pease, K. (1998) 'Criminology and school performance'. Database research at the University of Huddersfield.

Penny, V. (1998) 'Raising boys' achievement in English' in Bleach, K. (ed.) *Raising boys' achievement in schools*. Trentham Books.

Peters, T.J. and Waterman, R.H. (1982) *In search of excellence: lessons from America's best run companies*. Harper & Row.

Pickering, J. (1997) *Raising boys' achievement*. Network Educational Press.

Polyani, M. (1858) *Personal knowledge*. Routledge & Kegan Paul.

Posch, P. (1994) 'Changes in the culture of teaching and learning and implications for action research', *Educational Action Research*, Vol. 2, No. 2, pp. 149–161.

Pottage, T. (1999) 'The hidden disability', *Library Association Record*, Library Technology Issue, Vol. 4, No. 1, pp. 8–9.

Powney, J. (1993) OU course E271. Block D. Part 2. Open University.

Powney, J. and Watts, M. (1987) *Interviewing in educational research*. Routledge & Kegan Paul.

Pritchard, R.M.O. (1987) 'Boys' and girls' attitudes towards French and German', *Educational Research*, Vol. 29, No. 1, pp. 65–72.

Pyke, N. (1998) 'Boys will still lag in literacy stakes', *Times Educational Supplement*, 27 November, p. 5.

Qualifications and Curriculum Authority (1998) *Autumn statement*. QCA.

Qualifications and Curriculum Authority (1998) *Benchmarking*. QCA.

Qualifications and Curriculum Authority (1998) *Religious Education and the use of language*. QCA.

Reynolds, D. and Cuttance, P. (eds) (1992) *School effectiveness, research, policy and practice*. Cassell.

Reynolds, K. (1996) *Children and their books*. Roehampton Institute.

Ribbins, P. and Burridge, E. (eds) (1994) *Improving education. Promoting quality in schools*. Cassell.

Richardson, L.D. (1992) *Techniques of investigation: an introduction to research methods*. National Extension College.

Riddell, S. (1992) *Gender and the politics of the curriculum*. Routledge.

Riddell, S. and Brown, S. (eds) (1991) *School effectiveness research: its messages for school improvement, Edinburgh*. HMSO.

Roberts, G.L. (1992) *Questionnaire design*. University of Huddersfield.

Robson, C. (1993) *Real world research. A resource for social scientists and practitioner-researchers*. Blackwell.

Rogers, C. and Freiberg, H.J. (1994) *Freedom to learn* (3rd edn). Merrill.

Rosenberg, M. (1965) *Society and the adolescent self-image*. Princeton University Press, USA.

Royal Society of Arts (1998) *The effect and effectiveness of arts education in schools (interim report)*. Arts Matter Project/NFER.

Ruddock, J. (1994) *Developing a gender policy in secondary schools*. Open University Press.

Ruddock, J. et al. (eds) (1996) *School improvement. What can pupils tell us?* David Fulton.

Rudestam, K.E. and Newton, R.R. (1992) *Surviving your dissertation. A comprehensive guide to content and process*. Sage

Sammons, P. et al. (1995) *Key characteristics of effective schools: a review of school effectiveness*. HMSO.

Scheerens, J. (1992) *Effective schooling. Research, theory and practice*. Cassell.

Schofield, M. (1969) *Social research*. Heinemann.

Schön, A. (1983) *The reflective practitioner*. Temple-Smith.

Sewell, T. (1997) *Black masculinities and schooling. How black boys survive modern schooling*. Trentham Books.

Shaw, J. (1995) *Education, gender and anxiety*. Taylor & Francis.

Sherman, R.S. and Webb, R.B. (1988) *Qualitative research in education: focus and methods*. The Falmer Press.

Shipman, M. (1981) *The limitations of social research* (2nd edn). Longman.

Shipman, M. (ed.) (1985) *Educational research: principles, policies and practices*. The Falmer Press.

Short, J. (1997) 'Help at hand for under-achieving boys', *Managing Schools Today*, June/July.

Siann, G. *et al.* (1996) 'Motivation and attribution at secondary school: the role of ethnic groups and gender', *Gender and Education*, Vol. 8, No. 3, pp. 261–274.

Simons, H. (1979) 'Suggestions for a school self-evaluation based on democratic evaluation', *CRN Bulletin*, No. 3.

Siskin, L.S. (1994) *Realms of knowledge; academic departments in secondary schools*. The Falmer Press.

Skelton, C. (1996) 'Learning to be tough: the fostering of maleness in one primary school', *Gender and Education*, Vol. 8, No. 2, pp. 185–197.

Slavin, R.E. (1990) 'Achievement effects of ability groupings in secondary schools: a best evidence synthesis', *Review of Educational Research*, No. 60, pp. 471–490.

Somekh, B. (1994) 'Inhabiting each other's castles: towards knowledge and mutual growth through collaboration', *Educational Action Research*, Vol. 2, No. 3, pp. 357–381.

Somekh, B. (1995) 'The contribution of action research to development in social endeavours: a position paper on action research methodology', *British Educational Research Journal*, Vol. 21, No. 3, pp. 339–355.

Spear, M. (1989) 'Differences between the written work of boys and girls', *British Educational Research Journal*, Vol. 15, No. 3, pp. 271–277.

Spear, M. (1991) 'Sex differences in written work: a rejoinder', *British Educational Research Journal*, Vol. 17, No. 2, pp. 147–148.

Spender, D. (1982) *Invisible women. The schooling scandal*. Chameleon Books.

Staberg, E.-M. (1994) 'Gender and science in the Swedish compulsory school', *Gender and Education*, Vol. 6, No. 1, pp. 35–45.

Stables, A. (1990) 'Differences between pupils from mixed and single-sex schools in their enjoyment of school subjects and in their attitudes to science and to school', *Educational Review*, Vol. 42, No. 3, pp. 221–230.

Stenhouse, L. (1971) 'The humanities curriculum project: the rationale', *Theory into Practice*, No. 10, pp. 154–162.

Stenhouse, L. (1975) *An introduction to curriculum research and development*. Heinemann.

Stenhouse, L. (1981) 'What counts as research?', *British Journal of Educational Studies*, Vol. 29, No. 2, pp. 103–14.

Stobart, G. *et al.* (1992) 'Gender bias in examinations: how equal are the opportunities?', *British Educational Research Journal*, Vol. 18, No. 3, pp. 261–275.

Strauss, P. (1995) 'No easy answers: the dilemmas and challenges of teacher research', *Educational Action Research*, Vol. 3, No. 1, pp. 29–40.

Streatfield, D. and Markless, S. (1994) *Invisible learning? The contribution of school libraries to teaching and learning.* British Library Research Report.

Sumner, R. (1974) *Looking at school achievement.* NFER.

Sutcliffe, J. (1998) 'Age weakens thirst for knowledge', *Times Educational Supplement.*

Swann, J. and Graddol, D. (1988) 'Gender inequalities in classroom talk', *English in Education,* Vol. 22, No. 1, pp. 48–65.

Taylor, C. and Temple, G. (1996) *Combating copying: teaching enquiry and research skills.* Devon County Council Education Department.

Thomas, S. *et al.* (1993) *AMA project on putting exam. results in context.* AMA.

Topping, K. (1988) *The peer tutoring handbook.* Routledge.

TVEI Team – Kirklees (1994) 'TVEI in Kirklees and its impact on teaching and learning for 14–19 year olds'. A report presented by R. Vincent, Director of Education.

Underwood, G. and Jindal, N. (1994) 'Gender differences and effects of co-operation in a computer-based language task', *Educational Research,* Vol. 36, No. 1, pp. 63–74.

Walker, B. (1996) 'Young men behaving sadly', *Times Educational Supplement,* October.

Walker, R. (1985) *Doing research. A handbook for teachers.* Methuen.

Walkerdine, V. (1990) *Schoolgirl fictions.* Verso.

Wallace, C. and Cross, M. (eds) (1990) *Youth in transition: the sociology of youth and youth policy.* The Falmer Press.

Watson, G. (1987) *Writing a thesis. A guide to long essays and dissertations.* Longman.

Weindling, D. and Earley, P. (1986) *Secondary headship: the first years.* NFER/Nelson.

West, E. and Hunter, J. (1993) 'Parents' view on mixed and single-sex secondary schools', *British Educational Research Journal,* Vol. 19, No. 4, pp. 369–380.

West-Burnham, J. *et al.* (1994) *Leadership and strategic management.* Pitman Publishing.

Weston, P. and Mangan, C. (1988) *Learning to learn: helping pupils to improve their educational competence.* The Chameleon Press Ltd.

Whitehead, J. (1989) 'Creating a living educational theory from questions of the kind, "How do I improve my practice?"', *Cambridge Journal of Education,* Vol. 19, No. 1, pp. 41–52.

Whitehead, J. (1993) *The growth of educational knowledge. Creating your own living educational theories.* Hyde Publications.

Whitehead, J.M. (1994) 'Academically successful school-girls: a case of sex-role transcendence', *Research Papers in Education,* Vol. 9, No. 1, pp. 53–80.

Whitehead, J.M. (1996) 'Sex stereotypes, gender identity and subject-choice at 'A' level', *Educational Research,* Vol. 38, No. 2, pp. 147–160.

Whyld, J. (1986) 'Anti-sexist teaching with boys'. Published privately by the author.

Williams, E. (1995) 'Lapped by girls', *Times Educational Supplement,* 14 July, pp. 3–4.

Willms, J.D. (1992) *Monitoring school performance. A guide for educators.* The Falmer Press.

Winter, R. (1989) *Learning from experience. Principles and practice in action research.* The Falmer Press.

Woolnough, B.E. (1994) *Effective science teaching.* Open University Press.

Wragg, T. (1997) 'Oh boy!', *Times Educational Supplement,* 16 May, p. 4

Index